DEC 1 9 2019

3 1994 01583 7179

SANTA ANA PUBLIC LIBRARY

D0312601

The Best Advice I Ever Heard

Chicken Soup for the Soul: The Best Advice I Ever Heard
101 Stories of Epiphanies and Wise Words
Amy Newmark

Published by Chicken Soup for the Soul, LLC www.chickensoup.com
Copyright ©2018 by Chicken Soup for the Soul, LLC. All Rights Reserved.

No part of this publication may be reproduced, stored in a retrieval system or transmitted in any form or by any means, electronic, mechanical, photocopying, recording or otherwise, without the written permission of the publisher.

CSS, Chicken Soup for the Soul, and its Logo and Marks are trademarks of Chicken Soup for the Soul, LLC.

The publisher gratefully acknowledges the many publishers and individuals who granted Chicken Soup for the Soul permission to reprint the cited material.

Front cover photo courtesy of iStockphoto.com/ismagilov (©ismagilov)
Back cover and interior photo courtesy of iStockphoto.com/RichVintage (©RichVintage)
Photo of Amy Newmark courtesy of Susan Morrow at SwickPix

Cover and Interior by Daniel Zaccari

Distributed to the booktrade by Simon & Schuster. SAN: 200-2442

Publisher's Cataloging-In-Publication Data
(Prepared by The Donohue Group, Inc.)

Names: Newmark, Amy, compiler.
Title: Chicken soup for the soul : the best advice I ever heard : 101
    stories of epiphanies and wise words / [compiled by] Amy Newmark.
Other Titles: Best advice I ever heard : 101 stories about epiphanies and
    wise words
Description: [Cos Cob, Connecticut] : Chicken Soup for the Soul, LLC,
    [2018]
Identifiers: ISBN 9781611599848 | ISBN 9781611592849 (ebook)
Subjects: LCSH: Conduct of life--Literary collections. | Conduct of life--
    Anecdotes. | Wisdom--Literary collections. | Wisdom--Anecdotes. |
    Epiphanies--Literary collections. | Epiphanies--Anecdotes. | LCGFT:
    Anecdotes.
Classification: LCC BJ1595 .C45 2018 (print) | LCC BJ1595 (ebook) | DDC
    158.1--dc23

Library of Congress Control Number 2018956118

PRINTED IN THE UNITED STATES OF AMERICA
on acid∞free paper

25 24 23 22 21 20 19   03 04 05 06 07 08 09 10 11

Chicken Soup for the Soul.

The Best Advice I Ever Heard

158.1 CHI
Chicken soup for the soul

$14.95
CENTRAL   31994015837179

Amy Newmark

Chicken Soup for the Soul, LLC
Cos Cob, CT

Changing your life one story at a time®
www.chickensoup.com

Table of Contents

❸

~Why Didn't I Think of That?~

❹

~Maxims for Marriage~

❺

~Making Good Habits~

6

~Think Positive~

7

~Follow Your Heart~

8

~Take Care of Yourself~

9

~How to Be Happy~

10

~From Failing to Fabulous~

⑪

~Positive Parenting~

Introduction

This new *Chicken Soup for the Soul* collection started years ago, when we realized that so many of our writers were telling stories about how one piece of advice changed their lives. I was fascinated by the concept — that a few words, sometimes even from a stranger — could change everything. So, we asked the public to send us stories about the *one piece of advice* that reoriented them, solved a problem, or changed the trajectory of their lives.

As I was heading off to the Seattle airport today to fly to Burbank I knew that I would be writing this introduction on the plane. But I didn't expect that our Uber driver, Shad, would be such an inspiration and so relevant! When Shad heard that I was part of the Chicken Soup for the Soul team, he was thrilled, as he is a big fan of our books. And then he handed me a journal that he kept in his car. For years, Shad has been asking his riders to share their best advice. He's collected 3,500 handwritten entries so far.

As of this writing, I am on a publicity tour for our August book, *Chicken Soup for the Soul: The Power of Yes!*, I quickly scrawled, "The best advice I have for you is to use the power of yes to make a policy of saying yes to new things — every day — even if they scare you." I read it to Shad, and then he said, "What about saying no?" So I assured him that we believe in the power of "no" as well, and I added, "And use the power of no to eliminate the things that don't add value to your life."

I do have my own story about a piece of advice that changed my life, and you'll read it in this collection. It's story 27, and it's about a few words that were such an eye-opener to me that I still think about them every time I feel overwhelmed by the amount of work I have to do. They have been a critical part of my success as a multitasking writer, executive, parent, spouse and grown daughter.

You'll also read great advice in these pages about living life to the fullest, achieving success in your career or vocation, keeping your marriage fresh, and raising happy, healthy children. We also have plenty of stories containing great advice for making *yourself* happier and healthier, and for pursuing your passions and dreams. And if you take some missteps along the way we also have stories for that, with a chapter on how to turn failure into fabulous.

We've all been talking about these stories in our office, as all of us have been picking up new tips for our own lives. We are privileged to have jobs that let us sit in the front row for all the great advice that streams in from our writers. We are better for it — happier, healthier, more grounded and grateful for what we have, less anxious, and certainly having more fun. Because these stories are not just full of advice, they are great entertainment, too! We loved putting this collection together for you, and we look forward to hearing how the wise words in these pages improve your lives. Let me know what they do for you by sending an e-mail to amy@chickensoupforthesoul.com.

— Amy Newmark —
September 4, 2018

Chapter
1

Living Fully

How Sweet It Is

There is no better way to bring people together
than with desserts.
~Gail Simmons

The sign said "Going Out of Business Sale" and it drew me into a gravel parking lot streaked with overgrown grass. The dilapidated building and I had a lot in common. I was divorced; some of my children were acting out, one so severely he was in a delinquents' home. I felt like I was failing as a mother. The master's degree it took me eight years to earn had priced me out of the freelance market, and the senior housing project I'd been working for sold out, so I was jobless.

Something beckoned me inside. I strolled the picked-over aisles of the once-quaint gift shop. The rear wall was lined with plaques. One of them made me laugh out loud: *Life is uncertain. Eat dessert first.*

Seven months passed after that. The fifty résumés I sent out yielded two interviews and no job offers. My savings account was dwindling. I couldn't afford to eat out, but occasionally a friend or relative would treat me. I remembered the advice on that plaque and I always ordered dessert before — or instead of — dinner!

I got my family and friends to join me in eating dessert first. One time, my sister and I ordered an amazing chocolate creation. It was about ten inches tall, and elaborately decorated like a lighthouse, with a white chocolate beacon. It was scrumptious. Chris and I still talk about the buzz in the restaurant when we ate it first.

Another time, a friend and I drove from Milwaukee to a writing conference in Toledo, and then drove up to Detroit to visit Chris. She and her husband Mike took us out for my birthday. On the way into the restaurant, we passed the dessert cart. In its center was a three-inch chocolate rose, festooned with carved petals. "I'll have that," I told the hostess who seated us.

"That's not for sale; it's just decoration," she said.

Mike excused himself. Shortly after he came back, a waiter arrived with that rose on a fancy dessert plate, garnished with raspberry sauce.

"Mike!" I exclaimed. "That must have cost a fortune!"

"You don't want to know," he said.

I don't share well with others when it comes to chocolate. But that night, I offered to share my rose with Mike.

Finally, serendipity led me to a new career in the cosmetics industry. I was able to finance two of my sons' weddings. I was meeting great people and having fun. I replenished my savings account. And I could afford to buy myself those dinners — still ordering dessert first.

I made a new friend, Audrey. Neither of us noticed the fifteen-year difference in our ages and we became fast friends. We started having lunch together every Monday.

The wait staff laughed when we ordered dessert first, and then applauded our decision. We became regulars and went through the entire dessert menu, each ordering something different so we could share. We asked waitresses to cut each serving as equally as possible so we wouldn't "squabble" about who got the larger piece. We laughed a lot. We never ran out of things to talk about. Audrey was a fount of wisdom, and I shared my faith with her.

As time went on, Audrey's appetite waned. We shared one dessert instead of two. She took most of her lunch home for her husband. But we spent the same amount of time chatting. Waiters and waitresses from all across the restaurant came over to our table. "We knew you were here," they'd say. "We could hear you laughing."

As Audrey's health deteriorated, it became more difficult for her to get around. Nevertheless, we clung to our Monday lunches, with dessert first, until a few weeks before she died. I miss her. I miss our bonding over apple turnovers, hot lava cake or key lime pie.

I resolved not to let the dessert-first tradition die. One of my adult granddaughters and I get together for dinner several times a month, and we always have dessert first. We've gone through the dessert menu at one restaurant and have moved on to another. We talk and laugh and share the little details of our lives. I listen between the words for things she's not saying, and I ask God's guidance for how to respond to her needs without meddling.

> *Eating dessert first is about spontaneity and not taking ourselves too seriously.*

For my birthday this year, Shauna made me a plaque: "Life is short; eat dessert first." It dominates my "grandma wall." We both know the message is not really about eating sweets; eating dessert first is about connecting with those we love, listening with our hearts, and sharing the things we've learned. Eating dessert first is about spontaneity and not taking ourselves too seriously. It's about embracing change and living in the moment. And in those moments, in spite of their uncertainty or brevity, we glimpse how sweet life is.

— Diane C. Perrone —

don't know," I stammered.

Her smile widened as compassion and understanding shined from her like a porch light in the night, somehow dispelling my trepidation. "Okay, how about doing it for just a week? And really, all you have to do is one brave thing a day. Don't look at the whole week ahead; just look at today. All I ask is that you try for the next seven days to do one thing every day that takes you out of your comfort zone. Some of them may work; some may not. All I ask is that you try. Then, once you've done that one thing, I want you to call me and tell me what you did and how it turned out."

A week sounded more reasonable. And like she said, all I had to think about was today.

"Okay, I'll do it," I said, feeling happier already.

"Good," my friend said with a grin and nod of approval.

After she dropped me off at my apartment that afternoon, I pulled out my book of lists. Flipping through the pages, I found myself growing overwhelmed. I closed the book again, laid both hands on it and said aloud, "Help me, angels. I need to do just one brave thing. What should it be? One thing. Just one thing."

Immediately, the words "book signing" came to mind. The one thing I had been dreading most was putting myself out there as an author. Not giving myself time to think too much about what I was doing, I flipped to the page of possible book-signing locations. The list was complete with phone numbers. I grabbed my cell phone and dialed the local library.

Five minutes later, I hung up. My smile could not be contained. I had a date to speak to the library's teen reading group about my young-adult novel and my life as a writer.

I felt so excited about knocking that out of the park that I made three more calls and booked two more signing dates. Then I called my friend and thanked her.

Even now, thirteen years later, when I find myself stuck, I remind myself of what I now refer to as OBTAD. **One. B**rave. Thing. **A. D**ay.

— Susan Walker —

Put Enough Paint on the Brush

*Your work is to discover your work and then
with all your heart to give yourself to it.*
~Buddha

My grandfather was a house painter. No one could paint a wall like Grandpa. Consequently, he was always in demand. In his lifetime, he must have painted hundreds of houses inside and out. It wasn't hard to tell that he loved his work as well as his life. He was a happy, outgoing man who made friends easily.

Once, while in college, I helped Grandpa paint a house. While working inside, I noticed how skilled he was at giving a wall a quality coat of paint so quickly. As a matter of fact, he could carry on a conversation with the homeowner, laughing all the time, while painting three walls to my one.

At one point, he stopped to watch me. He noticed how I took my time dipping the brush in the paint bucket and how I carefully wiped off both sides of the brush as I pulled it out so as not to waste any paint. Then I spread the thin coat of paint on the wall without spilling a drop. It was a slow, tedious process, but I dared not laugh or "kid around" for fear of making a mess.

Finally, he gave me some advice. "Here, watch this," he said, as he took the brush from my hand and dipped it into the bucket. He pulled it out heaping with paint. "See, this is how you do it. Don't worry about spills and messes. They can always be cleaned up. Treat a wall the way you treat people. Be generous. Have fun. Always put enough paint on the brush."

With that, he turned and applied a thick coat of paint on the wall while resuming his conversation with the homeowner. Yes, he did spill a few drops, but I noticed how much better his wall looked than mine. I also noticed how much fun he was having.

I'll always remember the lesson my grandfather taught me that day.

Life is not always perfect. Some days, we spill very few drops; some days, we spill a lot. The only thing that really matters is what the wall looks like when we are done (and how much fun we had painting it). "Put enough paint on the brush!"

— Tom Krause —

What Would You Do If You Weren't Afraid?

Your life does not get better by chance.
It gets better by change.
~Jim Rohn

Most of my life, I let fear stop me from doing the things I wanted to do. I was always stopped by the "what ifs." I don't know how I managed to scratch my way out of a bad marriage. Blind determination, I suppose, driven by a desire to just get out.

My two best friends were always there for me through it all, each supporting me in different ways. One of them was my "girls' night out" gal, and we would go out for dinner and cocktails every other Friday night.

One night, we were trying a new restaurant. As we chatted, my friend leaned in to me and whispered, "The bartender keeps staring at you." I very discreetly looked over at the bar, and I practically fell out of my chair. The bartender was the most gorgeous man I'd ever seen! "We have to have a drink at the bar," I said. I was surprised these words came out of my mouth, as it was unusual for me to be so bold.

We proceeded to the bar, and the exchange of energy between the bartender and me was undeniable. He was so good-looking and emitted such good energy that I felt as though he was out of my league. Quite honestly, I didn't think I'd see him again, so when he messaged me a

One Brave Thing

*The biggest rewards in life are found outside your
comfort zone. Live with it. Fear and risk are
prerequisites if you want to enjoy
a life of success and adventure.*
~Jack Canfield

After separating from my husband in 2004, I descended into a dark hole of depression. I was living in the little box my husband's words and actions had built around me. I was not a brave soul, and at that point in my life I had no idea what was to come. Even though my second book had just been accepted for publication, I was stuck. I didn't know how to move forward with my life.

A good friend who had helped me grow strong enough to leave my husband took me out to lunch one day. After we placed our orders, she folded her hands together on the table and leaned in as if about to impart a tremendous secret.

"You're stuck," she said.

I blinked and nodded as tears began to fill my eyes. "Stuck and scared and not sure how to fix myself enough to get unstuck."

My friend smiled and nodded. "Been there, done that, burned the T-shirt. You need to do one brave thing."

For some reason, whenever the word "need" comes out of someone's mouth in relation to my life, I immediately start thinking of reasons why I can't do whatever the "You need to…" is.

Even as I began to shake my head, my friend leaned closer. "Stop. Right now. Just hear me out, okay?"

I nodded and leaned in, too.

"One brave thing a day. That's all you have to do. Just one small thing every day, and you'll be able to change your world forever."

As I sat and contemplated her words, she took a sip of her iced tea.

After nearly a minute, I asked, "But what is the one brave thing I should be doing?"

She smiled in a way that made me think of Yoda. "Whatever it is you're not doing now because you're afraid. You could make that phone call to the coffee shop asking to do a book signing, call the library and set up an appearance, submit another book, or just go next door and introduce yourself to the neighbors. All it takes is a minute of courage to start and then a deep breath to follow through. Just one thing. One brave thing. Every day. Think you can do that?"

> *"One brave thing a day. That's all you have to do."*

At that moment, the waitress arrived with our lunches, so I had a minute to process.

One thing.

Just one thing.

That shouldn't be too hard, I thought. And I had hundreds of things to choose from. My want-need-should list filled a dozen pages in a notebook I kept on my desk. I'd started the lists ages ago, and pulled out the notebook every couple of months to add to the lists or reprioritize the numerous entries. Rarely did I actually cross something off the list.

As I mixed my Cobb salad together and assured the waitress that everything looked fine, I gave serious thought to my never-ending to-do list.

One brave thing a day.

"I like it," I said finally. "And I think I can do it."

My friend smiled. "You might surprise yourself. Now, can you commit to me here and now that you will do one brave thing every day for the next month?"

A month? Thirty brave things. All at once the fear that had been my constant companion for most of my life kicked in once more. "I day later, I was floored. Throughout that week, he and I messaged back and forth. He invited me to come down while he was working, and said he'd buy me a drink. But then, the communication just dropped off. I assumed he had lost interest, but that invitation still gnawed at me.

That weekend, my other best friend, who never gets a chance to go out, made a once-in-a-blue-moon plan to meet me for drinks. I told her I really wanted to go back to where that bartender worked. Just as I was about to leave my house, she texted me. A snag had come up, and she wasn't sure she'd get there.

I really wanted to go to the restaurant, but by myself? My internal thoughts were not helpful. *What if she never shows? I can't walk into a bar alone. I'm afraid to do it. I don't even know if he's interested. I'll look like a fool.* I sat there paralyzed with fear, swaying radically between taking off my make-up and going to bed or standing up and getting in the car. I started scrolling through pictures on my phone, mostly screenshots of social-media memes I had saved for one reason or another. Then I landed on the meme that would change my life forever. It said, "What would you do if you weren't afraid?"

It was a simple question really, but extremely profound. *If I elimi-nate all my fears from the situation,* I asked myself, *what will I do?* The answer was exactly what I did. I got in the car and drove straight to the restaurant. I cast fear aside and did exactly what I wanted to do, despite the negative possibilities.

The result? He and I have been together for two years and share a wonderful home together. His love is beyond anything I could have dreamed of.

If I hadn't cast fear aside that night, I would have missed out on the love of my life. So now, when opportunities arise and I'm apprehensive or don't know quite what to do, I ask myself that one question:

> *If I hadn't cast fear aside that night, I would have missed out on the love of my life.*

"What would you do if you weren't afraid?" Whatever the outcome, at least I can say I didn't let fear hold me back.

— Sarafina Drake —

Remember Who You Are

*Always be a first rate version of yourself and not a
second rate version of someone else.*
~Judy Garland

My husband Ben and I watched as our daughter Jennifer pulled on her coat and headed out the door on a Saturday night. At sixteen, she was dating, and this was a movie night with a group of boys and girls.

As she reached for the knob, Ben called out, "Remember who you are!"

Jennifer grinned and nodded. Those words were like a warm cape she tossed onto her shoulders as she shut the door behind her.

To Jennifer, the phrase "Remember who you are" meant that she was a good person, a nice girl. She knew that every time she left the house, she represented her family to the world. Her behavior reflected on all of us. Jennifer wanted to make sure she told our family's story with her actions and words.

To me, it meant, "Remember that we love you. Remember that no matter what you do in life, our love is all encompassing. We will be there for you, through thick and thin. And remember you were chosen by a wonderful man to be a part of his life, and to carry on his legacy of kindness, goodness and dignity."

I was a single mom when I met Ben. I found his Southern humor and down-home phrases attractive. A bachelor in his mid-thirties, he often told me he was "a hard dog to keep under the porch." We started out as friends, but deeper feelings developed.

When Ben first asked me out on a date, I assumed it would be nothing more than a few hours of fun, not the beginning of a courtship. He thought I was a nice person, although I had experienced many difficulties in life and made plenty of mistakes. And he found Jennifer to be "most charming," as he would say.

We dated for a short while, and then he dropped off the radar. I was more than a little hurt. As quickly as he had stepped into our lives, he stepped out again. Jennifer often asked about him. She was only eleven, and I wanted to protect her from the ache that comes when romance falters and sputters out, so I did my best to hide my disappointment.

Much to my surprise, Ben called one evening several weeks later. He wanted to see us again. I reminded him that he had walked away abruptly before, and I wondered what had sparked his interest now. There was silence on the other end of the phone. Then Ben spoke.

"I knew when we met that you and Jennifer were a package deal," he began. "This would have to be a serious relationship right from the start because a child was involved. I needed to take time, think about everything, and decide if I was willing to be a part of your life and Jennifer's. I know now that this is what I want."

When Ben was a child, his grandmother often told him, "Remember who you are." This was a family motto, teaching Ben what it meant to be a person who could hold his head up in any storm, show respect and consideration for everyone, and not make promises he couldn't keep.

Ben remembered. And he stepped forward and made a promise to Jennifer and me that he planned to keep forever.

We married in a small church in Oregon. Ben was nervous that day. So was I. We were both well aware of the tremendous responsibility we were taking on. Jennifer was beaming with the innocent optimism of youth. She looked at me and grinned.

"Ben's the kind of dad you see on television," she said, which to her was the highest honor.

Together, we raised Jennifer. Ben was often astounded by the spats Jen and I had as we weathered the storms of junior high and high school. He said we sounded like "two Poodles barking." Then we would all laugh. Ben always brought harmony and peace. His was the voice of reason.

He never raised his voice to Jennifer, nor punished her for transgressions. When she flubbed some opportunities in college, I was angry and hurt, wanting to pull her out of school because college was not something to be taken lightly. But Ben was more understanding.

"My parents gave me chances," he said, "and we should do the same for Jennifer. I believe in her."

Through his gentle guidance and loving care, Jennifer finished college and earned a master's degree. She now enjoys a career in teaching and is a preschool director.

Throughout those years, Ben often smiled and reminded her, "Remember who you are." That phrase often caused good-natured eye rolling and laughter, but underneath it all was a declaration of love and respect, the foundation of our little family.

Ben was there for her wedding, there when our grandson Ronan was born, there to help decorate the nursery and take Jennifer and the baby to doctor check-ups.

But one day, a swift and cruel lesion in his brain sent him to the sidelines. The doctors gave him a year to live. We spent endless days at the hospital for surgery, radiation, chemotherapy, blood tests, and check-ups. No matter what the doctors tried, the cancer grew.

That last Christmas, Ben cradled Ronan gently in his arms. His disease now confined him to a wheelchair, and wide, angry scars tracked across his skull. The cancer was growing in the part of his brain that regulated speech. Ben could only say a few words, and sometimes they were garbled. But that Christmas Day, he laughed out loud when Jen looked at her baby son and said, "Remember who you are, Ronan." Ben knew his advice would carry on.

Somewhere in this vast universe, on the February day Ben took his final breath, I like to think he was ushered into heaven by a voice that said, "Ah, Ben. Welcome. I see you always remembered who you are."

— Sharon Frame Gay —

Walk Quietly

*Look at a tree, a flower, a plant. Let your awareness
rest upon it. How still they are, how deeply rooted in
Being. Allow nature to teach you stillness.*
~Eckhart Tolle, Stillness Speaks

On my third day of walking the Via de la Plata Camino de Santiago (a 1,000-kilometer — 625-mile — walking pilgrimage in Spain), I faced one of the greatest challenges of my life: an incredibly steep hill after a very long day of walking. Even months of preparation, which included walking hundreds of miles in and around the Las Vegas desert where I live, hadn't prepared me for the humidity of southern Spain. Before I realized what was happening, I got blisters on my feet, irritated by my damp wool socks. By the third day, the blisters had burst and each step produced horrible pain. I think the correct term for what happened is that my feet were "shredded."

So, here I was, facing the steepest climb I'd ever seen, and each step was so painful that I could barely move. I didn't think I could make it up the hill, and I didn't know what to do. The alternative was to walk back the way I'd come through the massive national park and then walk the level road into the next town — a 25-kilometer journey I knew I'd never get through.

Standing there, scared and desperate, I wondered why I had come on this seven-week walk. I'd been dreaming about the Camino de Santiago ever since I'd read Shirley MacLaine's book, *Out on a Limb*.

Years later, I watched the Emilio Estevez movie, *The Way*, about the Camino, and that encouraged me to go ahead with this journey. I planned, chose a route, and tried out different hiking clothes, sleeping bags, and backpacks. I walked four to ten miles every day for about six months — on tracks and through the hills and mountains surrounding Las Vegas. I read books and guides, and arranged my schedule to allow for nearly two months away from everything to have this experience of a lifetime. And now, on Day 3, I felt like a failure. How could I make it to the final destination — the Cathedral of Santiago de Compostela — if I couldn't get up this hill?

I took another few steps and stopped, panting through the pain. A few more steps, and more panting. Somehow, I held back the tears. Then, seemingly from nowhere, along came a fellow pilgrim I'd met the night before at the hostel. He smiled warmly when he saw me.

Jon, a retired accountant from Switzerland, was walking his twelfth Camino. He said "hello," asked how I was, and then listened to my fears. He was silent for a long moment and then said only two words: "Walk quietly." He smiled kindly again and then walked quickly up the steep hill and disappeared into the trees.

For the briefest of moments, I wondered if he'd actually been there in front of me or if I'd hallucinated the encounter because of the pain.

I took another two steps up the hill, and pain shot through me. I panted and tried to catch my breath. "Walk quietly" rang in my ears. *Walk quietly*. I allowed my breathing to return to normal. I prayed silently for help and strength, and Jon's words echoed in my head.

Part of my spiritual practice is a few minutes each day of quiet-mind meditation. So I breathed deeply and quieted my mind. I took a few more steps. Again, my breathing was labored, so I waited and quieted my mind. I realized that "walk quietly" meant without labored, noisy breathing. I took another step. It meant to walk without chastisement of myself in my own head. I took another step. This wasn't a race, but a long journey. Long journeys happen one step at a time. I took another step. If I walked quietly, I could hear the birds in the trees while I waited to regain my breath. I took another step. I could hear the negative thoughts pushing into my head. Once heard, I could release and quiet them. I took another step. I could hear the buzzing of the bees in the fields of wildflowers I'd passed through that spring day. I took another step.

I arrived at the summit, sat on a big rock on the belvedere, and drank most of my bottle of water. There, spread out before me as far as I could see, was the glorious vista of the massive national park with countless green trees and acres and acres of meadows where purple and white spring flowers swayed in the breeze. Somehow, I'd done it. My chest didn't fill with pride at my accomplishment; instead, I felt humbled as "Walk quietly" replayed in my mind.

Throughout the next seven weeks, Jon's words came back to me again and again. They didn't just help me climb that mountain. They changed the way I experienced my Camino de Santiago. I turned off the music in my headphones and listened for the cuckoos' calls. I walked with a quiet mind, letting go of the business that our lives are so filled with. If my breathing labored, I found a comfortable spot in soft grass to sit and rest for a while. I took off my boots and socks, letting my feet air and my socks dry before continuing. I listened to the wind in the trees and the tinkle of the bells on goats chomping Spanish hillsides. The words "walk quietly" provided solace and offered inspiration. They reminded me to live in the moment, and those quiet moments remind me now to walk quietly in *this* moment.

—Gregory A. Kompes—

Type Casting

Before anything great is really achieved,
your comfort zone must be disturbed.
~Ray Lewis

was delighted. "You've been cast as the Typist," read the text message.

I had only recently started applying for extra roles on films, and here I was getting cast as "the Typist" (my first-ever Screen Actors Guild role). The non-speaking part required typing on an old Remington typewriter.

When asked about my experience, I responded that I had earned a certificate of typing and steno from Katharine Gibbs — way back in 1983 — and had learned to type on an old Smith Corona typewriter. That (and a short video clip of me typing on my friend's father's typewriter) got me the job.

After several minutes of pure elation over getting the role, however, I panicked. It was only in a moment of courage that I had even submitted for the part, and now here I was… getting it!

Now I felt the weight of the unknown: *Why had I applied for this part with my very rusty skills? Was I really a good enough typist for the job? Why was I putting myself in such an uncomfortable situation in the first place?*

Typing well on an old metal typewriter is quite different from typing well on a modern computer. It requires finger strength and skill in order to type smooth keystrokes. One must keep a steady pace as well, so as not to jam the letter rods.

As the shooting date approached, my anxiety grew. However, thanks to YouTube, I was able to rekindle some of what I had known about old typewriters by watching numerous tutorials, including how to change typewriter ribbons, use margin releases, and adjust the key weight from light to heavy.

Still, I dreaded the new experience and wondered if I had acted too impulsively when I accepted the role.

I was a new empty nester and I wanted this to be the year I would step outside my comfort zone, but it felt scary. Why, I wondered, did the act of trying something new make me so uncomfortable? It wasn't until I spoke with a friend at church that Sunday that I had my answer.

"It's good that you feel uncomfortable," he said. "It means you're in your growth zone."

"What do you mean?" I asked.

"You have to remember," he continued, "that there's no growth in your comfort zone, and there's no comfort in your growth zone."

Growth zone? I didn't know there was such a thing! I was in a growth zone!

Being in that zone basically *required* feelings of inadequacy. In fact, feeling uncomfortable was a crucial element of being in a growth zone. It's like releasing the margins on a typewriter. With that in mind, I reasoned, feeling uncomfortable actually felt good!

That Monday and Tuesday, I played "the Typist" to the best of my ability. Only my hands were filmed, which made accuracy even more critical. Typing on a film set felt strange, but exciting, as one camera zoomed onto the page. The metal slugs steadily hit the ribbon while the director quipped, "Type faster here. Now, type faster here."

> *"There's no growth in your comfort zone, and there's no comfort in your growth zone."*

My heart raced as I prayed for precision. I was nervous and uncomfortable, but I was having fun! I was typing as fast as I could, uncomfortable as could be, in my new growth zone.

Accepting new challenges within the growth zone will always push me into a world of anxiety. But I liken it to plugging away on an old Remington typewriter. It takes a little strength, discomfort and, at times, precision. I may hit wrong keys every so often, go too fast, and even get myself all jammed up, but as long as I'm in the growth zone, it's to be expected. We all need to use a margin release every now and then.

—Mary C. M. Phillips—

What Would You Do If You Won the Lottery?

Life is a lottery that we've already won. But most
people have not cashed in their tickets.
~Louise L. Hay

I hated my job; all I did was complain about it. One day, I was whining about work to my brother. "I have no idea what I want to do. I cannot stand banking."

He had heard enough of my complaining and he responded with the clearest, most life changing question I had ever heard: "Imagine that you just won the lottery! What would be the first thing you'd do?"

Without thinking, I blurted out, "Oh my God! Move to Italy!" That had always been my dream — since childhood. But I hadn't thought about it in years. After all, I had my "good" job. With all my debt, I couldn't even afford to take a staycation, much less contemplate something as glorious as moving to Italy.

What a fantasy: *Italia*. The architecture, the little towns. I thought about all the mouthwatering food I would eat there. I imagined sending my boss a letter of resignation — in Italian… from Italy!

My brother brought me back to earth, "Then do it! Move. I'm sick of hearing that you hate your job. I'll come visit."

"I don't have the money. And I don't speak Italian."

My brother was relentless. "JC, if you wait until you learn the language, you'll never do it. Every day someone else is moving there and living your dream. Money, or lack thereof, has always been your obstacle. Why are you letting it hold you down?"

> *"Imagine that you just won the lottery! What would be the first thing you'd do?"*

I explained about my pile of debt, my responsibilities.

"Well then, do whatever it takes and get out of debt," my brother responded reasonably. "Start saving. Focus on moving to Italy."

I did it. I put aside my fear about the money and I concentrated on what I would do if I didn't have to worry about money. I set a goal; I would move to Milan before the end of the year. Then I threw myself into paying off my debt. I stopped spending money on anything but essentials. I canceled my magazine subscriptions, cable TV, even my tony health club membership. I stopped going out for meals and brought lunch to the office every day. Importantly, I also took daily steps to help me concentrate on my end goal. A picture of Italy went on my desk at work to remind me of my dream. I had an espresso at an Italian restaurant and met Italians who gave me fabulous travel advice. Library books were a great resource, as was talking to everyone I knew who had been there for their suggestions. Those positive actions changed it from being a dream to becoming that much closer to reality.

It worked. I paid off my debt and managed to move to Italy with $1200 in my pocket, more than I had ever saved. I had no idea what would happen, but it would be better than the life I had been living in Los Angeles: a bored, stressed-out, debt-ridden banker.

My imaginary lottery win forced me to listen to my inner voice, and that imaginary lottery ticket turned into a real plane ticket. Sean had said the magic words. It had never occurred to me before that I could remove money as the impediment to living the life I wanted. It was a turning point in my life, and since then I have continued to travel the world.

My time in Italy taught me I could do whatever I wanted if I put in the effort. Living in another country was never as scary again: I knew that when I grew tired of it, I could return home. A few years later, I lived in France and made incredible friends for life and learned so much. Knowing how to speak French helps me at the oddest times.

Then, I discovered hostels — their flexibility (let someone else handle the electricity, gas and related responsibilities!), maid service (I hate doing laundry!), and sense of community (amazing travel tips and fabulous excursions). Hosteling (you often can do it for just a few days or a long period of time) lets you sample different cities without tying yourself to a lease. Hostels are furnished, so when you leave, you simply grab your bag and you're on your way. When hosteling, my friends prefer to rent private rooms; I do dorm rooms, but either way is fun. That's how I lived in Colombia and Argentina.

All this happened thanks to a simple but life-altering question from my brother. To this day, when I need to make an important decision, I take money out of the equation. My journey is global, but now I'm back in LA and working as an actress. When I accept a role, I write down the reason I am doing it. And, you know what? It is never about the money.

— JC Sullivan —

Engage

This idea of shared humanity and the connections
that we make with one another — that's what, in fact,
makes life worth living.
~Clint Smith

The day my parents dropped me off at college, my dad gave me one word of advice: "engage." I nodded through the lump in my throat and kissed him goodbye.

I dutifully wrote the word "engage" in all lowercase letters on a blue Post-it note and stuck it to the wall above my desk. That night in my unfamiliar, narrow twin bed, I tried to muffle my crying. My roommate, Chelsea, heard me anyway and she handed me her stuffed puppy dog. I held it and cried myself to sleep.

My homesickness was a constant challenge. But as classes started, I mustered my courage and began to engage as best I could. I dropped a calculus class that I hated in favor of a psychology class that fascinated me. I auditioned for the prestigious Vassar Repertory Dance Theatre and for the student-run dance group FlyPeople. Although I wasn't a trained singer, I auditioned for the Christian a cappella group, Alive. I didn't make any of them, but for the first time in my life, I didn't let failure get to me. I shook back my hair and kept going. I was determined to find my place — the people, activities, and groups that would shape my college experience. And I was going to keep engaging with everything that looked remotely interesting until I found it.

I went to a few Catholic student group meetings, but they felt boring and perfunctory. I tried the more evangelical Christian Fellowship, and I loved the music and how friendly and passionate the students were. I went back for a second meeting, and a girl I didn't remember greeted me by name.

I went to Christian Fellowship regularly from that point on. The following year, I joined them for a weeklong service trip over spring break called the New York City Urban Project (NYCUP). I fell in love with New York City and the people we served there. Toward the end of that week, the program director, Tiffany, told us about an eight-week summer program. The next morning, I swayed on the subway next to one of the adult coordinators and said, "James, will you be here this summer?"

"I'm not sure yet," he said. Then he turned his piercing blue eyes on mine and said, "Why? Are you coming?"

I heard in that question an invitation to engage with my faith more deeply, in a way that scared and thrilled me. I had planned to return to my high-school restaurant job for the summer and to the camp in Scotland where I'd volunteered the previous year and made some close friends. Students who came to the summer NYCUP program in New York had to fundraise $3,000, and that thought terrified me.

Still, I remembered my dad's advice: engage. I decided to use my courage once again and do hard things. I sent letters to the church I'd grown up in, to my family and friends, and to the adults who'd run my high-school youth group. I raised more than the $3,000 program cost.

And so, on a Wednesday morning in midsummer, I found myself in the InterVarsity Christian Fellowship NYC offices listening to Tiffany read us a passage from Matthew 25: "For I was hungry and you gave me something to eat, I was thirsty and you gave me something to drink, I was a stranger and you invited me in, I needed clothes and you clothed me, I was sick and you looked after me, I was in prison and you came to visit me." The verses were familiar, but the assignment she gave us next was new: "I want you to partner with someone you haven't talked to much, and go out into the city and be Jesus for people."

No elaboration.

My heart was thumping. Be Jesus for people? That was weird. I did not want to engage in it. I wanted to sit back, be safe and anonymous, and not have to feel uncomfortable.

But everyone else was standing up and pairing off. It was obvious whom I should partner with — Simeon was the only person I'd hardly talked to at all. The two of us grabbed some bag lunches and headed out.

Simeon, it turned out, was easy to talk to. We talked about our experience with the summer so far, our volunteer work and our families. We stopped outside an apartment building and talked to an old man in a wheelchair who was sitting in the sunshine. When the old man went back inside, we continued walking until we found a park.

It was almost lunchtime, and the park was full of people sitting on benches and eating lunch, walking along the pathways, and chasing after kids. In the center was a patch of grass where several homeless people sat on pieces of cardboard. People averted their gaze.

I took a deep breath and followed Simeon as he walked right up to a homeless guy in his thirties who was playing a ukelele. His name was Jesse. We sat down and started talking to him. We opened our brown paper bags and shared our lunch.

Jesse told us he had dropped out of med school. He showed me the pharmacy textbook in his backpack. He told us the meaning of each of his tattoos. At one point, he stared into my eyes and said, "I like your eyes. They're just like mine."

He was right. We had the exact same shade of hazel eyes.

Clouds gathered as the afternoon waned, and it was time for us to leave to meet up with our group. We went to Subway and bought Jesse a sandwich for dinner. He thanked us, and we said goodbye. It started to rain as we walked down the street, and Simeon pulled a rain jacket out of his backpack and gave it to me.

That summer stands out in my mind as a testament to the power of what I can do if I choose to engage with the world instead of isolating myself. To press in — instead of pulling back. To do hard things that I've never done before.

That day in particular stands out as the best possible beginning to a future of engaging with the world. Simeon and I are still partners and still trying to be Jesus for people. We've been married for seven years. He serves as a pastor in the United Methodist Church, and we recently welcomed our son Elijah into the world.

— Brooke Adams Law —

10

Promise Me!

*A mentor is someone who sees more talent
and ability within you, than you see in yourself,
and helps bring it out of you.*
~Bob Proctor

The folding doors opened. I clambered up the short set of stairs, dropped my fare into the change receptacle, and then inched my way down the narrow aisle that divided the seats on either side of the city bus. When it jerked into motion, I grabbed hold of one of the leather hand loops that hung from the ceiling, swaying back and forth as the bus buzzed down the freeway and then zigzagged its way along the downtown streets. From the smudged glass windows, I watched the lavender early morning as it lit the steel and glass monoliths. Just before my destination, I pulled the wire signaling the driver to stop at the next corner. When the folding doors opened. I stepped down onto the sidewalk and stared up at the glistening giant that now stood before me.

I walked forward, but the sidewalk, damp from an earlier rainstorm, forced me into a child's game of leapfrog over small pools of water. I smiled, remembering the fun I had as a little girl, jumping in puddles and scattering water over my red rain boots. But those days were long past. I was seventeen going on eighteen, and it was the first day at my summer job working for an insurance company in downtown Dallas.

I checked my reflection in the huge plate-glass window, adjusted my dress, moistened my fingers, and smoothed my bangs. I slid through the revolving glass door and took the elevator to the tenth floor where Nancy, my supervisor, greeted me with her arms folded across her chest.

"You must be my new summer recruit," she said in a wheezy voice. Nancy twisted open her tattered cigarette case, retrieved a cigarette, and positioned it in the corner of her mouth. She struck a match and brought the tip of the match to the end of her cigarette, engulfing it in the match's tiny flame. She inhaled and then flicked her match onto the floor, extinguishing it underneath her shoe. Nancy did an about-face. "Follow me," she demanded, cigarette smoke billowing from her nostrils. She marched across the scuffed-up, gray linoleum floor. I stepped behind her, keeping my elbows tucked in as we paraded down the narrow strip of tiles between row upon row of army-green file cabinets that appeared to be standing at attention waiting for her next command.

"We use a color-coded, alphanumeric filing system. It's all explained in here." She handed me a weathered-looking booklet. "Understanding this system will help you pull files for insureds' whose policies are up for renewal. You pull files every morning. Once the policies are rated, typed, and mailed, then they're re-filed. Re-filing is done every after-noon. Don't leave until you've re-filed the files in your section. This," she pulled my time card from the clock-card machine, "is where you'll punch in. Remember to punch in every day, or you won't get paid. Be on time. No dilly-dallying in my department," she said with her lips tightly pursed. "And remember, the work we do here is important, so don't be sloppy."

Using one of her nicotine-stained fingers, Nancy tapped her cigarette ashes onto the floor and handed me a piece of paper. "Here's the list of files to pull this morning. Bring 'em to me once you're done. Lunch is from 12:00 to 12:30; you can bring your own lunch or eat in the cafeteria on the sixth floor. You get all that, recruit?"

"Yes, ma'am," I replied. I resisted the urge to salute.

"Now, get to work!" Nancy did another about-face and marched toward her office.

Thus began my first summer job. Despite Nancy's brusque personality, I liked working for her. Yes, she was direct. But she was clear and to the point, and I always knew where I stood with her. During the ensuing weeks, Nancy taught me some important office skills — typing, filing, time management, answering the telephone, problem solving, and handling conflict with strangers. As a result, I matured and became more confident.

When summer came to an end, I contemplated quitting high school and continuing to work. But when Nancy learned of my plan, she hailed me into her office. "Look at me," she huffed, her chest pushing out smoke in rapid, deliberate bursts. "I don't have a family. I don't have a career. I don't have beauty or a man. I don't have money, and I sure as hell don't have a future. Don't settle for life here like I did. Don't sell yourself short. Don't do it!" There was protest in her eyes. "You're smart as a whip and one of the smartest recruits I've ever had. You're sure as hell better than this place. Don't be mediocre. You'll trap yourself and become cynical like me. Leave this place! Graduate from high school. Go to college. Don't come back here. Promise me!" Nancy ground her smoldering cigarette into her ashtray. "Promise me that!"

"Okay, Nancy!" I agreed, rather shocked. "Okay! I promise."

And I was true to that promise, never forgetting the crusty woman who steered me away from a dead-end job and down the path toward high-school graduation and college. College was difficult, though, and I often doubted myself and my ability to continue. On more than one occasion, I wanted to quit. But in those moments when I struggled, Nancy's advice echoed in my mind, encouraging me and giving me the fortitude to carry on. I kept my promise to her and graduated from college, obtaining a teaching certificate with a major in business and English.

When I walked across the stage on graduation day and received my diploma, I looked out upon the crowd. For just a moment, I thought I saw Nancy applauding from a front-row seat. She wasn't there, of course, but she was there in spirit. To this day, I'm grateful for Nancy; her advice altered the course of my life and forever changed me. My college education strengthened me and led to a life rich with possibilities and adventures. I wouldn't have experienced any of it had

Nancy not been passionate enough and brave enough to challenge me to a promise — to claim a life beyond mediocrity.

— Sara Etgen-Baker —

Chapter
2

How to Be Successful

11

Like an Airport

I believe that if one always looked at the skies,
one would end up with wings.
~Gustave Flaubert

The best advice I've ever heard was given to me by one of my college professors. At the time, I was living in Chicago and attending a wonderful university there, majoring in writing. One of my professors was a highly successful author who had written many books for young people, something I aspired to do. I was grateful just to be in her class, but in a one-on-one after-class conference, she commented on how seriously I took my writing. From her perspective, writing was not just an interest or hobby for me; it was my greatest passion.

"Do you want to make a career of this?" she asked.

I'd known the answer to that question since I was thirteen.

"Definitely," I assured her.

"There's an approach you should take then," she said. "In order to launch a successful writing career and, more importantly, sustain it, you need to treat your career like an airport."

I was puzzled. "Connect with a lot of people?" I asked.

"Well, yes," she said, "but you need to have a writing project taking off, landing, and boarding—constantly."

Given I had spent a year of my younger life working for a commercial airline, I not only appreciated the analogy, I understood it. Movement and action produced results. I needed to be diligent as a writer. I needed to produce a lot of work in order to reach the level of success I was aiming for — and capable of. I needed to take what I was doing seriously and practice self-discipline.

Immediately, I took the advice and applied it to what was then a tiny spark of a career. I looked at the projects I had completed and my works-in-progress. I put together an action plan (or, as I came to call it, a flight plan). This included small, achievable goals, a solid timeline, and a short list of objectives (i.e., What did I hope to accomplish by completing my plan?).

I set my plan for take-off, and that's exactly what it did. My writing career ignited. Within the first month, an excerpt from one of my stage plays was published in an anthology. This led to theatre producers and teachers reaching out to me with interest in my script. This resulted in three productions of my play. One of the high schools invited me to come and speak to their young playwrights. A week after that, I was invited to attend a high-profile literary festival to discuss my work. There, I found out about a wonderful writing workshop in New York that was being instructed by one of my favorite playwrights. I applied to the workshop, and was not only accepted, but I submitted my script and received a workshop scholarship in response. While at the conference where the workshop was held, I made considerable contacts that led to more productions and professional opportunities. Once I got home, I immediately put together my next flight plan.

> "You need to have a writing project taking off, landing, and boarding— constantly."

Fast forward nearly two decades (and many flight plans later), and I'm still applying my professor's advice to my writing life every day. The results have been beneficial (and life-changing) beyond measure.

One of the many perks of being a writer is that I get to travel extensively. In truth, my writing has taken me around the world. As someone who spends a considerable amount of time in airports, travel time is never lost on me. On each occasion, I'm reminded of that fateful conversation I had years ago in Chicago that completely changed the trajectory of my life as a writer.

Every project that boards, takes off, and lands serves as the ultimate reminder to me to always be receptive to advice. You never know where expert co-piloting (guidance) will come from. I am eternally grateful to my professor (who has since written more than fifty books for young people), who saw something in me that inspired her to reach out and give me words of wisdom — the invisible wings I needed to fly.

— David-Matthew Barnes —

Hit by Lightning

Be who you are and say what you feel,
because those who mind don't matter,
and those who matter don't mind.
~Bernard M. Baruch

My son stared stoically out the window of the car. Looking closely, I saw the tracks of earlier tears on his cheeks. What had happened? He'd been fine when I dropped him off at school. What could have gone so wrong in the past seven hours? How could he possibly look so sad when he should be so happy?

Two weeks previously, my son had been selected for a scholarship to attend the college of his choice because of his academic accomplishments and community service. Our entire family had been in a celebratory mode. We were so grateful for the news. It was such a wonderful achievement and relief to know we would get financial assistance for his college education.

So what had gone wrong? Why such a sad face and downcast eyes?

I finally got the answer after a few hours of probing. I learned that my son's scholarship news had generated jealousy among his friends. Not only were these classmates unsupportive, but their comments reflected resentment that he was thinking about "going away" to college. Since he was "a nerd" and "so rich" now, they said he might as well go away, because he wasn't welcome with them anymore.

As his mother, I felt I should know how to make everything

better, but I didn't. The mocking and bullying didn't make sense to me. I kept wondering how something so positive had been twisted into something so negative. I searched for words of comfort, but nothing I said helped my son.

When the scholarship had first been announced, my son's school was as excited and proud as we were. The award reflected positively on the curriculum, teachers, and staff. The school had held a ceremony for the announcement. The news had been printed in the school paper, and a news release was sent to the media. I felt it must have been that publicity that triggered the recent comments — and, in the ensuing days, the negative rhetoric just kept coming.

For the first time in his life, my son did not want to go to school. He began saying he was not even sure he wanted to go to college. Nothing I said or did made any difference. Every day, he seemed more dispirited and downhearted. His sadness hung like a gray cloud over our whole family.

Nothing his teachers said had much impact either. Both his counselor and his principal offered words of encouragement, but there was not any change. The slump in his shoulders and the sadness in his eyes remained.

The taunts from his peers also kept coming.

After a few weeks, I felt my son was becoming seriously depressed. His world was crumbling. When he announced that he wanted to give up the scholarship, I knew something had to be done.

I decided to go up one more rung on the academic ladder and take him to visit the superintendent of schools. I didn't know the superintendent, having encountered him only at a few academic functions and community events, but no one else in the school system had been able to change my son's outlook. I was desperate.

The superintendent's office was in a separate administrative building, removed from the high-school campus. When we arrived, it was hard not to be impressed by the imposing and impressive surroundings. It was a very professional, successful atmosphere, and I felt fortunate this busy man had agreed to see us.

Our initial interaction centered around introductions, school activities, and congratulations on my son's scholarship. The superintendent, however, seemed to sense what was wrong and why we were there. He began to address my son directly and maintain eye contact only with him. They talked about the merits of education, how it was hard to change one's surroundings, and the benefits of new challenges. I can't recall his exact words, but it was something along the lines of the following:

"Whenever you decide to grow a little and extend yourself above the norm, there is always a danger you won't be the same. It's like the trees in the forest. When one tree decides to grow taller than all rest, that tree is most likely to get hit by lightning. It's a chance you take. When people are different, it seems like they're more likely to be attacked for those differences. I know this because when I was a teacher, I had no problems. I fit in with all the other teachers with whom I worked. I was surrounded by colleagues and friends. I wanted to be a principal, however, and when I achieved that goal, I found some of my colleagues and friends resented my advancement."

I remember wondering where he was going with this, but I noticed my son was sitting up in his chair and listening intently. He was obviously interested in this man's perspective, so the superintendent went on.

"When I decided to become the superintendent of all the schools in the system, it was even worse. I remember the resentment... the lack of encouragement. I know what you're feeling, but you can't let those feelings keep you from your goals — because I'll tell you a secret. You know those trees I mentioned, well, when you do grow taller, and you rise above all the other trees in the forest, you realize there is so much more to see. Your view is better than ever. You can see the sky, the stars, and everything else beyond your little local forest. Once you see what's out there, you realize you can't go back. You've seen it, and you're not the same. You want to grow taller and extend yourself even further because you want to see more. You want to do more. Don't be afraid to grow, son. In the long

> *"When you do grow taller, and you rise above all the other trees in the forest, you realize there is so much more to see."*

run, you won't regret it. I never have."

Well, I don't know if it was him, his words, the office, or the trees in the forest, but my son finally smiled. He shook hands with the superintendent, stood up a little taller, and, within a few days, returned to the bright, smiling, effervescent boy we'd always known.

In the weeks that followed, I tried to figure out what the difference was and why this man's advice had resonated. I believe my error was in downplaying the problem and telling my son that what other people said didn't matter. The superintendent knew that those words did matter to my son. He understood because he'd been there.

Years have passed, and my son is now a respected physician. I'm very proud of him, and I remain very grateful that one man took the time out of his busy day to give my son some personal and heartfelt advice that made all the difference.

— Billie Holladay Skelley —

Chicken Soup for the Soul

Strength and Surrender

You have power over your mind — not outside events.
Realize this, and you will find strength.
~Marcus Aurelius

My favorite yoga teacher is a woman named Wendy. I love her classes because she explores a "life philosophy" during each class, and years ago, she taught us a lesson that I still carry in my heart. While gently putting our class through the paces of downward dogs, warriors and cobras, Wendy advised us to "navigate life through the combination of strength and surrender."

Whether we're facing a medical issue, a career decision, or a personal choice, Wendy said we owe it to ourselves to use our strength to try to affect the outcome we want. She said we should use every resource available, and all the strength we have, to ferociously fight against illness, try and get the job we want, or maintain a relationship that's important to us.

Then she added, "But once all has been said and done — and you've explored every viable option — then it's time to surrender." She cautioned us that surrendering doesn't mean everything will turn out as you wish. It means it's now time to prepare a place in your heart to accept the outcome, come what may.

I've utilized this advice of "strength and surrender" many times, but two events stand prominently in my mind:

The first involved my career path. In my twenties, I worked in the entertainment business and had a successful career as a Visual Effects

Coordinator and Post Production Supervisor on music videos and commercials. As I worked on projects for Madonna, Michael Jackson and Eric Clapton, I knew how lucky I was to be given such fabulous opportunities, but I longed to work in television and film also. In particular, I wanted to work on a TV show or for National Geographic. I also wanted to work on a children's film. Most of all, I wanted to work on the Warner Bros. lot because I felt completely at peace every time I visited that studio.

I tried everything I could think of to get hired for my dream projects, but no doors would open. After many years of working on music videos and commercials, the ninety-hour workweeks began to feel tiring rather than exhilarating. I let my dreams of working in television and film go, left the business and surrendered to a gentler life working as an Event Coordinator at a comedy club. I worked at this job for three years and loved everything about it — especially my boss, Dana. When Dana announced she was leaving her position as General Manager, I reluctantly decided it was time for me to resign as well.

As fate would have it, a producer called and offered me a position on "a reality show that did well in the U.K., so they're going to try it here in America." Long story short, that TV show ended up being *American Idol*. So, out of the blue, there was the TV show I'd always wanted to work on! Oddly enough, what followed next was a film project for National Geographic and then a children's film on the Warner Bros. lot! I don't know why each of my career goals was fulfilled years after I stopped actively pursuing them, but I was grateful.

The second time I took Wendy's advice was when I started having health problems. I'd developed an autoimmune disease that attacked my eyes and knees. For quite a while, I had trouble walking and could only see shapes and colors. I'd heard the word "autoimmune" before, but I didn't really know what it meant. My doctors explained it's when the body erroneously identifies a body part as a "foreign object" and sends white blood cells to the area to attack the intruder. I repeated it back to my doctor because I couldn't believe it.

"My body thinks my eyes are foreign objects, so it is trying to destroy my eyes?"

The doctor said, "In a nutshell, yes."

My rheumatologist was able to find medication that eased the inflammation in my joints, but my ophthalmologist struggled to stop my body from attacking my eyes. As the weeks turned into months and my eyesight still had not returned, I began to worry. I told my ophthalmologist I needed a "realistic timetable" as to when my vision would return because I wasn't able to drive or work. When she said, "I don't know that your vision *will* return," I freaked out. I'd always assumed this was just a waiting game. Until that moment, it had never occurred to me that my eyesight might never return.

I called my husband Tom and my mom as the taxi drove me home. Tom said, "I know your doctor is incredible, but let's get a second opinion."

My mom said, "If your eyesight never returns, I'll learn Braille and teach it to you. I taught you to read when you were little, and I'll do it again if I have to. But let's not go down that path yet."

My mom and Tom researched the top ophthalmologists in the world and found that one of the leading experts was at the UCLA Stein Eye Institute near my apartment. At the Stein Eye Institute, the doctor did a thorough examination of my eyes and then took time to talk with me. He said he'd trained my doctor and she was one of the best he'd ever seen. He'd looked over her notes and was in complete agreement with her treatment course.

I said, "I know, I think she's phenomenal, too. But she said she doesn't know when, or even if, my eyesight will return, so I'm scared and want a second opinion."

The doctor took a deep breath and said, "The hardest thing in medicine, and in life, is that half the time, we can't predict the outcome. Sometimes, all we can do is vigorously treat the symptoms and hope for the best."

I went home, crawled into bed and cried. It was a deep, gut-wrenching, soul-cleansing cry because I knew I had shown strength and exhausted every possible avenue toward recovery. Now it was time to surrender.

The next morning, I felt sad but calm. I accepted that either my eyesight would return or it wouldn't. And if it didn't, my mom and Tom would be there to help me transition into my new lifestyle.

Tom continued to give me medicated eye drops around the clock, and I helped myself by resting and eating healthfully. Gradually, and to my relief, my eyesight eventually returned, and my life went back to normal.

I've been lucky so far. I've gotten the outcomes I've wanted in most cases. There are projects I'm currently working on that appear to be at a standstill or to have hit a dead end. There are doors that remain closed no matter how politely and persistently I knock. There are barriers I can't seem to get around and hurdles I can't seem to clear. But I quiet myself with the knowledge that I have chosen to walk through life trusting in the strange and often serendipitous dance of strength and surrender.

— Rebecca Hill —

14

Your Inner Circle

A friend knows the song in my heart and
sings it to me when my memory fails.
~Donna Roberts

While I was in college in my early twenties, I was given an assignment to interview someone in the mass communications industry. Fortunately, one of my older cousins, Mil, was a videographer and producer in the Atlanta area and agreed to help me. Mil is roughly eight years older than me, and at this point he had an amazing career. I really looked up to him and was in awe of his accomplishments.

As Mil and I sat down to lunch, he told me grand stories about his adventures, and I was totally enthralled. Then, out of nowhere, he became somber and said to me, "Elaine, you will meet three kinds of people: The ones who lift you up and inspire you. The ones who keep you grounded and remind you to be humble. And the ones who drag you down. Learn how to identify them. Find mentors and let them lead you. Know who loves you and will always be there to pick you up should you fall. But, most importantly, learn to recognize those who drag you down. They are always wanting from you, but never have anything to give back. That is the hardest one because sometimes the people who drag you down are the ones you love the most."

I could tell by the timbre of his voice and the look in his eyes that not only was he speaking from his heart, but from personal experience. I felt bad for him because I knew that someone he loved had left that hurtful imprint on his heart.

I was pretty young and didn't grasp exactly what he was saying to me until years later when I was in my mid-thirties and having some struggles in my life. People were hurting me and calling it love, but I was so loyal to them that I couldn't see it. One day I was at lunch with my boyfriend Bart, a very special man whom I will always love and respect. He looked me in the eyes and said, "When things go wrong in your life, always take a look at your inner circle. That's all you have to do. Take a hard look at the people you are allowing to influence your life. Ask yourself if they are a positive influence or a negative one. When you have your answer, make a change. You can control this situation, or stop it, by changing your inner circle."

> **"When things go wrong in your life, always take a look at your inner circle."**

I was blown away by the simple yet shrewd advice I was given. Bart's comment instantly took me back to that day with my cousin Mil over a decade earlier. Suddenly, I understood exactly what Mil was saying to me all those years ago, and what Bart was saying to me then. Thinking back, I see that this was a powerful message — so powerful that God sent it to me twice. First Mil, whom I looked up to as a young adult, planted the seed. Then Bart, whom I love and trust, made it grow.

Today, I am in my mid-forties, and this advice still sticks in my mind. I strive each day to keep my inner circle full of people who are going to lift me up or keep me humble, and I will not hesitate to cut ties to someone who tries to bring me down.

— Elaine Jolly —

15

Just Like Katey

If you set goals and go after them with all the
determination you can muster, your gifts
will take you places that will amaze you.
~Les Brown

School was starting soon, and I was nervous about my junior year of high school and the changes being an upperclassman might bring. I wanted to apply for the national honor society, become a member of the Tri-M Music Honor Society, and run for an officer position in Communications Club, an organization I had been involved with since sixth grade. But I didn't think I had enough talent for any of those positions and feared rejection.

My best friend Katey and I were meeting for dessert at Panera Bread. When we sat down at the table, I was quiet, and Katey could tell something was bothering me. When she asked me what was wrong, I opened up to her. I explained how nervous I was about starting eleventh grade, and about the things I feared I couldn't do. Then I asked Katey how she accomplished so much. I had always envied her because she seemed to get everything she wanted. She was a drum major in the school marching band and held first chair in the flute section in wind ensemble. Why couldn't I be like Katey?

Katey looked me straight in the eye and said, "Colleen, every year I set five goals for myself and work very hard to reach them."

I had to laugh at that. Katey got everything she wanted just by setting goals? That sounded absolutely ridiculous. Katey looked at me once more. "Colleen, I want you to set five goals for yourself this year." Even though I still thought the idea of setting goals was absurd, I said I would give it a try.

Later that night, I wrote down five goals for myself: to make Tri-M, be inducted into National Honor Society, become an officer of Communications Club, be more positive about myself, and get straight A's at least one term.

I still thought setting goals wouldn't help me achieve anything, but it was worth a shot. And I wanted to enjoy the kind of success that Katey had.

School started and I worked on achieving my five goals. In October, I wrote a speech about why I would be a good officer for the Communications Club. It was incredibly difficult for me to get up and recite my speech in front of my fellow club members because I was shy and not used to being the center of attention. However, I used every ounce of courage I had and I did it. I was elected to an officer position because of my entertaining and persuasive speech.

In November, I applied for Tri-M and was accepted. As part of the induction ceremony, I sang in a recital for all the new inductees. It was a surreal experience. I used to only sing in my room with the door shut and wouldn't even sing for my family and friends. Finally gaining the confidence to sing in front of people was truly indescribable.

After my success with Tri-M, I applied for the National Honor Society, which was a very long process. I had to collect signatures from the advisors of the clubs and activities I participated in and write an essay on why I should be a member of NHS. It was a lot of work but definitely worth it when I was inducted in December.

I had achieved my top three goals in only the first few months of eleventh grade. I continued to set goals for myself during my junior and senior years of high school and accomplished more than I ever dreamed I would. I got the lead role in a play, got a scholarship at the end of my senior year, and became vice president of Project Support, an organization that helps students with disabilities make friends.

Katey's advice to set five goals really worked. I learned to be self-confident and to reach for whatever I dreamed of, because it turned out that I could achieve way more than I had imagined. I could be just like Katey.

— Colleen Perisutti —

16

Turn On the Light

We worry about what a child will become tomorrow,
yet we forget that he is someone today.
~Stacia Tauscher

The spring before our son Hank was scheduled to enter kindergarten, we were invited to what the school called "Kindergarten Roundup." That somewhat rowdy title led me to believe that Hank and I would be enjoying an evening filled with cowboy themes and pretend rodeos — a fun night.

We arrived to find an inch-high stack of forms to complete and several on-the-spot tests to see where Hank ranked academically.

Somewhat nervously, I watched from the edge of a hard plastic chair as Hank recited the alphabet, counted as high as he could, bounced on both feet at different times and different speeds, and arranged blocks in a series of confusing patterns that lost me almost immediately. Hank did all right with the blocks, but bogged down when trying to identify a series of pictures. When the tester held up a drawing of a dress and asked him what it was, Hank didn't have a clue. "I barely wear dresses anymore," I whispered to her apologetically.

"That's all right," the tester said, dropping the dress card and looking at Hank with sympathy. "It isn't your fault, Hank," she added.

Sinking down in my blue jeans, I continued to watch the testing. Hank persevered, and half an hour later we were almost done with the Roundup.

"All right, Hank," the tester told him, "just a few easy questions, and you'll be all set for kindergarten." She glanced over at me and explained, "We're looking for logical conclusions. We want to hear what Hank thinks is the logical thing to do in each situation."

I smiled back at her, but inside I felt a fresh flash of panic. Suppose Hank couldn't reach any logical conclusions? Would they keep him out of kindergarten until he could? What if he never could? Visions of the two of us figuring out the logical conclusion to every move he might make for the rest of his life danced rapidly through my head.

Eating too much sugar? Tooth decay!

Skipping gym class without an excuse? Visit to the principal's office!

Forgetting to file your tax returns seven years in a row? Federal prison!

They were not heartwarming scenarios.

"What happens when the doorbell rings?" the woman asked.

"My mom answers it," Hank replied. My shoulders relaxed slightly. So far, so good.

"What do you do when your tummy growls?"

"I ask my mom for something to eat."

The woman giving the test nodded her head. "Okay, Hank, tell me what you'd do if you went into a dark room."

Thinking hard for a few seconds, Hank raised his head triumphantly. "Be brave," he said.

The tester waited a moment before prompting, "What else would you do? Wouldn't you turn on a light?"

"Oh, yeah," Hank said, "if I could reach it."

> **All I could think about was how many events awaited him when being brave right off the bat was going to be a huge help.**

Obviously, being brave wasn't the answer the school district wanted, but as I listened, all I could think about was how many events awaited him when being brave right off the bat was going to be a huge help. School. Job interviews. Marriage. Parenthood. Aging. While it's smart to turn on a light for illumination, it never hurts to be brave while you're waiting for your eyes to adjust to the glare. From the mouth of my own child, I realized that I'd been handed a nugget of advice that applied to my own life just as much as it did to my son's.

Hank and I left Kindergarten Roundup a bit more solemn than when we'd arrived. This kindergarten stuff involved more than either of us had expected. "Who's ready for ice cream?" I asked, thinking we both deserved a small reward.

"I am," Hank said. "Going to school is harder than I thought it would be, but I think it's going to be all right."

Smiling, I took his hand. Hank was going to be just fine. And so was I.

— Nell Musolf —

17

The Sensitive Plant

Life is inherently risky. There is only one
big risk you should avoid at all costs,
and that is the risk of doing nothing.
~Denis Waitley

ts scientific name is *mimosa pudica*, but my mother always called it the sensitive plant. It's a fern-like herb with rows of green, narrow leaves that fold together, like strips of tiny fingers, whenever the plant is touched or shaken. The plant is originally from more tropical climes, but it is now grown all over the world as a houseplant.

I don't remember a time when my mother didn't have her sensitive plant in the ceramic pot on the windowsill over the kitchen sink. It always got the afternoon sun and stayed the right temperature. My mother claimed the plant loved the extra humidity it received from the hot, steamy water when she washed dishes.

I loved to gently run my index finger along the plant's stems and watch the leaves quickly fold together.

"Somebody's been messing with my sensitive plant, David," my mother would joke when she found the plant's leaves all tucked tightly together. "I wonder who?"

The December when I came home from my first semester of college was a stressful time. I was upset with my performance so far, and although they tried not to dwell on my dismal grades, I know my parents were disappointed, too.

One morning after the holidays were over I was having a cup of coffee at the kitchen table when my mother wandered in and poured a steaming mug for herself.

"I've been thinking," I said. "I'm going to see if I can find a full-time job next week."

"What about school?" my mother asked as she sat down across from me and added a splash of cream to her mug.

"I don't think college is for me," I replied. I took a sip of my coffee and shook my head. "Especially after how last semester went. With my grades, I can't face going back there."

"David, you can't be serious," my mother said.

"I'd rather get a job than go back to college and risk another semester of disaster," I replied.

My mother shook her head. "You can't do anything in life, anything at all, without taking some risks. You'll even be taking risks if you get a job." She pointed to the windowsill over the sink. "You can't go through life like my sensitive plant."

"What?" I asked.

"You're a human being." She got up, went to the window, picked up her sensitive plant and placed it between us on the kitchen table. "You can't be like this plant," she said, sitting back down.

"What's wrong with your plant?"

"Nothing," she answered, toasting the sensitive plant with her mug of coffee. "I like this plant — but it's a plant, not a person."

I shrugged my shoulders. "I don't get it."

"Look," she said, as she reached out with her index finger and ran it along one of the plant stems. The fern-like leaves closed up tight. "That is what you're doing with college." She ran her finger along another stem. "And this is how you're dealing with those grades." She continued to touch the plant as she talked. "The plant doesn't want to risk anything, so it just closes up and hides. When it opens back up a few minutes from now, the plant will just close again and again every time it senses there's a risk."

"So, basically you're saying I'm just avoiding the situation," I said.

"Life for us isn't like it is for this sensitive plant," explained my mother. "We don't always get the afternoon sun. Sometimes, it's too hot or too cold. Even if we're afraid of risks, we can't just close ourselves off from life's uncertainties."

My mother and I sat silently at the table for a while. Slowly, the leaves of the plant began to open once again.

"You're saying that I should just deal with it and go back to college," I said. "Right?"

"That's what I'm saying," replied my mother. "And it seems the sensitive plant agrees with me." The leaves of the plant had once again opened up.

So, a few weeks later, I headed back to college. I did graduate eventually, thanks to some wise advice from my mother and the example of her sensitive plant.

—David Hull—

18

Two Kinds of People

Character is doing the right thing
when nobody's looking.
~J.C. Watts

Our boys had taken the recycling bin out to the street the night before, because our morning pickup was at the crack of dawn. The next morning, I discovered Old Man Winter's cruel joke. The relentless South Dakota wind had turned cardboard boxes into winter's version of tumbleweeds. They were scattered everywhere. I needed to run out and gather them before the collection truck pulled up. I zipped insulated coveralls over my PJs, added a parka and scarf, and then sealed myself up with mittens and a cap. I scurried out the door and zigzagged across the driveway like a chicken pecking for seeds.

In a few moments, I'd snagged the stray boxes and crammed them into the bin. It was a good thing. My face was quick to remind me that exposed skin in below-zero temperatures is not a good idea.

I was ready to dash back into the house when I spied it. One of the cardboard boxes had made its merry way to the park next door. I grimaced as I fought the temptation to leave it there. I stood frozen (figuratively and literally) as the words my father had spoken years before began to echo in my brain.

I could hear his voice as it carried over the sound of burgers sizzling from the heat of Kingsford charcoal briquets. In the background, cows were meandering and mooing as they made their way from the field to the stock tank. I sniffed the sweet smell of freshly cut alfalfa. I was sitting cross-legged on the picnic table as we made small talk. I asked him how his day at work had been.

He indicated it was fairly typical: conference calls, meetings, and paperwork. And then he caught himself and said that one interesting thing had happened. Someone in the hallway had walked past a piece of garbage.

He had my attention. *What was so important about a piece of garbage?* I thought.

He went on to describe the scenario. His place of business had rather long hallways. He said he noticed a wrapper at the end of the hall. He kept himself back and observed the number of people who walked past it. He could tell that some of the folks had seen it but chose not to stop. Eventually, someone picked up the wrapper and plopped it in the mouth of a waiting garbage can.

And then my dad said something that has stuck with me ever since.

"I learned today that there are two kinds of people in the world—the kind who, when they see garbage, will stop and pick it up… and the kind who won't."

He continued, "It made me realize that we all get to decide what kind of person we're going to be—a person who leaves the world better than how they found it, or a person who doesn't."

Then he looked at me with a smile and his penetrating, blue eyes. I knew that he was asking me, without saying it out loud, "What kind of person will you be?"

It's been forty years since that conversation. I've lost track of how many times his unspoken advice has affected the choices I've made. Some of those decisions were of major consequence; my career, my marriage, my callings… all of them were influenced by those words.

And yet, the truth is, those big decisions were shaped by hundreds of little choices that youth gave me the opportunity to make first:

Classmate being bullied? Stand up for him.

Money to spend? Save it up.

Litter in the street? Pick it up.

Want to give up? Pull yourself up.

Each time, I had a decision to make. And the backdrop for them all? "There are just two kinds of people in the world."

Today, my father's advice is finding its way into my kids' lives. Their choices regarding vocation and how they conduct themselves in relationships, as well as being of service to others, are being influenced by that unspoken challenge: "What kind of person will you be?"

I'm grateful for his words, but even more for the way he modeled what it looks like to leave the world better than how you found it.

Oh, and that renegade cardboard box? You already know what happened. Despite having all the mobility of a Michelin Man bubbled in layers of clothing, I ran to the park, snagged the box and, with a grin as broad as my frozen face would allow, slam-dunked it into the bin!

My dad's been gone for more than a decade now, but I still tell him I get it: *Two kinds of people, Dad… two kinds of people.*

— Cindy K. Krall —

Learning to Run My Own Race

*Don't rely on someone else for your happiness and
self-worth. Only you can be responsible for that.*
~Stacey Charter

A few years ago, I decided to take the plunge and start working from home. I was a stay-at-home mom with two young boys, feeling a bit lost after leaving the working world. I desperately wanted something to focus on that had nothing to do with diapers or sippy cups. I also longed for an excuse to connect with other adults on a regular basis.

Only a few weeks into my new adventure, I realized how quickly I was getting trapped in the comparison game. I found myself constantly comparing my progress (or lack thereof) with others on my team. I viewed their Facebook highlight reels as proof that this business was coming easily to everyone but me. Several times in those first few months, the crushing weight of comparison had me close to quitting.

Then one of the leaders on my team gave me some great advice: *Keep your blinders on.* You know the horses that wear blinders next to their eyes as they pull carriages around Central Park? They are there for a reason — to help the horses avoid distractions as they plod down the chosen path.

I took my leader's advice and put on my own blinders. I started to appreciate the little goals I was achieving in my business. I certainly wasn't making giant leaps and bounds like some others on my team, but as one small success led to another my confidence grew. I was proud of myself for doing something way outside my comfort zone.

Then I began to think about other dreams that had been buried deep inside my heart. I had always loved to write, and I had started a motherhood blog after my second son was born. But I had never been courageous enough to share any of my writing outside a small circle of friends and family. The thought of being compared and not measuring up to other mommy bloggers was crippling. But once again, those words of wisdom from my team leader crept into my head: *Keep your blinders on.* Don't let the distraction of comparison keep you from this dream.

So, with a hopeful heart, I submitted my first article to a parenting website. I was floored when it was accepted! I had other pieces published on other sites, and I was relieved not to be a one-hit wonder.

But then I found myself back in the comparison trap when my pieces didn't get quite as many "views" or "likes" as other pieces from other writers. The value I placed on my own words began to diminish. Maybe what I had to say really wasn't that important. I let the comparison game sap the joy that writing gave me and tarnish a dream I had held for over thirty years. I needed to put my blinders back on!

I've let comparison creep into other parts of my life as well. One of my biggest areas of struggle is motherhood. It is the petri dish for comparison. I often find myself gazing at another mom and thinking, *Look at her, keeping it all together with perfectly dressed children, a perfect mom body and not a hair out of place. Here I am with a baseball hat pulled down over my greasy hair, one kid with the remnants of breakfast still on his shirt, and the other with mismatched socks and crazy bed-head. I'm still trying to lose the baby weight, too. I am failing.*

Over the years, I've learned the hard way that comparing myself to others truly gets me nowhere. It thwarts my ambition and overshadows my successes. Whether in business, my writing, or motherhood, there will always be someone who is doing

> **I've learned the hard way that comparing myself to others truly gets me nowhere.**

it better. The truth is, I'm not running their race. I'm running my own. I have to keep going back to that advice: *Keep your blinders on.*

So, I focus on my own journey. I don't let others' accomplishments diminish my own. And I remind myself that it doesn't matter if I cross the finish line first or dead last. I'm in the race, and I'm enjoying it… at my own perfect pace.

— Mary Ann Blair —

20

Writers Are Powerful People

A word after a word after a word is power.
~Margaret Atwood

I was giving a talk at a writer's conference when a woman asked me how I found the courage to interview people for my articles. She said she would be too nervous to ask them questions.

It reminded me of myself when I first dared to think of becoming a writer. I always intended to write books for children, not for newspapers and magazines. I, too, thought I would be too afraid to ask questions of important people. Yet, in the course of my writing career, I have been in the presence of powerful people such as governors, senators, CEOs, corporate lawyers, and clergy. I have talked to big men who exerted physical power, and to bullies who claimed power through their nastiness. Sometimes I was so hesitant I thought of refusing an assignment, but I forced myself to do the interviews and get the stories.

How did I find the courage to interview those people? It was all due to a more seasoned writer, a friend who gave me some great advice at the beginning of my career. She told me to never forget my power.

My friend was small, soft-spoken, and kind. She didn't look like a powerful person and yet she was fearless with her writing, challenging accepted truths and shining a light on what readers deserved to know. Whatever qualms she might have had did not deter her from doing what she thought was important and right.

I assured the woman at the conference that it was okay to be nervous, but it needn't prevent her from doing her job. She had a unique voice that would help her structure her article and guide others to understand the subject. I could hear my friend's words flowing out as I continued. "Don't hold back," I said. "Writers are powerful people. We must fearlessly expose our deepest selves or the writing won't be good. A writer has to dig down into essentials, into principles and pain, into joy and delight, to engage the reader."

I also told her not to be afraid of rejection. It's inevitable that it will occur, but it is only a stepping-stone in one's career. A writer is someone who writes regardless of the obstacles.

I told her to respect her power, that writers influence the world. Our words galvanize political movements, change cultures, and excite passions. Whether writing fiction or non-fiction, poetry or essays, a writer puts into words emotions and perspectives that can spur others toward action or personal growth.

As I spoke, I saw her face brighten, her shoulders straighten, and her hopes rejuvenate. And when I told her about my children's books, about the dream that never faded and was realized, I could see that she was ready to claim her power.

I silently thanked my friend for the encouraging words that had so helped me and would now be instrumental in inspiring another writer's life.

— Ferida Wolff —

Chapter 3

Why Didn't I Think of That?

21

Gardening Again

Act as if what you do makes a difference. It does.
~William James

I am a great fan of gardening. My first solo experience with dirt was at eleven years old: a mix of flowers out by a big rock in the back of our yard. But even then I was too practical, reasoning that we could not eat flowers, so why grow them? So, until recently, my gardening had consisted of growing the vegetables of my foremothers. It's hard work, but life is always better with a garden.

During one of my gardenless (yes, that's a word) years as a middle-aged adult, I was back in college. I had reasoned that old people shouldn't take on loans for tuition. How would they live long enough and make enough money to pay them off? Educational loans are a young people's game, I decided. I actually knew people pushing sixty-five who had taken out loans in their young student years for college and were still making monthly loan payments.

So my practical, part-time college job was working as a school lunch lady at the local high school. When tuition and book charges were due, I knew I would still have at least one meal a day at school while awaiting my next paycheck.

One year I signed up for summer classes, and school was out. That meant no lunch-lady paychecks or free food. The lunch ladies I worked with gave me a going-away present: a five-pound jar of peanut butter. "You can always get day-old bread really cheap," they told me.

Summer school started. I stopped by the book window to buy

books before heading to the first class. I gave my list to the book lady, and she pulled what I needed from her shelves and ran the amounts through her cash register. She was probably familiar with students who nearly fainted when they heard the total. I gasped when she told me, and I turned to look out the large glass windows to compose myself. I had enough for books and nothing else. After putting gas in my car, paying rent and utilities, I wasn't going to eat all summer long.

Someone behind me spoke up. "If you like vegetables, our summer staff always leaves their fresh produce on that table you're standing near."

What has fresh produce got to do with the fact that I just emptied my bank account for summer-school books? I thought.

I looked at the table. There were some radishes and a bit of leaf lettuce—enough to make a salad—and a small collection of fresh herbs. I composed myself and turned to thank her before stuffing it all into my backpack. I scooped up my new books, smiled and started to leave.

"The season is just getting started, so you students can look forward to lots of fresh veggies," she called after me.

Every few days—and especially on Fridays—I took little bits of produce home, as did other students. Those vegetables were a lifesaver. If I hadn't had that produce and the peanut butter, my only other option would have been to stand in a food line at the local church every day, and that would have meant missing class.

One day near the end of the first summer-school session, the book lady was there and I asked her to pass on my thanks. "Please tell the gardening people I really appreciate the produce. It has been wonderful. I just don't understand why they bother."

The book lady smiled. "Never assume that people are doing fine," she said. "Always share whatever extra you have whenever you can." I didn't understand what that meant, but I thanked her again and went to class.

On the last day of the second summer session, I noticed a huge pile of produce and some beautiful garden flowers. The book lady was out, but it was the first time I suspected she was the one who was feeding me (and other students) all summer with fresh produce. The flowers were to celebrate.

My lunch-lady job started again the next week. I had done well in my classes and promptly forgot how difficult it could have been to eat that summer.

Years passed, and I resumed growing the occasional herb or random tomato plant. But last summer, I participated in a community garden project. In the very tiny space, a friend and I grew lettuce, chives, green beans, onions, carrots, and radishes. My friend insisted on some wildflowers, too.

I did most of the gardening because she had a busy summer, but there was enough for both of us. By midsummer, things started to get out of hand. We had too much of the lettuce, radishes, onions, etc. I figured I would just let the garden go to seed and turn it under. Of course, I had been bragging about my green thumb at work because we had all this produce.

> *"Never assume that people are doing fine."*

And then I thought about the new woman at work. She was kind of quiet and always went out to eat for lunch. "Would you like a few veggies?" I asked her.

She nodded. "I love veggies."

That evening, our garden needed a little water. I took home everything ripe, bringing the excess to work — green beans, lettuce, herbs and some wildflowers. When I gave the produce to my co-worker, I was embarrassed it was so little. She thanked me politely as we left for the day.

The next day, she caught me in the restroom. "I don't know that I thanked you adequately yesterday." Her eyes got misty. "We have been really struggling to put food on the table for a long time." I was speechless. "The night before you gave me the produce, we had to get food at the food bank." She stopped a minute to compose herself. "Those green beans were so sweet. We haven't had fresh stuff in so long. And the flowers…" She paused to compose herself. "People just assume you are doing fine. If they would just share that little bit extra whenever they could, it would have made our lives so much easier."

She was crying hard now. I was stunned by her words.

I realized I had heard what she was saying before… years before… from the book lady. She had fed me and other students for an entire summer because she had shared that little-bit-extra philosophy. I would have had to miss class and stand in a food line every day if it hadn't been for those fresh vegetables.

"You're welcome," I said to my co-worker, as I left her in the restroom. I realized that for the last two weeks since she had started work, she had gone without lunch, leaving the building so people would think she was eating elsewhere.

"Never assume that people are doing fine. Always share whatever extra you have whenever you can." That lesson was more important than all the classes I took that summer.

— Pamela A. Gilsenan —

22

Ask Them

Knowledge speaks, but wisdom listens.
~Jimi Hendrix

The best advice I ever got was from a "missionary" who'd previously been an executive for a large cosmetics company. I first met Larry when I helped out at a summer school in Mexico. We shared space in a church just across the border in a tiny Texas town. A fellow teacher and I spread our sleeping bags on the floor of the nursery every night during our two-week stay. Larry was living in a storage closet with no windows; there was barely room for a bed and some boxes of clothes and books.

Larry had been there for two years. Each morning, he got up and drove church groups across the border to build houses in the *colonias* (slum-like areas) on the outskirts of Matamoros. He was the crew boss and chief carpenter for the inexperienced teenage volunteers who arrived each week.

While we stayed at the church, Larry often joined us for the makeshift dinners we prepared in the church kitchen. Over mac and cheese, he shared his life story.

He explained that several years earlier, a church outreach program building inner-city houses got him started. He thought he'd seen poverty in Texas, but it was nothing like the slums surrounding Mexican cities just over the border.

"I decided," he said, "that while I was still young and strong enough, I had to do something to improve the lives of the poor peasants." He went on to explain how he'd found people willing to sponsor house-building expeditions into Mexico. Then the tiny church in Los Fresnos offered him a space to live.

We teased him about his untrained laborers. "Wouldn't it be easier," I asked, "just to build the houses yourself?"

Larry grinned. "Probably, but that's not the point. My crews receive even more than they give. Their experiences in the *colonias* change their hearts and challenge their attitudes. Besides," he explained, "each youth group brings with it enough money to pay for the supplies for a single house. We need the money as much as the manpower."

Larry's answer reminded me of a question I'd been meaning to ask him. I'd noticed that some of the homes were built from cinder blocks and others were framed from wood. "How do you decide," I asked, "which kind of house to build for each family?"

Larry gave me "the look." It was the look he gave to anyone he thought was being patronizing. He gave it often during the first few days of each group's visit.

Certainly, I hadn't meant to be patronizing. What had I said wrong? I tried again.

"Is it based on the amount of money a church group brings down or the kinds of supplies that are donated?"

Larry rolled his eyes again.

Thinking I'd missed something obvious, I pushed a bit. "No, really, Larry, how do you decide which type of house to build for a family?"

Larry looked straight at me and said, "You ask them."

When Larry worked for the cosmetics company, he respected his customers by asking them how they'd like to look. In the same way, he asked the families from the *colonias* how they'd like their homes to look.

Before meeting Larry, I often imposed my expectations on family members and the parents of my students. I didn't ask. Now I try to help them build the "houses" they dream of.

— Ellen Javernick —

23

Celebrating the Woman Who Did All the Work

*We often take for granted the very things
that most deserve our gratitude.*
~Cynthia Ozick

When I hung up the phone my heart sank as I thought about my mother, thousands of miles away. Her health had been steadily declining since we'd seen her during our last vacation. I reminded myself that we'd enjoyed her twenty-two years longer than the doctors had predicted. But I still found it hard to imagine my world without her.

With my birthday a week away, Mom had taken over the conversation that day, reliving every detail of my birth. I completely understood what those birthing memories meant to my mother because, when my children's birthdays rolled around each year, I always revisited every detail of their births. That's what mothers do.

Mom's birthday is twenty-two days after mine. If she made it that year, she'd turn eighty-nine. While I tried to remain positive, I needed to do something special for her "just in case," and I already knew what that was. I'd gotten the idea one night while folding laundry and listening to one of Amy Newmark's Chicken Soup for the Soul podcasts.

On this podcast, Amy told a great story by Peggy Purser Freeman called "Deconstructing My Birthday," from *Chicken Soup for the Soul: Think Possible*. In her story, Peggy finds a way to make her birthday more meaningful by giving to others. Amy then talked about how we should celebrate our mothers on our birthdays instead of ourselves. Why not? After all, they carried us for nine months and did all the work to get us here.

Amy's words really hit home. I've never cared much for celebrating my birthday, and I felt the same way Amy did. Not only had my mother gone through nine months of agony to carry me, but when it finally came time to deliver me, the doctor told her he'd have to knock her out cold. I was close to a ten-pounder, and Mom was tiny. I was trouble right away.

After a scary arrival, I mysteriously screamed day and night for several months, causing the doctors and my mother much concern. As a toddler and preschooler, I earned the nickname "Jill the Pill." As I grew, I earned my place as the black sheep of the family. Even though I thought I was a pretty decent kid, I'm probably responsible for almost every gray strand of hair on Mom's head. In fact, I'm sure I still cause her much worry.

If I wanted to pull off this idea by my birthday, I needed to get it out in the next day's mail. I grabbed a generic birthday card from my file box and wrote: "Dear Mom, Happy Birthday to Me!" In the card, I explained that my letter was a birthday present I was giving myself by celebrating the woman who had given birth to me.

> We should celebrate our mothers on our birthdays instead of ourselves.

My mother got her letter the day before my birthday. And while I knew she'd enjoy it, I was not prepared for her overwhelming response or the emotion in her voice. "You have no idea what a beautiful present you've given me," she said. "I've never received such a priceless gift in my life!"

Out of all the many thoughtful presents I'd given my mother over the years, none touched her so deeply. While I'd always expressed my love and appreciation to my mom, this time I'd gone into great detail, reminiscing about every single thing she had ever done for me as well as stellar moments in my life and even the horrendous times. Mom could see that my childhood wasn't all about me. I'd taken note of all the little as well as the big things that she had a hand in. She mattered a lot! I hadn't forgotten.

Months after my birthday, she was still thanking me. I even received a little note included with money she wasn't supposed to send that said, "Dear Jill, What a beautiful gift you sent me. I will cherish it always."

Not only did that little gift mean more than the world to my mother, it made a huge difference for me. When the day comes that my mother is no longer with me, at least I'll know that I celebrated her in the way that she deserved, and she received memories that meant more to her than any present on earth.

—Jill Burns—

The Possible Dream

*You are never too old to set another goal
or to dream a new dream.*
~C.S. Lewis

O n a warm spring day in 1976, I asked my college professor if we could talk after class. I revered Bob Barger. I had taken every history class he taught, whether I needed it to graduate or not. He was warm and personable, and brought each subject he taught to life. And, unlike many of the professors, he actually knew our names.

Although I was the oldest student in his class, I was attending college for the first time. During casual conversation before and after his lectures, I learned a little about his family and his values. If anyone could help me, he could. It was the end of the semester and the end of my classes with Dr. Barger. It was now or never.

I just had to know: Was my dream impossible? After the last student left, I asked Dr. Barger if he had a few minutes for me. As soon as he sat down, I took a deep breath and blurted out, as fast as I could: "I'd like to go to law school. What do you think?"

He didn't give me a quick answer. We talked about my hopes and what I wanted to accomplish. At the end of the conversation, he said, "You have the ability to do well in law school. You can do it." I had so many fears and doubts, and I paraded them out one by one.

"But there are hardly any women lawyers," I said.

"Then you can be one of the pioneers," he said.

"But I have three kids at home."

"You've managed to get your degree here. You can manage law school."

By then I was down to my last "but."

"But I'll be thirty-eight by the time I finish! I'll be so old."

Dr. Barger, who'd celebrated his thirty-eighth birthday at least twenty years ago, didn't laugh at me. Instead, he said, "In four years, you'll be thirty-eight anyway. Why not be thirty-eight as well as being a lawyer?"

Why not, indeed? That commonsense piece of advice changed my perspective and my life. I'd be older no matter what, so I might as well give law school a try. And so I did. It wasn't easy to juggle my family responsibilities, my studies, and, later, a job as a law clerk, but my children were good students and we did our homework together. I took law books with me to their swim meets, where a friend and neighbor whose children swam with mine was amazed that I was going to law school at my age.

To my surprise, I found that being older, with a supportive husband and family, gave me an advantage over younger people who were still finding their way. At thirty-eight, I graduated cum laude, passed the bar exam and started practicing law. Of course, I let Dr. Barger know that the advice he gave me hadn't been wasted.

I shared his advice and my own story with many others. Among them was a legal secretary who was considering law school. She wrote to thank me after she passed the bar exam. I gave Dr. Barger's advice to a friend with grown children who had always dreamed of being a schoolteacher. She had the same doubts that I'd had: She'd be too old to teach when she finished her education. She wasn't. She flourished as a teacher. "I never would have done it without your advice," she told me.

Not my advice — Dr. Barger's advice, repackaged and passed on. Oh, and my friend from swim meets? She followed my example, went back to school, and became a therapist.

Thirty-five years after I graduated, my college honored me and other graduates. Although Dr. Barger had been gone for many years,

I thanked him for his influence on my life. I like to imagine that he heard my thanks, and he knows that the advice he gave me has spread, like ripples on a lake, influencing many others and changing lives for the better.

—Josephine A. Fitzpatrick—

25

What You Is

Trust that in living true to yourself, you will attract
people that support and love you, just as you are.
~Jaeda deWalt

When I was in the fourth grade, many years ago, I had an autograph book. It was pink and white, with pinstripes. On the cover was a drawing of two old-fashioned, raggedy little girls. My best friend, Lisa, had given it to me. And, more than anything, I wanted Mamo, my grandmother, to sign it.

"Will you sign my book, Mamo?" I asked one Sunday afternoon. We were visiting in the living room, and the midday sun was falling across the carpet in long, gold bars.

"Why, I'd love to, baby," she said. I handed her the book, and she pawed through her handbag for a pen.

"Now let me think," she said, and she began to write. I remember watching her gentle, soft hands curl around the pen. Mamo always had manicured nails—and a heart of gold. She finished writing, closed the book, and handed it back to me. I could hardly wait to see what she'd written.

But I waited until evening when I was tucked tight into my bed. Then I reached over and snapped on the light. I opened the book to Mamo's page.

The words were captured in my grandmother's scrawl:

Be what you is, and not what you isn't. Because if you is what you isn't, you isn't what you is.

It was signed, *I love you, Mamo.*

"How odd," I whispered into the night. Somehow, I'd expected more. I didn't even understand the crazy, incorrect grammar. Mamo didn't talk like that. I was disappointed. I'd wanted something to touch my heart. I'd wanted something more.

Decades later, I found pleasure in the pursuit of words. I was finding success as a freelance writer, but I struggled with accepting my own voice. My own style. I'd find a favorite blogger, and I'd want to sound like her. I'd study how an author turned a phrase, and I'd want her voice. I fell in love with writer after writer and voice after voice, and I'd try to imitate those writers I loved.

> **Be what you is, and not what you isn't.**

Then one day, right after we'd moved into our old Victorian and cardboard boxes were stacked through the house like a tall, brown maze, I found the pink striped autograph book. Mamo had long passed away, but the book was nestled between old high-school yearbooks and my bedraggled childhood teddy bear.

I sat on the hardwood floor and opened it with careful hands.

And Mamo's page was right there. *Be what you is…*

Those words washed over me. Dear Mamo. When she'd written them with those kind, soft hands, on that long-lost afternoon, I'd been disappointed. I'd wanted more.

But as I read those words, washed in wisdom and time, they soaked into my soul. I could see Mamo, with her twinkling green eyes, her coiffed auburn hair, and a loving expression on her face. I could almost hear her. "Darling, use your own voice. Sound like yourself. Be who God made you to be. If you're trying to be someone else, you're losing out. You're losing you."

I've taken those words to heart, and I've found my own style. I still want to learn. I still want to grow. And I'll always admire others, too. But I'm happy to be who God made me to be.

There's joy and freedom in just being what I is.

— Shawnelle Eliasen —

26

The Third-Room Rule

Never settle for anything less than you want.
~PJ Harvey

learned many valuable things from my mother, a woman who developed a number of methods for coping with life's little challenges. Our family called the strategy she developed for checking into hotels "Mom's Third-Room Rule."

"Always hold out for the third room," she told us. "It's only after you reject the first two rooms that they realize you mean business and will give you a Good Room."

When you check into a hotel, she explained, the folks at the front desk size you up. Are you a business traveler in an expensive suit? You'll get the best the hotel has to offer. But our Midwestern family of four — Dad and Mom and two little girls — in two adjoining rooms? They probably figured that we'd settle for less.

Mom was never the kind of woman who'd settle for less. And she taught me well.

For instance? My recent stay at a resort hotel in California. When I checked in, the desk clerk gave me a room that had a pair of double beds, not the king-sized bed I'd requested. I was traveling alone; the last thing I needed was two beds. Plus, the beds were rather small — as, for that matter, was the room itself.

I returned to the front desk and politely asked for another room.

Room Number Two did have a king-sized bed, but the room faced a wall! The view from the window was of a vast expanse of cement.

I'd looked forward to a nice view of a lovely California town. But this room gave me a view of nothing but an alley. Plus, because of that vast wall, the room was rather dark. And it had a noisy air conditioner.

"The second room they give you will usually be worse than the one you've rejected," Mom always told us. Why? Perhaps to punish you for not just accepting that first room? Or maybe they assume that you'll give up and take what they've given you.

Not my mother!

I grew up watching Mom do the Three-Room Shuffle whenever the Warren family checked into a new hotel. (My dad, who wasn't persnickety about this kind of thing, wisely left these negotiations up to his wife.) As my sister and I got older and became more aware of the situation, it became a game to critique what was wrong with Rooms Number One and Two.

Our favorite place to play this out was at the Waldorf Astoria in New York City, where we stayed for a week each December while my dad attended a conference. In a classic hotel like this, the rooms within a price range can vary wildly. Our goal? To get good ones.

The first set of rooms they gave us was always mediocre. We promptly rejected them. "This won't do either," Mom would say after a brief look at their next offer. Once again, we'd troop back down to the front desk with all our luggage, where Mom's perseverance would finally be rewarded.

I have fond memories of our family—after turning down the first two sets of small, dark, noisy rooms we were offered—walking into an adjoining set of splendid, large, high-ceilinged hotel rooms with wonderful views.

"This is more like it," Mom would say happily. That was our signal to unpack and settle in.

With this in mind, I took one look at The Room That Faced a Wall and returned to the front desk. "Call me a *kvetch*," I told the desk clerk, "but a room that faces a cement wall doesn't say 'spa vacation' to me. It says 'incarceration.' Can we try again?"

As she handed me yet another room key, I thought of Goldilocks and the Three Bears. First room? Beds too small. Second room? Faces a wall. But the third room?

It turned out to be a large, quiet corner room on the fourth floor. There was a comfy-looking, king-sized bed, a lovely reading chair, and a view of Walnut Creek with the California hills in the distance.

Perfection!

Thanks, Mom, I thought, as I opened my suitcase and settled in.

— Roz Warren —

27

Just Do It

The most effective way to do it, is to do it.
~Amelia Earhart

I was always such a procrastinator. I remember it affecting my health and wellbeing even back in fifth grade. I still recall the autumn day that I was stuck inside working on a project about Canada while my brother was playing touch football with our neighbors. I loved touch football and I was so disappointed that I was missing the game. But I had waited until the last day before this project was due, even though it had been assigned a month earlier.

You would think I would have learned a lesson but I continued to procrastinate all the way through school. I didn't even finish all my college applications, driving my mother crazy. I only applied to three colleges, and had no safety school, because I did the applications on the last day they could be mailed out.

I continued doing things last minute, in a panic, in college. I recall one time that I called my brother and had him read one of my high school papers to me over the phone while I scrawled it down on paper. Then I typed it up and submitted it for a freshman year expository writing assignment. I would get to the end of a semester and have to do four months' worth of work in one week. That meant pulling all-nighters, not doing my best work, and, ultimately, getting sick because I was so exhausted.

Then, during my sophomore year, I was over at my boyfriend's, hanging out with his roommates and complaining about how I had one week left before the end of the term and I had to write three papers and study for two final exams. I was afraid I would never get it done. And yet I was frozen, so fearful that I hadn't even started to dig my way out of the mess I had made.

My boyfriend's roommate Aris, who was pre-med, must have been tired of my complaining. He looked at me and matter-of-factly said, "Just do it."

That seems so simple, right? But those three words, which were really the gentlest of rebukes, snapped me right out of my paralysis. And I thought, *He's right. I can complain about it, or I can just do it. I need to pick one thing and get started, and then I'll do the next thing and the next thing and they will all get done.*

> *I can complain about it, or I can just do it. I need to pick one thing and get started.*

Aris's simple words cut through my logjam. I went back to my dorm room and I got to work, methodically starting and finishing each of my long-delayed projects. And I never treated my workload the same way again. I've been repeating those words to myself for more than forty years now: *Just do it.* With the underlying message, *Stop feeling sorry for yourself. You signed up for this. You can get it done. But getting it* done *involves* doing it!

People say I'm a machine now. And they ask how I get so much done. I owe it all to those simple words, and their underlying message that I should stop thinking about it, and just power through whatever impossible tasks I've taken on. "Just do it" was my personal mantra long before it became a popular corporate slogan. Sorry, Nike.

— Amy Newmark —

28

Photographs and Memories

We are making photographs to understand
what our lives mean to us.
~Ralph Hattersley

Several years ago, I attended a memorial service for a friend's mom. As people eulogized her, I kept looking at the framed picture perched on an easel beside the closed casket. It was an old, grainy, black-and-white shot taken when she was about twenty. The photo was faded and the young women in it had posed with a solemn look on her face. She bore no resemblance to the vibrant elderly lady I'd known, with her bright eyes, sculpted features, and laugh lines that were a testament to a life well lived.

I gazed at it for a long time, wondering why the family would select such an outdated photo since most of us attending the service could not relate to the young woman staring back at us.

It wasn't until weeks later when I was helping my friend go through her mother's home and possessions that I dared to ask why she'd opted to display a picture that was taken so long ago.

"We didn't have a lot of photos of my mother," my friend confessed regretfully. "Mom always ran away from the camera. I wish I had more pictures to remember her by, but there was only a handful in a small shoebox to choose from."

"You come from such a large family," I pointed out, surprised. "Surely some of you must have had a few pictures you took over the years."

"We looked," she admitted, lowering her eyes to fold a lace blouse lovingly before she placed it in a pile to donate. "We went through dozens of albums, and there was nothing. When the camera came out, Mom always found an excuse to leave the room. Even when we asked her to pose for a group shot, she'd refuse. She claimed she wasn't photogenic and didn't want to ruin the picture." The sadness in her voice touched my heart, and a chill of shame ran through me.

When we were finished and I was about to leave, I hugged my friend and, again, expressed my condolences.

"Do yourself and your family a favor, Marya," she told me wistfully as we pulled apart. "I know you hide from the camera, too — but stop. Leave something for your son to look at when he's missing you years from now — something he can show his own kids when he talks about you. Give future generations a face to go with the name."

> *"I know you hide from the camera, too — but stop."*

Her words stayed with me on the long bus ride home. That night, I waited until everyone was in bed before I took out my photo albums. I leafed through the pictures that memorialized the last thirty years of my life, knowing what I'd find. I was saddened by how few there were of me. The ones where I did appear were close-ups of my averted face or a protesting hand trying to cover the lens. Others showed me with my head bowed or my hair falling forward to hide my features.

The last picture I reluctantly posed for was at my son's christening. There were plenty dated before then, but when it became evident I wouldn't lose my "baby fat" I began to avoid the camera. I became the photographer instead of the subject, seizing every opportunity to avoid yet another gruesome picture of my flabby thighs or protruding tummy.

I continued turning the laminated pages that held hundreds of images of my loved ones. Some were good, some bad, some downright awful, capturing them in unflattering angles and grimaces, yet each one was precious to me because of the many tender memories. Whatever made me think that similar ones of me wouldn't mean as much to those I love?

I recalled my friend's bittersweet smile when she explained her mother's shortage of photographs. I realized my vain, distorted perception of no longer having the perfect face or body made me guilty of the same transgression.

I cringed with remorse when I remembered how many times I'd reached into a batch of newly developed pictures and torn up the ones I believed fell short of perfection. When we bought our first digital camera, I was ecstatic to find I could delete my "ugly" image with just a touch of a finger, and I did so with a vengeance, ignoring the protests of everyone around me. I never considered that, by being visually absent in years of Christmas, birthday party, picnic, graduation, and vacation snapshots, I deprived my family of treasured memories.

I closed the album slowly. Regret and the clarity of hindsight filled me with shame. If only I could turn back time and jump from behind the lens into the midst of the photographs splayed out before me, hamming it up with my family and friends. If only I could superimpose myself so that I could stand proudly at my son's side when he took his first steps, graduated, and every milestone in-between. Instead, I'd insisted on playing photographer, and those opportunities were gone forever.

"It's not too late," I murmured to myself as I got up to place the albums back on the shelf. Quietly, I slipped into bed beside my sleeping husband. Before I dozed off, I made a silent vow, determined to keep it no matter how self-conscious I was.

Now, when there's an occasion to take pictures, I willingly surrender the camera to someone else while I pose with my family. I'm still critical of myself, wincing at the images of my chubby body and aging face. I ignore the exasperated sighs of everyone within earshot when I complain loudly about how awful my hair looks. But the pictures, no matter how awful they look, remain and make their way into brand-new, bulging albums. They hang on walls, fill frames, and are duplicated to hand out to anyone who wants them.

No one knows what tomorrow will bring, but I can be sure of one thing that won't happen: My son will never have to say, "I wish I had a picture to remember her by."

— Marya Morin —

29

The Eleventh Door

You can't just sit there and wait for people to give you that golden dream. You've got to get out there and make it happen for yourself.

~Diana Ross

Our house search was going nowhere. Nearly a year had passed since the sale of our first home. We were renting an apartment until we could find the right place. That was proving to be no easy task. There were plenty of homes on the market, but none fulfilled our long list of specifications. As with our previous home, my husband and I would be joint owners with my grandmother and brother, so we were looking for a two-family house with a big yard in a nice neighborhood. It had to have some vintage architectural charm, like porches, maybe a fireplace, bay windows, hardwood floors, or French doors. On top of everything, the price had to fit our limited budget.

We looked at numerous places, many in deplorable condition or congested areas. Some had been converted from single-family homes, with unequal space and peculiar layouts. The glowing descriptions from eager brokers never seemed to match what we found when we got there. It became so discouraging that we were ready to stop looking.

During our house-hunting lull, my grandmother blurted out of the blue, "Why don't you go find it yourselves?"

"How?" I asked.

"Just go where you like the neighborhood and knock on doors.

Somebody might be thinking of selling."

My husband and I looked at each other and shrugged. Maybe it wasn't such a crazy idea.

We came up with a simple plan. Arek would take an afternoon off from work, and we would canvas door to door. We chose a sunny day and set out on foot from our apartment. We had come to appreciate the area, with its quiet, leafy streets lined with capes and duplexes, and just a short walk to the conveniences of the compact downtown. I carried a clipboard and pen to list every home we called at. The folks who came to the door politely listened to our well-rehearsed speech: "We're looking to buy a two-family house. Interested in selling?"

We heard an assortment of answers: "I hope not" (spoken by a tenant). "Maybe next year." "Where would I go?" I carefully noted each response before moving on to the next possibility. The eleventh house we tried, the most imposing we'd come upon, was dark gray with white trim and resplendent with porches and balconies. We rang the bell and stepped back. A middle-aged lady with carefully coifed hair and rimless glasses came to the door. After our little speech, she paused for a minute, and then asked if we could come back at eight o'clock that evening after they'd finished dinner. What could it mean? We weren't sure, but we halted our search for the day and headed home, giddy as two kids on the last day of school.

We arranged for my brother to join us for the eight o'clock meeting. Trying to keep our expectations in check, the three of us trooped back to the big duplex, aglow now with porch light and twin lampposts guiding us. We were ushered inside to a flurry of handshakes and introductions. The lady then led us on a quick tour, chattering endlessly about their lives in this house: the children they raised who were off at college; the christenings and graduation parties; the accommodations made for her aged mother; the Italian cooking supplemented by French Canadian specialties. As she rambled on, I marveled at the high ceilings, the crown moldings, the front and back staircases, and the vast back yard. Finally, she blurted, "This place isn't right for you — it's too big."

Immediately, we assured her that was not the case.

The man of the house offered his input next. He had lived there for forty years, first on one side of the duplex and then, upon marrying, on the other.

"Anthony," his wife reminded him, "you know that house I've always loved, the one with the columns? It's for sale!"

He rubbed his chin and shook his head. "So all that praying might be paying off?"

She turned to me with the inside story. "Last night, I made a novena."

Anthony knew he was beat. With a sigh, he named his price and said there would be no negotiation. "Take it or leave it."

We froze. After exchanging no more than a quick look and a nod, we took it.

"Are you sure?" they asked again when Anthony returned, holding a wine bottle. Yes, we were sure, though a dizzying sense of unreality came over us. The bottle was uncorked to seal the deal. Yet even as we clinked glasses all around, it seemed too good to be true.

Claire and Anthony bought the house with the columns, and we bought theirs. Thirty-three years later, we are still here. We, too, have hosted our share of holidays and cookouts. We raised our son here. We put all that space to good use, starting our printing business here. We put in an herb garden and grape arbor, and still plant a vegetable garden every spring.

Eleven proved to be the lucky number in our house search, but it never would have come to light if not for my grandmother's straightforward advice to just go after what we were looking for. Over the years, that approach has worked for us in all kinds of situations. And, like Grandma herself, it's something we've never forgotten.

— Lisa Loosigian —

30

The Secret to Being a Good Hostess

The ornaments of your home are the people who smile upon entering time and time again.
~Maralee McKee, Manners That Matter for Mom

I remember the day my mother made the comment, "She's learned the secret to being a good hostess." I wanted in on the secret. I was, after all, a grown-up; I had been married for two years.

As a new bride, I had pictured us throwing fantastic parties and delicious sit-down dinners. Tom and I had new dishes, new silverware, new everything. I wanted to entertain. I wanted to have friends over for fancy meals.

I imagined perfect table settings, fresh bouquets of flowers, and tapered candles. I dreamed of memorable dinner parties with gourmet meals like Beef Wellington or Chicken Cordon Bleu. I had never tried those foods, but they sounded classy to me.

One of the hurdles to such entertaining was the fact I was not a great cook. I had not learned the art of having all the components of a meal come out at the same time. Often, our choice was to eat the potatoes hot and the meat later, because cold mashed potatoes are not tasty. Adding to my inadequate cooking ability was the fact we were still in college and couldn't afford fresh flowers to adorn our table. And the only candles we had were those left over from our wedding.

As time wore on, my cooking improved. We managed to have a

few people into our home, but each time was stressful for me. I spent hours cleaning the house. I worried over every detail before our guests arrived, fussed about every detail while they were there, and fell into bed exhausted after our guests left.

Then, a few months after moving into a new house, a young couple in our neighborhood invited us over for dinner. They had two small children. Although the house was clean, we had to step over a few toys in the living room. Dinner wasn't quite ready, so Mary Jane asked if I could set the table while the men watched the children. She had made a meatloaf and macaroni and cheese. I watched as she heated green beans from a can in a saucepan and poured a can of peaches into a bowl. After dinner, I covered the leftovers while the men cleared the table and Mary Jane put the children to bed. We all enjoyed the evening talking, laughing, and playing a board game.

"It's funny," I told my mom the next day, "she didn't make anything special, but we had such a good time."

"She's learned the secret of being a good hostess," my mother told me. "Treat your family like company and your company like family."

I took my mother's words to heart. In the forty-plus years my husband and I have been married, I have enjoyed setting our antique dining room table with beautiful linens and interesting centerpieces for our family gatherings. Our daughters, sons-in-law, and grandchildren seem to truly appreciate the time and effort I put into making those occasions special.

> **"Treat your family like company and your company like family."**

But the feet under our kitchen table have belonged to good friends from all walks of life and all over the world. We have entertained everybody from business leaders to local farmers, from square dancers to ministers. We have welcomed friends from China, Korea, Finland, Italy, New Zealand, and India. I've served everything from pot roast to potpies.

Recently, when we needed to meet with a man to discuss publicity for an upcoming convention we were planning, I invited him and his wife to our home for dinner. They had never been to our house before.

We made the final arrangements via e-mail.

"How about coming at 6:00?" I typed. "We are taking care of our granddaughter for a few days, and she will need to get to bed early. Just be prepared to step over toys and be treated like family." Again, we had a fun, productive, and memorable evening.

Mary Jane and Mom, did I ever say, "Thank you"?

— Rebecca Waters —

Chapter 4

Maxims for Marriage

31

Love Him Unconditionally

Love is patient; love is kind. It bears all things, hopes
all things, endures all things. Love never fails.
~1 Corinthians 13:4-8

My husband and I were returning home from taking our daughter, Chelsea, to college. We had been through this three years earlier when we took our son to college, but then we still had Chelsea at home. Now the house would be quiet; no more kids around.

I asked myself: *What's next in our lives? Where do we go from here?*

As the weeks passed, Chuck and I became moody. I cried easily when reminded of Chelsea, and I purposely avoided her bedroom — too many girly things around. Chelsea was a daddy's girl and it was obvious my husband was sorely missing his little buddy, his sidekick, too.

The pain seemed to be getting worse. Yet, I thought, *Shouldn't we be finding comfort in each other over our mutual loss? Shouldn't it be easy now to turn to each other?*

I had thought the same thing after my stepson died when he was seventeen. As we struggled through that nightmare, I could understand how couples divorced following the loss of a child. Our current situation was similar, but the grief was on a much smaller scale. Still, when both parties are hurting deeply, it is hard to be there for one another, to show interest in the other person.

One day when Chuck came home from work, I greeted him with a perfunctory kiss and asked halfheartedly, "How was your day?"

"Good, how was yours?" he asked, feigning interest.

"It was okay, except the dishwasher's still not working right. And, thankfully, there weren't any phone calls, so I got some writing done. That was nice — no interruptions."

"Hmm," was his only response.

That's it, a "hmm?"

Gone were the days of announcing to our kids, "Daddy's home!" and watching them run to greet him at the door, jumping up and down, begging for him to scoop them up and throw them on the waterbed, one at a time. How they loved that! And how he must've enjoyed that, too....

Now he came home to a wife who talked about the dishwasher and the telephone. Hmm.

Suddenly, I recalled how short I'd been with him the other night and the hurt I'd seen on his face. He'd been looking more tired lately, too.

In my own grief, I had been focusing on how moody he had been. I had not considered what I might be like to come home to. Quickly, I prayed one of those intensely painful prayers, asking God to show me how I come across to others. I knew, for the sake of my marriage, that I had to face the painful truth: How had I changed over the years? What was I like to live with?

Suddenly, a short conversation from years ago was crystal clear in my mind. When our kids were preschoolers, Chuck and I were going through a tough time in our marriage. I knew we needed help, but I thought people who sought counseling were weak. So, instead of personal counseling, I chose to go to church, hoping a sermon would give me the answer. And, wouldn't you know it, that Sunday the pastor said, "We all need counseling at times from wise people. It is usually pride, though, that keeps us from seeking the help we need."

Ugh.

I called the church the next day for an appointment with the pastor. When I arrived, I was certain that, once he heard my story, he would readily agree with me — divorce was the only answer. I was sure of it.

Imagine my surprise then, after pouring out my heart to this kind man, when he responded with: "You need to love him unconditionally."

I stared at him. What?

The pastor continued, "Love him the way *you* want to be loved—with no strings attached."

That was it. Three words: "Love him unconditionally." Three words that changed the course of our marriage. Three words I have never forgotten. Three words that still have the power to change hearts.

Suddenly, I remembered something else I'd heard years ago: "If you want to be treated like a queen, you need to treat your man like a king."

I had not been treating my man like a king. I'd been pouting over not being needed as a mother on a daily basis. I had not been showing my husband the love that *I* had been craving.

What could I do to improve this next chapter of our lives? How could I get us out of this rut?

> *"Love him the way you want to be loved."*

The answers came daily. First, I began my mornings reading about the love God has for us and wants us to have for others. I saturated my mind and heart with it. Then, I purposely began hugging Chuck more. Judging by his shocked reaction, I realized just how far apart we had grown. I started listening to him more intently, and he reciprocated. As I did more things to please him, such as make his favorite foods and choose his favorite movies, he voluntarily helped with the housework. I even began watching some of his favorite shows with him instead of staying on the computer in the evenings, and he began handing me the remote, willing to watch the shows that *I* liked.

Gradually, our marriage became better than ever. A spark had been rekindled. We started talking about the future. Our twenty-fifth wedding anniversary was around the corner. We decided to splurge and take a cruise to Hawaii. After all, we had reached a milestone — it was time to focus on ourselves. And from the moment we boarded the ship, we were like two kids in a candy store, having the time of our lives!

That old principle once again held true: When we show love to another, especially when we don't feel like it, our feelings will catch up. It's a mystery, but when we love those who seem hard to love, we are actually teaching them to love us back. Here's to the next twenty-five years of loving unconditionally.

— Connie Cameron Smith —

32

Twenty Years from Now

*A great marriage is not when the "perfect couple"
comes together. It is when an imperfect couple
learns to enjoy their differences.*
~Dave Meurer

ike most young couples eager for their marriage to succeed,
my future husband and I looked for any advice we could get.
We read books, went to pre-marital counseling, and talked to
friends who had been married. While most of those resources
proved useful, the best piece of advice came from a dear friend at my
bridal shower.

During the shower, the hostess asked the guests to give me their
best marriage advice. Some provided housekeeping tips: "Don't leave
the dishes until tomorrow. They will still be there, and everything will
be dried on." Some gave relational advice: "Remember your husband
doesn't think the same way you do." Or, "Don't go to bed angry; you
will just wake up grumpy." While these were all useful, the advice that
had the most impact came from my friend Dawn.

Dawn began by telling us, "When Mike and I got married, someone
told me, 'In the middle of the argument, or the thing you are about to
get angry about, stop and ask yourself, *Twenty years from now, is this
going to matter?*"

That simple statement caused everyone to think. Most arguments
are over temporary things: clothing left out of the hamper or someone
cutting us off in traffic. Other things might have more of a long-term

effect: a bounced check, forgetting to pick someone up, a speeding ticket. But if you think about it, while they might warrant a difficult conversation, they aren't worth damaging a relationship through harsh words.

> *Twenty years from now, is this going to matter?*

It's been more than twenty-five years since my bridal shower, and while most of the advice has fallen by the wayside (especially the advice about dirty dishes,) I have tried to follow Dawn's advice by choosing my battles wisely. I always ask myself, *Twenty years from now, will this matter?* While I can't say it has saved my husband and me from all arguments, it has definitely reduced them to the ones that just can't be avoided.

— Betsy Burnett —

33

Making My House His Home

A house is made of walls and beams;
a home is built with love and dreams.
~Author Unknown

Widowhood was lonely, especially on weekends when my friends were enjoying activities with their families. Since my children live far away from me, I sometimes took myself to a movie or fussed with my dog. And I was surrounded by familiar possessions, helping me remember the life I had once lived. I felt no need for a man in my life, as that would be too complicated.

However, I had joined a widowed people's group where I met an intriguing man. "How would you like to go to dinner with me?" he asked one day. Our friendship quickly became romantic, despite the fact that my dog barked each time he hugged me. We saw each other every day. Eventually, my dog even grew to love him, too, because we walked her together.

My married children thought I was being hasty by dating this man exclusively. "Mom, you need to slow down. Date some more," they cautioned. I ignored their advice.

They had returned to their lives after their father's funeral while I searched for a life of my own. I was in my seventies, as was my new love interest. We didn't want to waste time. You might say it was a whirlwind romance, and it was, because we were both sure. We knew we had fallen in love.

About a month and a half after we met, he knelt on one knee

in my dining room and asked, "Will you marry me?" I grinned and said, "Yes." And then I asked if he needed help getting back up with his arthritic knee.

Where would we live? I owned the house that had been built for my maternal great-grandparents. He was renting, so it seemed logical that he would move into my house.

I already had a houseful of furniture, but he had an equal amount. We had to decide what we wanted to keep and what we no longer needed. It was a challenge to discard belongings that held meaning and family history for each of us.

One day, I went to his apartment and showed him the items I hoped we could keep. "I'd love to have this in our home." Then a friend who had remarried after her first husband died gave me some great advice: "Try to make your house his home, too. Don't let him feel like a guest in your house." After a minute, she added, "I made that mistake when I remarried. My second husband told me he felt like a visitor in my house. There was very little of him in any of the rooms. And he didn't know where he could put his things."

I recognized that my friend had given me advice I needed to take to heart. My husband-to-be is a pilot and owns various artifacts related to flying. We found a place for his airplane propeller in the office we would share. That was a good beginning.

He received a huge print of a biplane when he retired from IBM. I removed the painting I had hung over my fireplace and hung the biplane print there instead. On the mantel, we placed his big sculpture of a seagull, which represents the character from Richard Bach's book, *Jonathan Livingston Seagull*. On a wall that had no ornamentation, we hung his photos of Waterford, Ireland, from which his ancestors had come.

All my old television room furniture went in a garage sale, replaced by my fiancé's bookcases, television, television stand, and futon. We also hung photos of his parents on the wall. Sometimes, I would walk into a room and not recognize it as being in my home because of the "new" arrangement of furnishings and decorations.

After we married, I easily grew accustomed to my home, and my husband did, as well. Not long ago, he said to me, "I really feel as if this is my home."

I am so grateful to my friend who offered me such good advice from her personal experience. Just as she suggested, I have made my husband feel at home here and not like a visitor. The things we owned aren't as important as the love we share and the home we've made.

— Sandy McPherson Carrubba Geary —

34

Just Three Things

What greater thing is there for two human souls
than to feel that they are joined…
to strengthen each other…
~George Eliot

I smiled when I heard the car door slam. "Daddy's home," I told the two little girls who'd snuggled into bed beside me for a story. I kept reading, expecting to see my husband any moment. But ten minutes later, he still hadn't come upstairs. My son came in, and I asked him what Dad was doing.

"He's sweeping the floor," he answered.

Immediately, I felt ashamed. My husband had just worked a twelve-hour shift, and now he had to come home and sweep the floor. I'd been home all day. I should have done it myself.

I expected Eric to be irritated when he finally came upstairs. After all, I'd be annoyed to come home to a messy house every day. But when he saw me snuggled in our bed with our daughters, he smiled and said, "Hi, baby. How was your day?"

Before I could answer, the girls jumped on his back and squealed, "Tickle me, Daddy!"

He played with the girls for a few minutes, and then we tucked them into bed together. We repeated the process with our two sons.

When we were finally alone, Eric sat down to eat dinner. It was after 9:00. I'd eaten hours earlier with the kids, but I always sat with him so we could talk.

"How was your day?" he asked again.

"Good," I said. "Busy. I still haven't gotten used to taking care of twice as many kids every day." Eric and I had only been married for a few months. We'd each brought two children into the marriage, and for the time being at least, I was a stay-at-home mom to all four of them. It was wonderful but exhausting.

Eric nodded with understanding. "Kids are a lot of work."

"I'm sorry you had to sweep the floor when you got home. The girls asked me to read to them and…"

"That's no problem," Eric interrupted. "I know you're busy with the kids."

Eric's words were kind, but I still felt guilty. I was busy all day, but I never felt as though I had accomplished much. I hated that my husband had to come home from a very demanding job and do housework that I should've found time to do myself.

Don't misunderstand me. I think men should do their share of the housework, especially if their wives work outside the home. As a stay-at-home mom, I wanted Eric to help, but I didn't want to *need* his help. I wanted to be able to get the basics done during the day while he was at work.

But no matter how hard I tried, I couldn't do it all.

The next night, Eric came home from his twelve-hour shift and unloaded the dishwasher. The night after that, he put a load of laundry in the washer.

I appreciated his help, but needing it made me feel like a failure. I kept expecting Eric to express frustration about my lack of domestic skills, but he never did. Every night, he just seemed happy to be home with the kids and me.

But I knew an explosion was coming. Eventually, he'd grow tired of the messy house and get upset with me about it. The honeymoon would be over.

I fretted constantly about my inability to do it all. I wanted to be a great mom and stepmom, a loving wife, and a perfect cook and housekeeper. But there just didn't seem to be enough hours in the day.

I felt like a failure.

One day, I ran across some great advice by author Lysa TerKeurst. Like me, Lysa expressed the desire to be a "good wife." But she often felt overwhelmed by the demands she assumed that entailed. Like me, she had a self-imposed list of responsibilities that "good wives" do, and anything less than that equaled failure.

I could so relate.

Lysa went to her husband and said, "I can't be a perfect wife. Just tell me three things that are really important to you, and I'll try to do those things well."

Her husband told her the things that mattered most to him, and they didn't include having a spotless home. Lysa realized that she'd been stressing out over things that didn't even matter to her husband. She'd been trying to please him in ways that weren't important to him.

Was it possible that I was doing the same thing?

That night, after Eric and I put the kids to bed, I told him how I'd been feeling. "I hate that I'm letting you down," I said through tears.

Eric was shocked. "You think I'm disappointed in you? I'm not at all. I love coming home from work and seeing you reading to our girls. I love when the boys tell me that you played board games with them while I was at work. I was a single dad before I met you, and I didn't have a lot of time to play with the kids. I'm just happy that they're happy again." He stroked my hair. "You're doing a great job. And, honey, the house isn't perfect, but it's way cleaner now than when I was on my own with the kids."

Tears streamed down my cheeks at his words. I'd needed to hear them so badly.

I told him about the article I'd read. "So what matters most to you?" I asked.

Eric's expectations of me were so much more achievable than the ones I'd set for myself. His three things had nothing to do with perfect housekeeping and five-course dinners.

They had everything to do with loving my new family—something I could definitely do.

Some simple advice, followed by an important conversation, and I was set free from my feelings of guilt and failure.

There's no such thing as a perfect wife, and Wonder Woman is a fictional character.

But three things? That I can do.

—Diane Stark—

35

Putting Up

Keep your eyes wide open before marriage,
half-shut afterwards.
~Benjamin Franklin

Our neighbor across the street hosted a small birthday party for her eighty-nine-year-old mother and called a few of the ladies on our street to celebrate with her. Her friends were long gone by this age, and for undisclosed reasons, the few extended family members were estranged. So, armed with a few pretty packages, my friends and I happily attended.

Upon first glance, Mary looked like the quintessential silver-haired, sweater-wearing grandmother. Short curls framed her wrinkled face, which lit up in a broad smile when she saw us. Her sweet, high-pitched voice was reminiscent of a tiny, magical fairy with a tinkling laugh. It was always a joy to be with her. As she sat in her rocker, her fingers nimbly twisting and tangling yarn into yet another afghan, she shocked us with stories of how she rebeled against her parents' wishes and traveled to dangerous places around the world at a time when young women were expected to settle down and have kids. After she married, she rode on the back of her husband's motorcycle until she got one of her own.

When she spoke of her husband, her eyes moistened. He had passed away more than a decade earlier, but she still talked about him all the time. At the party, we sang the birthday song, and she blew out the candles. "George would be ninety-five if he were alive today," she said. We all marveled with our mouths full of buttercream.

"Yes," she continued. "We were married for fifty years." Fifty years. If we had marveled before, we positively gushed over this major accomplishment. Most of us had been married for only ten or fifteen years and had contemplated divorce at one time or another. I was going through a rough patch with my own husband at the time.

Being married for fifty years seemed inconceivable. I couldn't resist asking this sage wife how she had managed to stay married so long. "Mary," I whispered. "What is your secret for a long and happy marriage?" I didn't want just a long marriage. I wanted a happy one, too, and her marriage had been both.

The old woman looked at me for a long time. Finally, she quietly put down her cake plate, leaned forward out of her rocking chair and, with a bony hand, beckoned me closer.

"To be married for as long as I was," she whispered, "you have to put up with a lot of crap." And then she fell back into her chair. It took me a while to process what she had said, and then I began to giggle. Oh, the simple truth! As I shared her words of wisdom with the rest of the party, everyone laughed and laughed as Mary sat there with her eyes twinkling.

> "To be married for as long as I was," she whispered, "you have to put up with a lot of crap."

"I need to cross-stitch that and hang it over my fireplace!" one of the ladies exclaimed. As seemingly crass as the words might sound at first, they really put things into perspective. In our grandmothers' day, the phrase "putting up" meant either of two things: 1) They stored their food through canning, pickling or drying. 2) They endured or suffered in silence during situations that they didn't particularly like. It is true that when we're married — or in any type of interpersonal relationship, for that matter — we will not like everything about the other person, and most definitely will not like everything that happens or everything he does or says. But is that a good reason to end a relationship? Is it divorce-worthy?

Those words have stuck with me ever since. When we really love someone, do we put strings on our love? Do we require perfection from the other person in order to deserve their love? I do not like everything about my husband, and I can assure you that he doesn't like everything about me. But we put up with that sort of stuff because we love each other. Love outweighs the petty annoyances, the maddening frustrations, and even the bitter disappointments. Love does not require perfection, and to be married for a long time like Mary, we have to put up with some things we don't like.

It was the best marital advice I'd ever heard. Now, I have a happy and long marriage, too. We've been married for over thirty-three years, and if we live long enough, I know that we'll make it to fifty years like Mary. Because as you put up with some of the less-than-perfect stuff, your marriage undergoes a deep and meaningful transformation, and suddenly you discover what unconditional love is all about. And it may not be easy, but it is so worth it.

— Lori Phillips —

36

Ten Times a Day

To love is nothing. To be loved is something.
But to love and be loved, that's everything.
~T. Tolis

I n February 2003, I was moving to Hawaii to marry my boyfriend of four months. At only nineteen years old, I got quite a lot of advice before I made this huge life decision.

Most of the advice could be summed up in three words: "Don't do it." This was said to me in various ways, "You're too young…" "You haven't dated long enough…" "It's been long distance, so you don't really know each other…" But I was headstrong. Determined. Young and in love. So, I went through with my plan.

My boyfriend Matt was a Marine. He had been put on "stop loss," which is a military term meaning that his unit was under the possibility of deploying, and no one was allowed to leave their duty station. Because of this, we could only get married if I moved to Hawaii. It wasn't a terribly hard decision to make. On February 12, 2003, Matt asked me to marry him. On February 13, 2003, I put in my notice at work. Two weeks later, I was saying goodbye to a job and people I loved.

Most of the advice I had received about this marriage came unsolicited. And much of it was rather condescending. Despite this, the people I worked with at the sheriff's office were truly wonderful people. On that last night of work, they presented me with a few gifts, a card and a collection of cash they had pooled together. I *oohed* and *aahed* over the presents, pocketed the money, and glanced at the card. The messages were fairly standard—"Good luck" or "Best wishes"—but one person, one of my sergeants, wrote out a really thoughtful, detailed message. The message, in a nutshell, said that despite our young age, our brief dating time and our short engagement, our marriage could work if we worked for our marriage. She went on to say that during her marriage, she had come to find "these ten pieces of advice the most useful." Then she went on to list those ten pieces of advice.

Now, I don't remember all ten, and since I'm not a terribly sentimental person, I didn't save the card, so I can't go back and reread them. I only remember one of them, and it was the best advice I have ever been given. It was number seven in her list of ten, which I remember only because seven is my favorite number. It said, "#7: Say 'I love you' to each other no less than ten times a day."

Matt and I put this advice to use immediately in our short engagement and our marriage. In the beginning, we would make a joke of it. "How many times did I tell you that I love you today? Only seven? Here are three more." But over time, saying "I love you" became a habit—a lovely, endearing habit. We tend to say it far more than ten times a day. We say it when either of us leaves the house. We say it when we hang up the phone. We say it in texts more times than I can count. We say it randomly when nothing else is going on. We say it in intimate moments and public moments. We say it in a teasing, playful manner, and in a serious, romantic manner. We say it before we go to sleep. Sometimes, we say it at what we think is the end of a conversation, and then we continue the conversation and say it again a few minutes later.

We say it so much that our youngest son once bragged that he knows we are happily married because "you are *always* saying you love each other." We say it frequently, not only to each other, but to our three children who, having picked up on the habit, say it frequently to us as well as to other important family members. However, it is not just something we say; it is something we act on and feel deeply about. While it has become somewhat routine, it is never said lightly.

Those many "I love yous"—too many to count over fifteen years—have carried us through so much. Through dumb fights and through fits of laughter, through difficult times in our life, through triumphant times, through deployments and welcome homes, through births and through loss, through mundane days and through exciting moments. When my husband can't be home because the military calls him away, when he can't call, when he can't get online, when he isn't there to say "I love you," I have a thousand memories of him saying it to hold in my heart.

That simple piece of advice in that card was the best advice I have ever received. There is nothing more important than letting the people that we love *know* that we love them. Whether it is with words or not, say "I love you." Say it and mean it, and don't wait for a "perfect" moment.

—Jacqueline Chovan—

37

Nurture It Tenderly

In the enriching of marriage the big things are the little things. It is a constant appreciation for each other and a thoughtful demonstration of gratitude.
~James E. Faust

When I was growing up, my best friend lived across the street from me. I was at her house so often that I was like a member of the family. I loved my friend's mom almost as much as I loved my own. Mrs. Shepard was a cake-baking, cigarette-smoking, romance-novel-reading, stay-at-home mom. I especially loved her spectacular flower garden. My friend had no interest in the garden, but I was enchanted by it.

I spent hours — ultimately, years — helping Mrs. Shepard tend her flowers. Her back yard was a delight to my senses. The vibrant colors, the floral scents sitting heavy upon the air, and the buzz of the pollen-drunk bees made the garden feel alive; it was a heartbeat I felt inside my chest. I treasured my time in her garden and dreamed of the day I would have my own.

I will never forget the morning my friend's father packed his bags and left home for a "new life." I found Mrs. Shepard on the bench swing in the middle of her beloved blooms. She gave me a tremulous smile as I approached, wiped the tears from her cheeks, and made room for me to sit beside her.

As we swung together, I said, "Maybe he'll come back."

"No, he won't," she said sadly. "He's gone. He made it pretty clear that he doesn't love me anymore."

"How can that be?" I asked with an aching heart. "How could he just stop loving you?"

She sighed. "He didn't 'just stop' loving me. Love's been slipping away from us for a long time. I was sitting here thinking that marriage really is a lot like a garden; you know better than anyone how much energy it takes to care for it. For all the hours I spent keeping things alive out here, I never acknowledged the fact that my marriage was dying in there," she said, nodding toward the house.

"Let me give you a piece of advice," she continued. "When you get married—not only at the beginning, but when you're deep into the years—treat your relationship like a garden. Nurture it tenderly every day." I sensed the wisdom of those words and tucked them into my heart for safekeeping.

My husband and I invest a lot of time and energy in coaxing beauty from the land around our mountain home. We cherish the time we spend with our flowers, shrubs and vegetables. Throughout our marriage, we have tried to stay mindful of the fact that our garden is the perfect metaphor for our marriage. While others have compared the two, we have tried to live it with intention by applying the basic tenets of successful gardening to our lives together.

> *"Treat your relationship like a garden. Nurture it tenderly every day."*

Start with Good Soil: Because the root of any living thing is dependent upon a strong foundation to thrive, good soil is our most important purchase each spring. Before we committed to marriage, we planted our roots in a friendship based on mutual respect. We made sure that we had the same values and priorities. We laugh often, fight fairly and accept each other's imperfections.

Create a Plan: Before we put anything in the ground, we map out a blueprint to give each individual plant the optimal amount of sun, shade, rain and drainage that it needs. This gives it the best chance for success. In the same way, we took steps to pre-plan the most important aspects of our lives. We defined our career, financial, parenting, fitness and leisure goals before we walked down the aisle. We even had to figure out how to handle the inevitable conflict. We believed that our plans didn't take the spontaneity out of a marriage, just the unwelcome surprises that could tear it apart.

Nurture: Planting the seedlings is the fun part. It's the fancy dress, champagne toast, first dance, and exotic honeymoon phase of marriage. But the real commitment to those seedlings begins later — often under a hot sun — and continues. It's in the day-in, day-out grind that a marriage finds success, as well. My husband and I think of ourselves as a team. We run errands, work on household projects and volunteer our time to good causes together. We nurse each other through the inevitable illnesses. Our devotion to each other in the moments that aren't glamorous fortify our commitment to each other.

Sunshine: Few flowers will thrive without the benefit of the sun. My husband and I believe that a marriage must also be rooted in prayer, faith and trust.

Pruning: Deadheading is essential for preventing spent blooms from robbing a plant of much-needed energy. It also helps make way for new flowers to grow. In our home, we "prune" to check in and see how we're doing. We take time to listen, express concerns or get rid of hurt feelings before they can rob us of our energy. It's amazing how the removal of old distractions clears the air and renews our marriage.

Spice It Up: My husband and I spiced up our property with soft lighting, quirky ornaments and Adirondack chairs around a fire pit. We go hiking every week. We go on adventures and we share the excitement — and renewed love — when we kayak a rapid, horseback ride in the desert, hike in grizzly country, or dog-sled over snowy terrain. Of course, it doesn't have to be "death-defying." It just has to be fun!

Vase Arrangements: The best part of gardening is the beautiful finished product. An artfully arranged vase of flowers on our dining room table gives us a wonderful sense of accomplishment, as well as great joy. For our marriage, this means we set aside time to celebrate our love. Like a stunning bouquet, it's a gift to be treasured. We pack a picnic on a sunny day, hold hands at the theater, watch a sunset on a sandy beach or linger with our novels on a rainy morning. Most importantly, we express our love in a dozen different ways each day.

Mrs. Shepard and I remained close until her death several years ago. I think of her fondly when I'm tending my flowers in the cool of a summer morning. On my wedding day, she gave me a basket of gardening tools and an assortment of flower seeds with a note that read: "Nurture your gardens tenderly; the one that grows under the sun, as well as the one that grows inside your hearts." I keep her wise words of advice framed on my bedside table so I can always stay mindful of them.

My husband and I will celebrate our thirtieth anniversary in a few months. We have tended to our marriage as lovingly as we have tended our garden. I believe Mrs. Shepard would approve!

—Vicki Kitchner—

Chapter
5

Making Good Habits

Always Be a Friend

*A good friend is a connection to life — a tie to the past,
a road to the future, the key to sanity
in a totally insane world.*
~Lois Wyse

Sitting in church pews all my life, I've listened intently to dire warnings about the war between good and evil. How we as fallen humans are evil by nature, and good only by the grace of God. How we must fight daily against the evil we are inclined to do.

Frankly, it's a message that's hard to digest because, really, do any of us think of ourselves as evil? I have to admit, I don't. I've never stolen from anyone, picked up a knife or gun to harm anyone, or even reported anyone to the IRS. I pay my bills on time, volunteer at the library and recycle.

But some years ago, I stumbled across a brief essay that made clear to me what all those preachers were talking about.

One day on the NPR radio show, *This I Believe*, Deirdre Sullivan read her essay, "Always Go to the Funeral." In it, she relates how her father made her attend the funeral of her fifth-grade math teacher. Just sixteen years old and uneasy about death, Deirdre tried to get out of going to the service — the condolence line was just too uncomfortable to contemplate.

"Deirdre," her father said, "you're going. Always go to the funeral. Do it for the family."

Like Deirdre, I feared these encounters. I'm great on paper — I write a good and genuinely sincere sympathy note — but standing face-to-face with a grieving person and saying something meaningful? I stumble and stutter. I'd rather just sign the guest book and slip out the back door.

But then, four years ago, my best friend died. I had met Rebecca after she and her husband started attending our church. We became close rapidly — she had an only child, a son, and so did I. She was outgoing and loved a good laugh. Our friendship grew deep over coffee, movie nights and long phone conversations.

> "Always go to the funeral. Do it for the family."

Rebecca suffered a massive heart attack one night and died instantly. She was only in her fifties, but her family genes had claimed her. Her husband called us that morning, choking on his tears, and asked my husband and me to come over. There, I perched awkwardly on the couch, trying to think of what to say and coming up with nothing. I felt so inadequate.

Rebecca and her husband lived hundreds of miles away from their families and had only been in the area for a few years, so when it came to the memorial service, I was worried that no would have known her well enough to say anything. I realized that I needed to say something.

For days, I prepared what I was going to say. I memorized and rehearsed it. Still, I was afraid nerves would get the better of me, and my mind would go blank.

On the day of the service, I took my seat and waited for the invitation to share memories. My skin was ice cold, and my heart raced. My hands trembled, and the strength drained from my knees. I desperately wanted to back out. But I thought about the advice Deirdre Sullivan's father had given her — do it for the family — and found my courage.

I opened by recounting how Rebecca and I had been planning an outing to shop for swimsuits. To me, that was the best way to show how close we were — only a really good friend can be trusted to tell you the truth in that dressing room.

I went on to share how Rebecca lavished her time on others and bestowed her friendship generously. She encouraged others and lifted their spirits. In closing, I recited words about true friendship from the Scottish author George MacDonald: "If instead of a gem, or even a flower, we should cast the gift of a loving thought into the heart of a friend, that would be giving as the angels give."

As I spoke, I heard sobs from Rebecca's son in the front row. His pain made my heart ache. But I sat down certain I had done right by my friend.

In truth, Deirdre Sullivan's message isn't just that we ought to go to the funeral. Her message is a call to not give in to laziness and indifference. "In my humdrum life," she says, "the daily battle hasn't been good versus evil. It's hardly so epic. Most days, my real battle is doing good versus doing nothing."

That's it! I thought when I first heard those words. Evil suddenly made sense to me. Doing nothing — nothing to comfort the grieving, nothing to alleviate suffering, nothing to bring a smile to someone's face, nothing to make someone's life better — is a kind of evil. It's a selfishness that elevates our own desires above everything else. It's a miserliness of spirit that deprives others of the love and attention they crave from us.

To me, "always go to the funeral" means doing that thing you don't want to do when that inner voice nudges you to act. Do it when you'd rather queue up another show on Netflix. Do it when you'd rather scroll through your Facebook feed. Do it when you'd rather do nothing at all. Always write the note; always make the phone call; always extend a kind word; always offer up a listening ear. Always be a friend.

— Nancy B. Kennedy —

White Walls

*There's no straighter road to success than exceeding
expectations one day at a time.*
~Robin Crow

don't remember much from my time in the hospital but I remember a lot of white — white floors, white sheets and the four white walls that surrounded me.

At thirteen, I was spending my grade-eight year at in-hospital treatment for a severe eating disorder. Doctors referred to me as a textbook-case anorexic. I was driven, stubborn, and followed a dangerously rigid pattern of thinking. After spending almost two months in the hospital and hours in counseling, it seemed that nothing could change my mind. Though I had gained a marginal amount of weight, I continued to gravitate toward old patterns of thinking. Deep down, I knew that what I needed was beyond what any psychologist could offer. I needed a shift in mindset, a reason to change the way I had been living my life.

One day, my change finally came with the help of a few simple words. It was nearing Christmas and my three-month anniversary in the hospital. I went to bed miserably, watching the snow fall outside my window, and wondering when I would be able to escape the four white walls around me. The next morning, I woke to find my breakfast placed on the table beside me as usual. This time, I noticed something different: A piece of paper was folded and tucked under my spoon. Carefully, I unfolded the paper and read aloud the message:

Try this: Eat this meal for this moment. Then let the moment pass. Everything will be all right. Just live for now.

I stared at the message as the words jumped off the paper and planted in my conscience. *Live for now.* This meal was just for this moment, and then this moment would pass. I closed my eyes, took a deep breath and told myself to eat this meal for this moment, then let the moment pass and not worry about the rest. An amazing thing happened that morning: I ate my breakfast in full. No complaints, no fuss. And I did not think about it later.

For the rest of the meals that day, there were no notes, but I continued this experiment. I ate without allowing my mind to wander into the past or the future. Living for now. It became easier to break down the larger task of recovery into single meals, and then into single moments. I enjoyed the experiment enough to allow myself to practice it throughout the next week. And then the next. Eventually, I found myself using this technique in all areas of my life, from conversations with my doctor to watching TV. In every task, I would simply remind myself to remain present.

After four months of treatment, I was told I had finally reached a healthy weight for discharge. I could tell my doctors did not understand where my sudden willingness to recover had come from. I never found out who sent me that message or why it resonated with me. Before I left that morning, I promised myself that no matter what situation arose in life, I would always remember to live for now. I swear those white walls turned a bit brighter that day.

— Mannat Sharma —

Tiny Habits

What prompts us to action is desire; and desire has
three forms — appetite, passion, wish.
~Aristotle

"Honey, I received a promotional e-mail from a hotel chain today," my husband Eric said. "Because we've stayed in their hotels before, they offered us a vacation package in Hawaii. It's a really good deal."

"Hawaii?" I asked.

He nodded. "Maui, to be exact."

It sounded like a dream come true. "Let me see the e-mail," I said.

Eric showed me, and I could hardly believe that a vacation like that could actually be within our budget.

"Do you want me to call them?" he asked. "We can book it for next winter."

"That sounds great," I said. "I'm so excited!"

But within minutes, my excitement waned because I realized that vacationing in a tropical paradise required wearing a swimsuit, and my body was not exactly swimsuit-ready.

I sighed. My husband had asked me to go to Maui with him. I should have been thrilled. But the extra weight I carried made me feel embarrassed and ashamed, and it dampened my excitement about the trip.

For years, I'd tried to eat better and exercise, but my efforts were always short-lived. I'd do really well for a few days, sometimes even a few weeks, but then something stressful would happen, and I'd be right back to my old habits.

But with this dream vacation coming, I really wanted to drop the extra weight — to look better, but more importantly, to feel better. To enjoy a trip with my husband without worrying about my body.

But I'd tried and failed so many times before. It seemed unlikely that this time would be any different.

The next day, I was watching one of the morning news programs, and an author named James Clear came on. He writes about "tiny habits" and how important it is to just start moving in the right direction, even if the step we take is infinitesimal.

Then he explained something I'll never forget. "Each action you take is like a vote for the type of person you want to become. Each time you write, you become a writer. Each time you play the violin, you become a musician. Each time you exercise, you become an athlete."

I didn't want to become an athlete. I just wanted to be the type of person who could wholeheartedly enjoy going to Hawaii with her husband.

What actions could I take to become that type of person? I could make promises to myself that involved working out for an hour every single day and never eating chocolate again in my life. I could promise to eat salads every day and never even look at another French fry.

But I'd tried that all-or-nothing approach before, and it didn't work for me. The first time I messed up — and I always did — I'd give up.

Then I remembered James Clear's advice about tiny habits and the importance of taking just one step in the right direction.

What tiny actions could I take to become the type of person who could feel confident enough in a swimsuit to enjoy a vacation?

The next morning, as soon as I got up, I put on my walking shoes. Although I hadn't done any actual exercise yet, putting on the shoes was a tiny habit that made it more likely that I would.

After I got my kids off to school, I decided I would walk just to my mailbox, another tiny habit. The idea was to make the next action so small that I couldn't say "no" to doing it. When I got to the mailbox, I decided to walk to the end of my street. When I got there, I walked a bit farther before turning around and heading home.

It wasn't the hour of rigorous exercise I used to shoot for, but it was a sustainable habit. And continuous small steps in the right direction were better than giving up after only a few days because I'd set an unrealistic goal.

I went to the grocery store to buy some healthy food. But this time, instead of aiming for perfection, I looked for tiny habits I could incorporate into my everyday life. I bought Greek yogurt, almonds, and cheese sticks. I figured if I could eat those things instead of my usual unhealthy snacks, it would be another tiny yet sustainable habit.

I bought an insulated water bottle because I've found my intake increases if the water is very cold. Another tiny habit.

As the days went on, I walked a little, drank a lot of water, and ate my healthy snacks. I remembered that every healthy choice was like a vote for the type of person I wanted to become, and each vote drew me a tiny bit closer to my goal.

> *I remembered that every healthy choice was like a vote for the type of person I wanted to become.*

Unlike previous attempts, I didn't even aim for perfection. It wasn't possible anyway, and all it did was leave me feeling discouraged.

But my tiny habits were easy. And after a few weeks, I noticed that my jeans were a bit looser. The tiny changes I'd made were adding up. I kept going, and over the next few months, I noticed even more progress.

Today, our vacation is right around the corner. I recently purchased a new swimsuit, and I actually feel pretty good about it.

I wanted to enjoy our vacation without insecurity or embarrassment, and thanks to some great advice about tiny habits, I've become the type of person who is going to do just that.

— Diane Stark —

41

What This Virginian Learned about OHIO

One good mother is worth a hundred schoolmasters.
~George Herbert

My mom is the most positive person I know. She has an encouraging spirit, sees the good in all people, and always sees the silver lining in any situation. The world needs more people like my mom to view a glass as "half full" rather than "half empty." I grew up in a loving, positive home environment, where there were always family activities and lots of laughter.

I have fond memories of my mom taking us to volunteer at a food pantry every other Saturday morning. While my brother and I would have rather stayed in bed or watched cartoons on our day off from school, she had us tag along with her for her volunteer shift of interviewing and counseling people in Roanoke, Virginia who needed groceries to feed their families. While she did her service role, we helped in the food pantry, sorting, stocking and preparing bags of food. Surprisingly, this got to be something we looked forward to! My brother and I made a game out of filling each food bag for the families, and we always left feeling good about what we did.

My sweet mom even made household chores enjoyable. The best advice I learned from her that sticks with me today is "O-H-I-O." Growing up, my mom would hand me a stack of clean clothes, and I would immediately set them on the floor, promising to put them away later. My mom would say, "Kids, you've got to remember: OHIO! That means Only Handle It Once. When I give you clothes, put them away in your drawers as soon as I give them to you so they are only in your hands once." It got to be annoying during my high-school years when having a messy room was the norm. She'd gently remind my brother and me, "Kids, OHIO!" and we knew exactly what that meant. She said it in such a sing-songy tone, too, that it was hard *not* to follow her instructions since OHIO is so sensible!

Sadly, I never got the neat gene, if there is one. My college dorm room, my first apartment, and my current house are never that tidy. It is easy to forget this simple piece of advice my mom gave to me and leave stacks of mail or clothes lying around. Today, as a forty-two-year-old wife and stepmom, when I pick up my mail or bring clean, folded laundry to my room, I hear my sweet mom's voice in my head: "Remember, OHIO!" Most of the time, I take those extra two minutes to handle things only once and put them in their proper place. Who knew that this girl from Virginia would learn such a valuable lesson about OHIO that stays with me still today? Thanks, Mom!

— Kate Tanis McKinnie —

42

The Power of a Word

Words create worlds.
~Pierre du Plessis

I am a hair puller. I have trichotillomania, an impulsive control disorder where I pull out my hair. I remember being teased about my bald spot in eighth grade, when I was thirteen — which didn't help, considering that one of the causes of the disorder is poor self-image.

I learned to brush my hair so it wasn't as noticeable, but I was never able to completely cover my thin hair on top. I learned to cut my own hair so I could avoid salons. It was easy with my natural curly hair. The curls cover up uneven edges.

I tried to stop many times, but failed. That changed when I read about a study that showed the phrase "I don't" provided more empowerment than "I can't." For example, it would be more effective to say "I don't eat cake" than to say "I can't eat that cake."

After thirty-seven years with the disorder, I saw the possibility of a solution. What if I told myself, "I *don't* pull my hair anymore" instead of "I *can't* stop pulling hair?"

It's a completely different mentality. It gave me control over the impulse immediately. I could see a change in my hair in about three weeks.

It has been three-and-a-half months, and my hair is getting thicker every week. I still have the urge, but I remind myself *I don't do that anymore*. Who knew one little word — "don't" — could change a lifetime of impulsive behavior?

— Sandy Newman —

43

Tell Them You Love Them Now

I love you and that's the beginning
and end of everything.
~F. Scott Fitzgerald

A s a preteen, I loved inspirational stories. I devoured *Reader's Digest* and *Guideposts*. I treasured any heartwarming tale that gave me something to think about and I tried to incorporate the lessons I learned into my life.

One memorable story was about a person whose parent died suddenly. The last words spoken between them had been words of anger. This was not an unfamiliar situation to someone my age. As we try to establish our individuality, we push back against the people with whom we feel safe, the people we know won't turn away.

But it had never occurred to me that my parents could die suddenly. My mother and I were close, but she was the rule keeper in our house, so we argued at times.

But it wasn't Mom I thought about; it was my dad. Dad was a drinker and not one to share his feelings other than the anger or humor he sometimes revealed when he was in a storytelling mood. I started to think about my dad and his life, and the emotional distance between him and his family. My dad went to work in the mines at age thirteen, after his much-loved dad was killed in a mining accident. He had grown up too fast and too hard.

I decided that every night, before I went to bed, I would tell my dad I loved him. He was not a hugger, so I decided that when I said, "I love you," I would kiss him on the top of his bald head.

The first night I did this, he jerked his head away and looked at me like I was a crazy person. I was undeterred. Every night, it was "Good night Dad, I love you" and a kiss on his head. After a while, I noticed he stopped pulling away and began to lean in a bit. Encouraged by this, I began to add a small hug. He did not resist.

Then one night, weeks into the process, he said gruffly, "I love you, too." I paused for just a moment, struck by the wonder of it. I turned away quickly because I was not sure how Dad might respond to the tears spilling down my cheeks.

> *I decided that every night, before I went to bed, I would tell my dad I loved him.*

This changed how I saw my dad. He was not the scary guy who drank too much and had unpredictable flashes of anger. He was the guy sitting at the kitchen table every night with a beer in front of him, often with his head in his hands, who told me he loved me.

I began to sit with him on those nights he seemed talkative. As we shared a love of dogs, I got him to tell me stories about his favorite dogs, especially Mike, who followed Dad down to the mines every day. These stories revealed the tenderhearted side of my dad.

Many years later, after I was long married and living in another state, my father began to have some health problems. He refused to go to the doctor. My mother called and asked me to come home to "talk some sense into him; he'll listen to you."

I had already reserved my flight when she called to say, "Never mind, your father made a doctor's appointment." I decided to go home anyway and asked her not to tell Dad because I wanted to surprise him.

When he found me in the house, sitting at the kitchen table in "his spot," he was startled. In his usual brusque way, he blurted out, "What are you doing here?"

"Mom said you weren't feeling well, so I came home." He turned toward me and looked me straight in the eyes.

"Well, now I know I am loved." There was no hugging or overt emotion, just words from the heart.

Now he knows he is loved! I do not think he could have made such a vulnerable statement if we had not had those years of nightly "I love you's." After he turned and left the room, my mother expressed her amazement as well.

"Jude, you were right to come anyway. Your father needed you."

That doctor's appointment was the beginning of the end for my dad. He had fought off colon cancer more than twenty years before, but now was in a cancer fight that he couldn't win. Though he had surgery and we thought we had time left together, he died unexpectedly.

Fortunately, I knew what my final words to him were. I had stopped at the hospital on my way to the airport. I was returning to my home to check on my family, planning to bring them back with me to have time with Dad.

He was sound asleep. His nurse offered to wake him up, but I said "no." I wanted to carry with me this image of him sleeping so peacefully. So I just leaned in, kissed his warm head, rosy from the sponge bath she had just given him, and said, "I love you, Dad."

When I got to the funeral home and saw him in his casket, it didn't seem real. But when I leaned in and gave him a kiss on the top of his bald head to say one more "I love you," the coldness of his skin made it clear he was truly gone.

What was not gone is what I know: I am loved. I know he went to his grave knowing he was loved, too. And I'm eternally grateful to that long-ago author who wrote the story that got me to say it now, not to wait. I say "I love you" all the time — to my son and my beloved dogs, to my extended family and my friends. The beautiful thing is, most of them say it back. Often, like with my dad, they don't say it right away. But once we hit our stride, the rhythm is steady.

— Jude Walsh —

44

Sit With It

Holding on is believing that there's only a past;
letting go is knowing that there's a future.
~Daphne Rose Kingma

t was a random Monday afternoon, about two years after my forty-six-year-old husband's sudden death from cardiac arrest. I was sitting in my grief counselor's office, as I had been every Monday, when she asked innocently, "So how are you doing with the whole relationship thing? Have you thought about it at all? Have you thought about the idea of 'someone else' yet?"

I started sobbing. I felt like I had lost the ability to say words, so I just stared at her, as if searching for some explanation for everything.

She looked at me like she truly felt empathy for me and wanted to say the right thing that would fix it all. "I think it might be a very long time before you are ready to even be able to consider this as a possibility in your life. And that is totally okay. You aren't ready. But that doesn't mean you won't be one day."

Her words made sense, but I felt so stuck. "But why am I *still* in so much pain? When is the pain going to stop? Every time I try to move forward, I just miss him more. But then I'm so lonely, and I don't want to be alone forever. But I want my husband back, and that can't ever happen. I'm in love with a dead guy, but dead guys can't hug or kiss or answer me back in conversation. So what on earth am I supposed to do with all of that?"

She sat there for a moment, and then she said the three words that would first anger me, and then later change my life.

"Sit with it."

"Huh? What does that mean? Sit with what?"

"With all of it. The pain. The confusing emotions. The grief. Your feelings of love for your husband who died. Your fears about the future. You're not ready to go forward when it comes to dating, and you can't go back to the past. So you need to process all of it, marinate in it, and become friends with it. You need to sit with it until it shifts into something else."

Hmm. Interesting. "How long will that take?" I asked impatiently.

"It takes as long as it takes. Just sit with it."

At the time, in that moment, her advice and her words made me angry. It felt like she was saying to just do nothing. But now, four years later, I have come to realize that is the furthest thing from the truth.

Four years later, I have found love again, after finally being ready to open my heart to someone new. And that came as a direct result of working through many fears, hurt and pain.

I had to just sit with it.

In my life today, this piece of simple yet profound advice works in almost every situation. Trying to make a big work decision? Not sure whether or not you want to go back to school for your master's? Don't know where you should live or what comes next? When you are unable to make a decision about something or when you feel stuck, it usually means that your heart just isn't ready yet for this next thing. It needs a little time to process. To think it through.

Sometimes, you just need to sit with it.

— Kelley Lynn —

45

Is This Just a Cape Thing?

Yesterday I was clever, so I wanted to change the world.
Today I am wise, so I am changing myself.
~Rumi

I acquired a very valuable piece of advice in my forties. This came from Amy Newmark's book, *Simply Happy*. The book is a collection of the helpful advice that Amy has given and received throughout her life. The story that stood out to me involves Amy letting her children wear whatever they wanted to wear to school, including capes. She said her son dressed as Superman and wore a red cape to nursery school for months! Amy said she noticed things went better when she gave her kids "control over the unimportant things, such as how they styled their hair or what clothes they wore." Her thinking was that she'd save the "you must do it this way" conversation for the situations where it really mattered.

That made a big impression on me. Whenever I start thinking critical thoughts about a person who is doing something differently than I would, I stop and ask myself, "Is this just a cape thing?" In other words, are they doing something wrong, or are they simply doing something differently? And is it actually detrimental or just not my style?

So, here's the deal: I'm having a hard time at my job right now. I work at a beautiful hotel near the ocean in California. I've worked at this hotel for almost a decade. I have loved everything about it — the way it's decorated, the way it smells of freshly baked cookies, and the positive feedback I've received from the guests on a nightly basis.

Were things ever perfect? No, probably not. But, even so, for years my husband would say, "I've never seen someone so happy to go to work as you!" But these days my husband says, "I'm sorry you're so unhappy, hon. But you know that's how most people feel about their jobs. Most people don't like going to work; they simply do it because they have bills to pay."

Is that true? Do most people dislike going to their job?

Things at the hotel started changing about six months ago. The hotel hired several new staff members and a new interior-decorating team to "freshen up" some of the guest rooms. I was open to all of this because new people often bring wonderful insights and fresh energy to the situation. I hoped the new staff would bring great ideas. In terms of the interior decorators, I liked the hotel as it was. But things do need to evolve; otherwise, we'd all still be sleeping in caves with bear blankets!

Given that I felt open to change, it caught me off guard when I got teary-eyed as the hotel's antique wood hutch was wheeled away to make room for a bigger, more efficient, blue-and-white buffet. My emotions were so strong that I explored them as I drove home from work. Why did I cry when the antique breakfast buffet was removed? It was simply a piece of wood, right? Well, not exactly. In the silence of my car, I realized it was where I'd taken hundreds of photos of happy guests over the years. (The way the light bounced off the antique wood always gave the guests a beautiful glow, which is why I often photographed them in front of it.) I realized the tearing-up was nostalgia and appreciation for all of the beautiful experiences I've witnessed, and sometimes photographed, over the years.

It took me about a month, but I came to really like the new breakfast buffet. I liked that it gave the guests more flexibility in terms of when and where they could eat. With the larger, more efficient design of the new buffet, we were able to add a microwave for the guests to use. And now we had shelves for glasses, teacups, plates, bowls and silverware. I noticed guests started ordering dinner to be delivered to the hotel much more often, and it made me happy when I saw them enjoying a meal in the quietness and beauty of the hotel.

Next came the new staff members. One of them did bring a new, interesting perspective, but the other one was very loud and quite different from the hotel's norm. For weeks, I tried to be open to the louder staff member's approach. As she blared loud music and engaged our front-desk and housekeeping staff in boisterous conversations, I kept asking myself, "Is this just a cape thing?" When it became clear that her behavior was having a negative impact on the guests' experience, I concluded this was not "just a cape thing," and I was relieved when she was let go.

She was replaced by a new employee who has a fantastic personality but is also not the hotel's norm. This new employee is in her twenties and texts *all the time*! It bothers me because I feel she isn't fully paying attention, and therefore is being disrespectful to the guests and me by being so obsessed with her phone. But it's not just her. When Millennials check out my purchases at the grocery store, they often glance at their phone while they're waiting for the receipt to print. Last night, at the movie theater, the young person behind the counter texted continuously as I decided which size popcorn and what candy to buy. And that's when I realized that when it comes to texting, it's "just a cape thing." I need to let it go.

As for the updated guest rooms, it's a big change. Where we used to have a seaside shabby-chic décor, the new rooms have a minimalist, modern feel. I've noticed something very interesting. If guests have a long history with the hotel, they usually do not like the new rooms. But if guests are new to our hotel, they often say, "I love this room! It's so fresh and modern!"

So, for me, the hotel's repeat guests and any of you who are having trouble with change, we must ask ourselves: "Is it just a cape thing?" It usually is.

— Rachel Flynn Walker —

46

Three Choices

As I am sure you know, when people say, "It's my
pleasure," they usually mean something along the lines
of, "There's nothing on Earth I would rather do less."
~Lemony Snicket, The Penultimate Peril

"It all comes down to three choices." These were the wise words I heard one day while watching a daytime talk show. At the time of this "light bulb moment" I was consumed by a very busy vocation that involved pleasing a lot of people and I was also a single mom of three teenagers. Any given day contained more requests for my time than I could count, and I usually felt I needed to give an answer right away. That answer was usually "yes." Consequently I felt overwhelmed.

Then, on a rare day when I was home in the afternoon, one of my favorite talk show hosts talked about the "three choices." She had been prone to saying yes more than she should, and she talked about how overwhelmed she felt. However, she had learned that she didn't have to answer a request right away. If she didn't feel ready to say yes or no, she discovered that there was a third option she'd not previously employed: "Let me get back to you." She related that by giving herself time to think about how she wanted to respond, she often declined requests that she might have previously — and prematurely — said yes to. Now she was giving herself breathing room to consider her schedule, and more importantly, her desires and priorities. And she noted that it was important to have the integrity to follow up with your answer later.

It was a great idea, and in the many years since, this has been my practice. It has brought me great peace, as well as the feeling of greater control over my schedule. If you want to simplify your life, this is a beautiful tool to use. The next time someone asks something of you, remember that you have three choices. You can say yes. You can say no. Or you can say, "Let me get back to you." Consider your priorities and your desires. And then, with integrity, give your answer.

> *You can say yes.*
> *You can say no.*
> *Or you can say,*
> *"Let me get back*
> *to you."*

—Kimberly Ross—

Chapter
6

Think Positive

47

What Is Wrong with You?

Once you replace negative thoughts with positive ones,
you'll start having positive results.
~Willie Nelson

Four years after the dot-com bust, I shuttered my technology writing and consulting business. Fortunately, I soon found a new client — just one — but it was a start. At the time, I wondered if it was too good to be true. By the second month, something didn't seem right, and I developed a bad feeling about the client and the work.

When the third month's check didn't arrive on time, I sent the client an e-mail to find out what was going on. I sent another e-mail, and another, and another. The check never arrived, and I never heard from the client again.

With no prospects in sight, I hit rock bottom. Panic replaced cautious optimism along with my last shred of self-confidence. Anxious and immobilized, I hid from friends, quit answering the phone, and locked myself in my room.

One night, the phone rang, and Caller ID displayed the number of a high school friend. Even thought the last thing I wanted to do was admit my failure, I answered the phone because we had always been there to console each other during tough times. It would be good to hear a sympathetic voice on the other end of the line.

After the opening pleasantries, I launched into my laundry list of problems, knowing my friend would offer words to soothe my pain as she commiserated with me. Instead, she torpedoed my pity party with a rapid-fire soliloquy. I was too stunned to return her fire, so I just listened.

"What is wrong with you? You can do anything you want to do," she bellowed into the phone. "You are a writer, so start writing. Write for magazines."

"Write for magazines? Are you out of your mind? I don't know the first thing about writing for magazines, let alone what I could write that anyone would want to read. You have to know what you're doing just to submit a query, and I am clueless. Where would I even send the query — to what magazine and to what editor?" I yelled back at her.

"Figure it out," she said. "You were the one who concocted all the schemes to get us out of trouble when we were in high school, and you're in trouble now. Do for yourself what you always did for us. Just do it. You have always been a writer. Remember when you wrote all my papers in high school?" It had slipped my mind, but she was right.

She ended by repeating, "What is wrong with you? Get off your butt and just do it." And then she slammed down the phone. No "goodbye," no nothing!

I was furious with my friend and thought for a minute about crossing her off my list. I thought, *What is wrong with her? That's the thanks I get for all the support I've given her over the years?*

I fumed to myself. With nowhere left to turn, I fired up Google, my only remaining friend, to start the futile search for magazines that would accept a query by e-mail. In those days, most editors accepted queries only by U.S. mail, but I thought someone, somewhere must accept them by e-mail.

I found a magazine called *Low Carb Energy* that was looking for submissions. Bingo! Back in the mid-1970s, I had to lose twenty pounds in a little over a month for a flight attendant interview. I stumbled upon the Atkins Diet, reached my goal, and got the job. I had maintained my hiring weight since then thanks to watching carbs like a hawk. I was a walking encyclopedia about the low-carb lifestyle, and I was passionate about it.

I will always remember the day Dr. Atkins died; I cried uncontrollably.

Without his diet, I would never have been able to see the world and get paid to do it. If I could write about anything, it would be this. More important, that was a time when I had done something I would have thought impossible—just like now. Maybe I could pull off the impossible again.

Google returned successful query examples, so I went to work. I crafted one that combined the best of the examples. I copied and pasted the perfected query into an e-mail to the editor and hit Send. That was the last I thought about the query because I had done this exercise just to prove my friend wrong.

Imagine my surprise when, twenty-four hours later, I received an assignment. Now I had to get through the writing part of the exercise. I conducted interviews and then wrote the article in one sitting, editing it as if my life depended on it.

The article was not only accepted without a rewrite but also ended up on the cover! I went on to write for that magazine and others, not knowing that one day I would end up as editor-in-chief of a magazine and make a living as a freelance writer, editor, and author.

None of this would have happened if I had ignored my friend's advice. If not for her tough love, I might not have learned one of life's most important lessons: What was wrong with me was *me*. She made me realize the answer had to come from me—the change I needed to make was never going to come from the outside.

— MJ Plaster —

48

Exit Forward

The truth is, unless you let go, unless you forgive
yourself, unless you forgive the situation,
unless you realize that the situation is over,
you cannot move forward.
~Steve Maraboli

My therapist closed the door behind me firmly. I stood on the sidewalk, facing the lines of cars in the parking lot outside the professional office building. I blinked in the bright sunlight through eyes still damp with tears. I turned to re-enter the therapist's office, but the door through which I had exited had no doorknob or handle. My therapist had ushered me out the door of no return!

Puzzled and dazed, my one thought was, *How did I get here?*

Eight days earlier, I had dissolved at work in a well-attended staff meeting. Usually logical, dependable, and emotionally stable, all my pent-up anxieties, fears and resentments about my decision to divorce my husband gushed out in a very inappropriate setting. Jaws unhinged. I fled the staff meeting, horrified at my outburst. My long-time friend followed me and slipped into my office before I locked the door. I had isolated myself and felt so much shame that I had not even opened up to her about the end of my twenty-seven year marriage.

She listened. She left briefly and returned with a list of social workers and therapists covered by our Employee Assistance Program. "Make an appointment," she advised. I made an appointment for the following day with a therapist named Diane.

Diane welcomed me into her office. I plopped down on the couch and blurted out a jumble of fears, anger, resentment, grief and loneliness.

"What do you expect me to do?" Diane asked.

"Help me find my strengths."

Diane assigned me homework. I was to write a letter to my father, who had passed away, explaining why I was divorcing my husband. She scheduled me to return in one week.

That was an eventful week! I moved out of our home, taking only my clothing, music, photographs, bed linens and computer. I telephoned my mother and told her about leaving my husband. I stopped pretending everything was all right in my marriage. I called my grown daughters, who lived far from me. Those phone calls were more difficult than anything else. I wanted their understanding, but realized that was not realistic. I needed to be honest and accept the consequences.

Tearfully, I wrote and re-wrote the letter to my father, as Diane directed. I discovered that I still carried much grief and anger over his unexpected death.

I kept my appointment with Diane the following week. Diane wrote on her yellow pad as I talked. Calmly, I explained the actions I had taken to physically separate from my husband, and the weekly meetings he and I had set up to fill out the paperwork for an uncontested divorce. I shared how I had broken my isolation from my family. I cried softly as I told her about the letter I wrote to my dad.

Diane stood up from her desk and placed her notes into my file. She walked to a door across the room from where I had entered.

"You don't need me anymore. You have the strengths you need to go on with your life." She opened the door and I saw that it led outside. She motioned for me to leave.

I was flabbergasted. I did not budge from the couch.

"Go ahead," she directed, closing my file.

"But what about healing my relationship with my daughters?" I protested. "How about establishing another intimate relationship? How can I ever do that?"

Diane was adamant. She gestured to me once again to go out the door. "You'll figure it out."

In disbelief, I stood up reluctantly from the couch.

"But, but, but…" I edged out the door.

My therapist closed the door behind me firmly.

I did not expect this! First, I felt disbelief. Second, I felt abandoned. Third, I felt empowered. After all, Diane was paid to listen to people like me who had meltdowns at work. In her clinical judgment, she had decided that I had the strengths to rebuild my life.

So maybe I did.

I needed to find and use tools to heal myself. I realized I couldn't do that alone, but neither could I rely on someone else to do the work for me.

Acknowledging and releasing my negative feelings from so many years of a failing marriage was not accomplished in two brief counseling sessions. I needed an outlet for my pent-up feelings, and my adult daughters were not appropriate confidantes as they had their own feelings to work through.

So I blurted my feelings out to Mother Nature, finding solace and relief in pounding the sand beaches of the Gulf of Mexico. The beaches provided a private place for me to feel and release my anger, sorrow, fears and resentments. The vast beauty of the waters always comforted me, making me feel part of something larger and more important than me. The ever-changing Gulf waters mirrored my mix of emotions. The beach walks seemed safe and cleansing. With the brisk walk in the sand and release of emotions, I finally slept at night.

I needed to reconnect with people whom I had avoided, ashamed about my failing marriage. My mother and I talked on the telephone weekly. She was supportive even though she did not understand the reasons for my divorce. My sister, Nancy, who was also divorced, called me and sent little note cards. I was grateful to reconnect with Mom and Nancy.

Besides the emotional work of the divorce, there was the legal process. I met weekly with my ex-husband to complete the legal forms for an uncontested divorce. We sat across from each other at our kitchen table. With sadness and honesty, we admitted that we had failed each other as spouses. Week by week, in two-hour increments, we completed the paperwork to end our marriage. Together, we closed the door on our college courtship and long marriage.

I learned that I always have choices when a door is closed behind me. I can choose to turn back and futilely bang on that door, demanding it re-open. Or I can choose to acknowledge the emotions I feel and express them appropriately to nonjudgmental listeners. Now, when a door closes behind me, I know how to go forward.

— Mary Beth Sturgis —

49

The Right Basket

When you are grateful — when you can see what you
have — you unlock blessings to flow in your life.
~Suze Orman

"**W**hy do you have a man's lunchbox on your bookshelf?" I had noticed the old, black metal lunch pail over the years, and had just assumed it was my mother's attempt at decoration.

"Did I never tell you about the lunch pail?" she asked, surprised.

My father had passed away several years earlier, and occasionally I made the four-hour drive to spend a night with Mom and take her to dinner. This was one of those occasions.

"Shortly after your dad passed away, I struggled to make ends meet. I was paid monthly, and no matter how well I budgeted, it seemed I always came up short with a few days left till payday. No milk, no bread, nothing for sandwiches. I probably missed coffee the most."

She went on to explain how she tried to pretend she was doing some healthy dieting routine instead of having nothing. But one month, she was battling an illness right about the same time she ran out of provisions. She needed something to eat!

Before she left for work, she paused to pray, "God, I'm not asking for much — just something to help me make it until payday."

Then, as she walked to her car in the driveway, a pickup truck came hurtling by. She heard a clanking sound. She looked up to see a black lunch pail fly off the back of the truck.

She backed out of the driveway and drove down to retrieve the pail, thinking she would catch up to the truck around the corner at a red light. But he was gone. She looked down side streets and never saw his truck. On the drive to work, she couldn't resist peeking inside the lunch pail.

Two sandwiches, just like she would have made! An apple and a bag of chips. And… a Thermos of hot coffee! *Oh, Lord,* she thought, *surely you won't consider this stealing.*

So she drank the coffee and saved the food, doling it out over the next two days. She never saw the worker's truck again, so she put the lunch pail on her shelf to remind her that God has strange ways to provide, but He does provide.

I was angry when she finished her story. Mom had four grown children who would never have let their mother go without a meal.

"Every time I phoned you, I asked how you were, and you always said, 'I'm fine!' I asked if you needed anything, and you always said 'no!' So you were just lying to me!"

I continued to fuss at her. Finally, she just laughed and waved me off with her hand, saying, "Oh, son, remember the two baskets I always told you about."

The two baskets. Mom had a philosophy that everyone is given two baskets in life: a "blessing basket" and a "cursing basket."

> Mom had a philosophy that everyone is given two baskets in life: a "blessing basket" and a "cursing basket."

"Now, your 'blessing basket' is always bigger than your 'cursing basket,'" she would explain. "The secret to happiness in life is simple: Always carry your blessing basket." And with that, she would pick up a basket and wrap her arms around it in front of her chest.

"Just put the cursing basket over there somewhere," she would nod with her head. "Then, when anyone asks you how you're doing, just look down — into your blessing basket — and say, 'I'm fine!' You're not lying. You're just looking in the right basket!"

To this day, when anyone asks me how I'm doing, I respond simply, "I'm wonderful!"

It's in the basket I choose to hold.

—Danny Carpenter—

50

Be Flexible

*A flexible mind has a better chance to think differently
and take a unique path in the life journey.*
~Pearl Zhu

A few years ago, I stepped out of my comfort zone and signed up to go on a mission trip to Guatemala. It seemed like a good idea at the time, but as the departure date neared, I started to wonder what I had gotten myself into. Why in the world had I thought it would be a good idea to go to a strange country with people I hardly knew to do construction work at an orphanage?

To prepare for my trip, I spoke to a long-time missionary. "What advice can you give me?" I asked.

She merely responded, "Be flexible."

Huh? I was expecting deep words of wisdom that would equip me to face the challenges ahead. But it turned out those two words were the best advice I have ever received about mission trips and, in fact, life in general.

Being flexible is difficult for me. I am a planner, follower of schedules and maker of to-do lists. The idea of flexibility is to stretch without breaking. To my surprise, this trip revealed how much I could stretch and how much I enjoyed doing so.

As a planner, I normally like to envision what is ahead and prepare myself for it. Last-minute changes are unwelcome and disconcerting. However, I had not even made it to the Guatemalan orphanage when a huge change was thrust upon me. I had been steeling myself for dorm living with my female team members. Having experienced dorm living in college years before, I had some idea what those arrangements might be like. But on the way from the airport to the orphanage, our leader announced that the group was so large that not all the females could fit in the available dorm space. Volunteers were sought to stay in an apartment in another building. As an adult in a group made up mostly of teens and young adults, I felt compelled to raise my hand.

My willingness to be flexible with sleeping arrangements paid huge dividends. I was placed in a small apartment with two other women. There was a stunning view outside the apartment window. I only had to share the bathroom with two people instead of more than thirty. I became friends with the two ladies who were in the apartment with me. Best of all, the place was quiet and allowed me the alone time I craved as an introvert.

Now that lodging was in place, on to the work at hand. What were we going to do, and when were we going to do it? Sadly, no itineraries were distributed. Things were pretty free-flowing. I was stressed about how to be productive.

Work assignments were addressed at a group meeting on our first day. A request was made for volunteers to work in the kitchen. Unsurprisingly, no young people were interested; construction work on the hill was more exciting to them. Once again, I acted responsibly and raised my hand. I was sent off to the kitchen, where none of the workers spoke English. I did not speak Spanish. How was this going to work?

Flexibility paid off again. I was paired in the kitchen with another volunteer who became a good friend. Since then, we have gone on another mission trip together. I love to cook, so it was fun to be in the kitchen, even if I didn't always know what we were making. Kitchen duty was less physically demanding than playing mountain goat and carrying large concrete blocks up the hill to help with construction. I picked up a little bit of Spanish listening to the Guatemalan women in the kitchen. I learned that, despite a language barrier, we were able to communicate with each other on a basic level. And, of course, laughter and smiles are universal.

Meals at the orphanage provided yet another chance to work on my flexibility. It was not fine dining; there was no choice of entrees and usually no meat. Good thing I liked rice and beans! I was introduced to new dishes that, I have to admit, were very tasty. Let's take *pupusas*, for example; only by being flexible did I get to taste one. Upon my return home, I tried a Central American restaurant that served *pupusas*. Beats eating a fast-food burger any day!

I could have continued in my comfort zone sorting clothes in the orphanage's main lobby, but I agreed to carry a large box of T-shirts down the hill to the orphanage's school. I didn't know exactly where I was going, and it wasn't all that comfortable to maneuver the terrain with that box, but I was richly rewarded for my efforts. As I was leaving after dropping off the box, a small girl from the school approached and looked up at me. She began walking beside me as I headed back to the orphanage. I didn't speak Spanish, and she didn't speak English. We smiled at each other, which spoke more than words, and she shyly took my hand and held it as we walked. Had I been rigid and remained sorting clothes, I would have missed one of the sweetest encounters I ever had in my life. Thinking of it brings tears to my eyes.

My adventures on this trip gave me an appreciation for flexibility. Now I push myself to try new dishes and new experiences. Who knows? I might like them. I try to be open to Plan B if things don't go exactly how I had envisioned they would. Who knows? It might be more exciting that way. "Be flexible" wasn't just great advice for my mission trip. It's advice I now apply to everything I do.

— Alice H. Murray —

51

All the World Is a Playground

Each time we face our fear, we gain strength, courage,
and confidence in the doing.
~Theodore Roosevelt

G rowing up, I hated every girl who could skip. I sat inside at recess, watching all the skippers. No matter how hard I tried or cried, I just couldn't get the steps and rhythm right.

I felt so uncoordinated. So clumsy. My older sister tried to teach me, to no avail. And when I asked one of the girls at school to show me? Let's just say the snickering stopped me from asking again. Childhood can be brutal.

So can adulthood. I miss steps. I misstep. I watch others breeze by with more talent, connections, looks, and likes. I watch all the skippers skip by. Skipping.

Now in midlife, I am still tempted sometimes to stay inside at recess. I'm inclined to draw smaller, safer circles where I won't get hurt. It's tempting to believe I'm better off there.

But the fears never last long, thanks to the no-nonsense, no-frills fifth grade teacher named Miss Lyon who stopped all that in its tracks for me when I was just a kid. Miss Lyon was actually my older sister's teacher, but she was having none of my recess rejection. She sat down in the hallway during recess with me one day and said, "It can be rough out there, can't it?"

I nodded, holding back my tears.

She took the cue. We sat silently.

The sounds of bouncing balls, whistles and squeaking swing sets from outside punctuated the quiet. It sounded so far away. I had to admit, it also sounded like so much fun.

After a few minutes, she looked at me and promised I would find my people. Then she gave me some advice that I have never forgotten: "Walk out onto that playground like it's yours." And she opened the door to the outside and beckoned me through.

I bit my lip, smoothed my shirt and stepped onto the playground. Before my eyes even adjusted to the sunlight, an out-of-breath, sweaty boy named Mike Bowen blurted out an invitation. Batman, Superman and Aqua Man were over at the eagle's nest kicking butt and fighting crime. They needed a Wonder Woman.

They needed me.

They didn't care that I couldn't skip. They'd seen me climb to the top of the monkey bars like a pro. They needed an Amazon Princess who could pilot their invisible monkey bar plane with aplomb. In one fluid, coordinated motion, I grabbed the first monkey bar, hoisted myself up, through and onto the top of my invisible jet, and turned over the ignition. "Skippers, get out of my way," my spirit screamed. "I AM A FIERCE AMAZON WARRIOR. I fight cosmic foes so your playground is safe enough for you to skip."

How perfect. Imaginative, plot-spinning boys taught me to soar. And Miss Lyon taught me to roar.

It's been forty years now, but looking back I realize Miss Lyon knew something I didn't. Hallways at recess are empty. They are echo chambers that bounce our fears and failures back to us.

Oh, for all I know, maybe she really just wanted to get to the teachers' lounge and needed to clear the hallway. But my greater hunch is that she saw an opportunity to pour life and purpose into a lonely young person who was just one kind word away from finding her bravery.

"Walk out onto that playground like it's yours."

As a high school senior, I landed the lead role in *Oklahoma!* Even though other girls in my class had sturdier, steadier soprano voices than me, I learned my lines, practiced with a voice coach and walked onto that stage like it was mine.

At my first real newspaper job interview — which I flubbed in almost every conceivable way — I walked into the boardroom like it was mine. And I got the job.

> *"Walk out onto that playground like it's yours."*

A couple of years into my journalism career, my city editor told me to grab my notepad because I needed to head over to a United Way event for an interview. "Who am I interviewing?" I asked.

"First Lady Laura Bush," he said, waiting for a reaction. He didn't get one. I had learned years earlier to walk into any room like it was mine.

At my first-ever public-speaking engagement last year, I walked up onto the stage with that same confidence. I got tongue-twisted a few times. But the audience responded with laughter and attentiveness, and a line a dozen-deep when I was done talking.

At my church, where I lead a D-group — our churchy hip term for discipleship group — I walk weekly into a room filled with high school students. I try to understand what makes them tick. I hope that I'm helping. I don't always wear the latest fashion, but I walk into the room like it's mine.

And you know what one of the girls said to me a few weeks back? "How do you do it? You have such confidence, but it doesn't come off as arrogance. Someday, I hope I'll carry myself that way."

"You want to know the trick?" I asked her.

"You bet," she said.

"Just walk out onto the playground like it's yours," I said, telling her a story about a hallway, a teacher and a little girl who had ninja-level monkey bar skills. We walked out arm-in-arm and enjoyed a good laugh. And she promised me she would never forget the words.

— Laurie Davies —

Annie's Legacy

The first recipe for happiness is:
Avoid too lengthy meditation on the past.
~André Maurois

A s I drove to Annie's cottage, my mind was filled with worry. A
relationship that had seemed promising had ended. My company was downsizing, and I didn't know if my job was safe. I
was already overextended on my mortgage, and now my small
house needed work, which meant dipping into my ever-decreasing
savings once again.

Accelerating around the bend, I could see her cottage at the end
of the lane. At that moment, a shaft of sunlight hit my windscreen,
and for a moment I was blinded. Narrowly missing an old stone wall,
I slowed down. *I need to focus,* I scolded myself, but it was difficult to
stop the thoughts that were chasing around my head. I was worrying
about the past and trying to predict the future, and I didn't know
which problem to focus on first. I needed advice.

Some would say that my aunt — who was well known in the
village for her eccentricities — was not the best person to give advice
on matters of the heart or finances. But Annie had never failed me in
the past, and she had somehow managed to scratch out a living alone
on this small farm for years.

Leaving my car on her drive and walking around to the back of
her cottage, I found her feeding the chickens. A frayed dress hung
loosely on her small frame, tied neatly at the waist with string. Hens

clucked around her feet. She saw me and made her way to the gate. As she drew closer, I could see the fatigue around her eyes. I felt a surge of affection and admiration at how, despite her age, she managed to keep her small farm going.

Half an hour later, each of us holding mugs of tea, I filled her in on the details. Annie and I had a somewhat novel way of problem solving that involved a pack of well-thumbed playing cards from which she would "tell my fortune." As a child, I had believed we found the future in the cards. Later, I realised it was a clever form of analysis, but we still liked to play the game.

That day, though, the cards were not much help and seemed to be adding to the muddle in my head. After throwing ideas around for a while and feeling a bit despondent, I got up to make another cup of tea. But then Annie stopped me. Quite forcefully, she put her hand over my arm and said, "How long are you going to keep worrying over the past and the future?" I had to admit for the past few days I had thought of little else. She carried on, "You cannot change the past. We cannot predict the future. The only advice I can give you is to live in the moment. If you don't, before you know it, all those moments will be gone, and you won't even have the memories because you wasted them thinking about what *has* happened and worrying about what *could* be."

I think she realised she had spoken a little harshly as she carried on more softly, "Don't let yesterday and tomorrow take away today."

As I made more tea, I thought it through and had to agree that I had been spending too much time worrying over things for which, at the moment, there was no solution. Outside, it was a beautiful spring day. The beach was a mere fifteen-minute drive away. Annie's face lit up when I suggested we take a picnic to the beach.

On the shoreline, it was slightly breezy but warm enough. Gulls swooped close by and landed on the wall. The sea, though quite far out, was blue and clear. Dog walkers threw sticks, and a couple of horse riders cantered along the shoreline. People smiled as they passed, relaxed by the calm, wide-open space.

We walked for a while until we found a bench with a great view.

Annie headed off towards a beach shop. I guessed she was going for ice cream. However, when she returned, she was carrying two oblong shapes that looked like sticks. With a secretive grin, she started to undo the packages. I laughed when I realised she had bought a couple of kites.

> **"Don't let yesterday and tomorrow take away today."**

We took the kites onto the top of the sea defences. After one or two false starts, the breeze caught them. Before long, we could not think of anything but controlling the kites as they skipped and bounced in the sky, making us run forward or dash quickly backwards. Out of the corner of my eye, I could see people stop and smile, enjoying the view of two women in billowing clothes, running around, bumping into each other, and laughing wildly.

When we finally ran out of steam, we sat on the grass and looked up at the sky. I looked at Annie. On her face was an expression of pure pleasure. I was glad she and I hadn't spent the afternoon trying to find answers to my problems, but had instead enjoyed the day.

A couple of weeks later, I decided to pay Annie another visit. She had been right about telling me not to worry too much. Things had already improved. My job was once again safe, and some quotes for repairing my house weren't as high as I expected. So it was with excitement one evening after work that I put a little camping stove in the car and drove out to her place. It was a great evening for supper on the beach.

As I turned out of the bend at the top of the lane to Annie's cottage, I reflected on how just a short time ago I had been so lost in worry that I nearly crashed my car. I could see Annie's cottage at the end of the lane, welcoming as it always was.

But then my stomach gave a jolt. In front of Annie's cottage stood an ambulance, its engine idling. I could just make out the uniforms of two paramedics as they crossed the garden.

I left the hospital later that evening holding a small carrier bag containing Annie's belongings. The heart attack had been mercifully swift. She didn't suffer, I was told by the neighbour who had been visiting and called the ambulance.

Over the weeks and months, as I came to terms with my grief at losing my friend and confidante, Annie's advice often came to mind.

We could have sat in the cottage on that beautiful spring day drinking tea and trying to solve my problems, but instead we chose to enjoy the time at the beach. I will always be grateful for Annie's advice and that day we spent together, even flying kites together like young girls.

Her legacy to me is the beautiful piece of wisdom that will stay with me always: "Don't let yesterday and tomorrow take away today."

—Michelle Emery—

53

Two Words

Love cures people, both the ones who give it
and the ones who receive it.
~Karl A. Menninger

The only thing harder than being married to a competitive spouse is divorcing one. My husband was unbelievably charming as long as he got his way, but divorce to him meant war.

The war was underway one Christmas Eve, and I felt about as low as I could possibly get. I didn't know where we would live or what would happen to the children, or even our dog.

I found a church in the phonebook and took my two teenagers with me. I don't remember the sermon. I don't even remember the context. All I remember is that it was there, on that Christmas Eve, where the minister said something that felt so much like the gentle, whispering words of God that it was all I could do to keep from crumbling to the ground in a heap of tears.

He said simply, "Love wins."

Love wins.

Those were exactly the words I needed to hear. They were the words that kept me going that night and many nights after. Those are the words I still whisper to myself like a chant when I need strength.

Love wins. Not my husband. Not I. Love. Love wins.

When I told my husband I was divorcing him, he announced that he would punish me by getting custody of the children, because he had the financial wherewithall to do so. But in the end, the children didn't fall for it and refused to be bought. They stood firm. I stood firm. And I got full physical and legal custody.

Love wins.

A friend of mine, who didn't know that my soon-to-be-ex-spouse was trying to control me through money, suggested someone who could help me with my taxes. This wonderful man was more help than a lawyer ever could have been. When my husband became angry that he could no longer control my money, he tried to accuse me of breaking the law in a tax matter. This sparked an investigation that ended up bringing his own financial dishonesty to light in court papers while simultaneously exonerating me, all thanks to the caring of a friend.

Love wins.

My husband did everything he could to make it harder for me to leave. He spent money I'd inherited. So I turned to my first love, writing, with renewed enthusiasm. He tried to keep me from writing, too, but that was one thing he couldn't take away. In fact, in a sense he inspired me all the more to pen the words that soothe my spirit and replenish my soul, "Love wins."

It's not about conquering. Love never attacks. It rarely wins riches. It often doesn't win right away. Sometimes, it takes years and is attacked mercilessly in the meantime. But it withstands, waiting sure and strong and true, refusing to budge. And through enduring, love wins. If the intentions are humble and honest and sincere, love wins.

It hasn't been easy. I fail often. We still struggle, the children and I. But I look at these loving, wonderful young people, and I know the truth of those words. I know it when I pet our dog or look out the window of our home at our little garden. I didn't do this. Love did. And love wins.

Just knowing that fills me with happiness that there really is a form of natural justice in the world, and that alone makes the point all over again. Knowing that love wins makes love win.

What a paradox that it took a man who doesn't know love to push me, stumbling, up the path to this wonderful truth. No matter what I encounter, I will try to remember and be grateful, because love wins.

— T. Powell Pryce —

54

A Lesson in Perspective

Life is 10% what happens to us and 90%
how we react to it.
~Dennis P. Kimbro

The breath left her body as her chest hit the concrete. Her knees stung. And when my friend looked at her scraped arm, she noticed the purse that had dangled from it was gone. It was Hannah's first day in California. And as she picked herself up off the ground, she thought, *I'm going to like it here.*

The mugging happened in an instant, but Hannah's reaction to it has stuck with me always.

Hannah came to the Golden State for college. She had a sweet nature and calm, quiet style that reflected her Midwestern roots. When I met her, I was immediately attracted to her optimistic nature. I had to work at being positive, and I found it exhausting. I thought being negative was an innate part of my character. So I surrounded myself with positive people, trying to absorb their optimism by osmosis. Their joyful dispositions made me feel good when I was around them.

We were having dinner when Hannah told the story about her mugging. Several of us at the table were transplants to Southern California, and the conversation had turned to our first experiences in the state. Hannah was smiling as she talked about the excitement she felt when she moved to the West Coast. She said that when she decided to take a stroll around the college campus, she did so with happy abandon. And that might be what made her so ripe for a hard-hearted handbag thief.

After visiting the bookstore, she continued to the student housing area, admiring the palm trees and brightly colored flowers so different from fall back in Missouri. Other students were out enjoying the perfect Southern California weather — walking, skateboarding, playing Frisbee, and sitting on the balconies of their dorm rooms. That seemingly safe environment was just the type of atmosphere for a purse purloiner to find unsuspecting prey — like Hannah.

Hannah didn't hear him coming up behind her. She just felt a tug on her arm, and suddenly she was on the ground, skidding across the concrete. When she lifted her head, she saw a man running away with her purse. A shout went up to her left, and two students leaped over their balcony railing and chased the thief. But he was too far ahead. Her purse — with her money, credit card and ID — was never recovered.

"What a welcome to California," I said.

And that's when she said it — that incongruous line that has stuck with me ever since. "Yeah," she said, "that's when I decided I was going to like it here."

My jaw dropped. I was being sarcastic, but she wasn't. How could two friends see the same event from completely different perspectives?

"What?" I said, incredulously.

"What a great place — where two complete strangers risked their safety to help me," Hannah said.

Whoa. Wait a minute. I never would have seen the situation like that. I was focused on the purse snatcher: the negative. She focused on the men who tried to help: the positive. I had totally missed it.

> *"What a great place—where two complete strangers risked their safety to help me."*

That simple moment, sitting at the dinner table, was life changing for this glass-half-empty person. Happiness, it seems, is a matter of perspective. The silver lining. The bright side. The power of positive thinking. Seeing the good in the bad. That's the well Hannah dips into for her happiness. And we all have the ability to exercise that inner strength — even me.

I felt the weight of negativity lift. The simplicity of it was a lasting — and contagious — awakening.

"Pass the wine," I said. "My glass is half full."

— Martha M. Everett —

55

Back on the Horse

Failure is only the opportunity more
intelligently to begin again.
~Henry Ford

When I was nine years old, I badly wanted a dog, but my sister was allergic. Knowing my love for animals, my parents allowed me to graduate straight from caring for gerbils and walking the neighbor's dog to getting a pony. Bonnie was a dappled brown Shetland pony with a blond mane and tail.

While I was a lucky child, I was not a pampered child. I paid for Bonnie with my allowance and money I'd earned from doing extra chores. I had no previous horse experience, and I had to learn everything about Bonnie's needs because she was my responsibility. I learned how to feed, water and care for her every day. I hauled bales of hay, sacks of feed and buckets of water. I cleaned her stall, wielding a pitchfork and pushing a wheelbarrow. I learned how to brush Bonnie and pick the stones out of her hooves without getting kicked or stepped on.

My parents had no previous experience with horses either, so we learned together. They helped by hauling the grain and hay from the feed mill, and scheduling Bonnie's regular hoof trims and veterinary exams. We learned how to properly fit Bonnie's bridle and strap on her saddle.

My first riding lesson on Bonnie was in an outdoor arena with a wood fence. The painted white boards that circled the ring were nailed to the outsides of wooden posts.

I was feeling fine in the saddle, riding around the oval ring, when Bonnie bolted suddenly. Those horizontal boards were mounted low so as to stop a full-size horse from exiting, but Bonnie was short enough to duck her head and run under one of the boards. She fit, but I did not. Hanging on for dear life, I slammed into the board and knocked it off the posts to which it was nailed. The force of the blow knocked me off Bonnie. As I slid off her right side, the saddle spun around until it was hanging upside down from her belly with my left foot stuck in the stirrup. Bonnie, now at a gallop, dragged me along the ground by my left foot. I still remember the ground scraping along my back as my head bounced up and down and the sky appeared and disappeared. Mercifully, my left foot finally came free. I was left lying on my back with the wind knocked out of me, the dust from Bonnie's hasty retreat clouding up all around.

Mom and Dad hurried over to assess the damage. Fortunately, I was a sturdy child. Although I was covered with dust and would soon be black and blue, I wasn't bleeding profusely and didn't have any broken bones. We didn't wear helmets in those days, and I was a bit dazed, but my skull was intact, and my head seemed to be okay. Mom tended to me as I caught my breath, while Dad hiked off to the far pasture to retrieve Bonnie and the saddle that was hanging upside down from her belly.

What had spooked Bonnie so suddenly? We hadn't seen or heard anything. Dad said that he'd found a nail protruding from the underside of the saddle. The jab from the nail must have penetrated the saddle blanket and startled Bonnie. Dad fixed the nail so it didn't protrude and re-secured the saddle on Bonnie's back.

Once Bonnie and I had calmed down and were reassured, trying again was the only option. It was presented humanely, with plenty of support and an explanation for why the ride would be much smoother the second time — the nail had been fixed! It helped that Bonnie was exhausted from her gallop to the far corner of the pasture, and that Dad held the reins and led Bonnie around the ring with me back up in the saddle.

Bonnie and I learned that trying again could change things. Most people have heard the old saying, "Get back on the horse that threw you." People usually use that saying figuratively, but I learned it quite literally. As an impressionable nine-year-old, I learned without a doubt that something that had spun completely out of control into terrifying chaos just a few minutes earlier could turn out to be quite enjoyable the second time. We had survived the chaos! I learned to try again, and to try *differently* the next time to achieve a better result.

That experience had an enormously positive effect on my life. I think of all the times since then when something went terribly wrong, and I knew viscerally that I could try again and expect a completely different outcome. Like when I was in graduate school and my professor told me I wasn't graduate school material. I was stunned, but I didn't give up. I fired him as my advisor, found an advisor who believed in me, and earned two graduate degrees. Or when I lost my job due to a corporate acquisition and layoff. Instead of panicking, I took time to write a book and think about what I really wanted to do. Then I found a better job at a higher salary.

> *I learned to try again, and to try differently the next time to achieve a better result.*

My wise parents helped Bonnie learn the lesson well, too. From then on, Bonnie and I were friends, exploring many happy trails together while the saddle and I stayed up top!

I never saw the nail. Over the years, I've sometimes wondered if the "nail under the saddle" was a parental white lie to help get me back on the horse... a way to convince me to mount Bonnie and try again, with Dad holding the reins. Recently, almost fifty years later, I asked my parents if there really had been a nail sticking out. They both agreed emphatically that there was, and Dad told me more about how he had fixed it.

And that is why my family says, "Get back on the horse that threw you... but check under the saddle for a nail first!" This great advice has served me well for most of my life.

— Jenny Pavlovic —

56

The Way I See It

*A positive attitude gives you power over your
circumstances instead of your circumstances
having power over you.*
~Joyce Meyer

In my early forties, I was diagnosed with late-stage breast cancer. As a non-smoker who ate the right foods and exercised daily, all I could think was, *Why me?* My dread of the long journey ahead—surgery, chemotherapy and radiation—restricted me from seeing a bright side.

A few months later, my neighbor Greg fell off a roof and was paralyzed from the waist down. Only thirty at the time, he was an avid outdoorsman, plus he had a six-week-old baby. I could only imagine his despair. In a matter of seconds, he went from being an active young man to being helpless. I thought about visiting him, but didn't know if he felt up to company. Worse, I didn't know what to say.

Each time I passed his house, childhood memories surfaced of my dad and me fishing, playing catch, ice skating, sleigh riding—all the things Greg would never be able to do with his daughter.

Later that fall, hoping to take advantage of the balmy, sunny day, I decided to go for a short walk. But chemo had taken its toll, and now radiation had sapped the last of my energy. Dejected, I had turned around to go back home when Greg drove by honking and waving as if he hadn't a care in the world. To say the least, I was shocked to see he'd made his truck handicapped accessible.

Feeling guilty for not visiting sooner, I whipped up a homemade cinnamon coffeecake the following weekend. Before I could ring the doorbell, I heard wheels rolling on the hardwood.

In a cheery voice, Greg yelled, "Come on in. Enjoying the weather?"

Without thinking, I replied, "It's a great day for a walk." No sooner were the words out of my mouth than I felt my face turn red.

He grinned and added, "Or a roll."

He pointed to the fresh pot of coffee brewing and told me to grab two mugs off the counter. We sat down, and I worked up the courage to ask him how he was doing.

He answered, "I'm not gonna lie. At first, all I did was mope, making not only myself but everyone around me miserable. As far as I was concerned, my life was over, and nothing anyone said or did could alter my mood. Then one day, my dad, a retired Marine whose motto is 'Improvise, Adapt, Overcome,' stopped by and had a talk with me. He said, 'Son, you're looking at this all wrong. You need to focus on what you *can* do instead of what you *can't*.'"

Greg said he resented his dad's remarks, thinking he couldn't possibly understand what it was like to be confined to a chair.

"Dad continued, 'You still have your mind, don't you? Your hands still work, right? You can see and hear and speak.'"

Greg paused and said, "Dad summed up his pep talk with, 'The way I see it, the only thing different is your mode of transportation.'"

The muscles in Greg's chin trembled. "Dad's advice changed my life. The list of things I could still do was much longer than the things I couldn't. Thanks to his words, I had my truck made wheelchair accessible. And with my new lift, there was no reason I couldn't go back to my job as a body-shop technician. I've always loved boating, so I plan on getting back on the lake next summer."

When I got ready to leave, I hugged Greg and told him I admired his courage.

Although my mode of transportation hadn't been affected, my vehicle's exterior had changed considerably. Greg's inspiring story started me down the path of acceptance. No more wasting precious time and energy obsessing over hair loss or a damaged headlight that wouldn't hamper my life in any way.

Twenty-three years later, I'm still in remission, and Greg is doing well. The last time we spoke, he told me he was thinking of retiring in a few years so he could travel.

The way I see it, we're both cruising down the road of life just fine.

—Alice Muschany—

Chapter 7

Follow Your Heart

57

Time of My Life

How wrong we are to ignore our hearts
to follow the familiar path.
~Nikki Rowe

"Teach a life-skills class in an inner-city school?" I asked during a staff meeting. "Why in the world would I do that?"

A single woman in my thirties, I had a comfortable workload and didn't want to add another job responsibility. Besides, what did I know about teaching? I had no interest in public education; I didn't even have children!

"As employees in the community development department, our mission is to make the city a healthier place to live," my boss explained.

How this goal would be accomplished by teaching a room full of high school kids was beyond my comprehension. But my boss wanted "Life Management" to start the next month, so I began compiling a curriculum.

My duties as a community development specialist in an Oklahoma City hospital were mundane compared to the career I'd abandoned eleven years earlier in journalism and broadcasting. Though routine, my job was simple, and the salary was excellent. I had settled for security instead of continuing to challenge myself.

Little did I know that in going back to school as a teacher, I would be the one getting an education.

My first day at the high school, I felt as apprehensive as a child beginning kindergarten. Walking down the locker-lined hall, I remembered the hope of youth — that feeling of having my whole life ahead of me. At sixteen, my future seemed full of promise. Twenty years later, I was in that "future." Yet, I had given up my dreams, which required hard work, when I settled for the secure job I now had.

I walked into the classroom and found myself in a different world. One boy's dyed orange hair was tipped with green. Another sported large tattoos on his neck, ankles, shoulders and forearms. Two pregnant girls sat together in the second row, their stomachs bulging behind the desk.

Life Management won't help these misfits, I thought.

I made it easy on myself by having guest speakers talk to the class about topics like careers, managing money, making responsible choices, and setting goals. As the semester wore on, my view of those students changed. I saw them as children in need of encouragement and acceptance.

"That was an excellent question you asked, Maria," I praised the Hispanic girl with gang symbols on her hands. "You really paid attention today."

The corners of her mouth turned upward. "I liked the way that lady talked to us," she said. "Someday, I want to be a counselor and help people the way she does."

The speakers were making a difference for some students, but I never imagined that I, too, would be changed by one of the lectures.

Halfway into the semester, a guest walked into the classroom with an air of charisma that captivated us. Dr. Johnny Griggs looked more like an NFL linebacker than a neonatal intensive care pediatrician. Dr. Griggs's compassionate eyes belied his imposing frame. Immediately, the students seemed mesmerized by the soft-spoken black man in green surgical scrubs.

"None of you is here today by accident," he said, scanning the room and making eye contact with each student. "You all have a purpose for being alive on this earth. It's up to you to discover your destiny."

Dr. Griggs explained the importance of making every day count.

"Think of your life as the face of a clock. Most people live to be about eighty years old, so that would be the twelve o'clock position.

You are almost twenty years old, and that puts you at three o'clock, so a quarter of your life is gone."

His shiny, black eyes glowed with excitement as he said, "Choose wisely how you spend the time you have left."

We were spellbound as we listened, until the buzzing of his beeper broke our trance. Dr. Griggs had to get back to the hospital, but he'd left us with enough to think about for a lifetime.

On the way home, I realized the hands on my clock were approaching six! For all practical purposes, my life was half over. I had put aside my dream of a journalism and broadcasting career, and instead, I was living a safe, mediocre life.

That evening, I wrote in my journal about the regret I felt because I gave up on my dream of writing and broadcasting. As the words poured onto the pages, it became evident that I should go back into journalism.

Almost daily, I remembered the clock analogy and thought about writing. Soon, a concept for a book emerged, and I began waking up at 5:00 a.m. to write before going to work. Not a morning person, I felt energized by my passion. What a contrast from the lethargy and apathy I felt doing the job at the hospital.

> *"Think of your life as the face of a clock."*

Months later, I told a co-worker about my morning routine and the few opportunities I had to write. "They're going to have to fire me before I have enough time to finish that book," I joked.

Twenty minutes later, my boss called me into her office. A reduction-in-force had eliminated my job! But thanks to Dr. Griggs, I realized there was a plan for my life. The hospital's severance package allowed me to launch my career. I had time and money to follow my dream.

Never again would I comb the help-wanted ads and accept an easy or meaningless way to make a living. No longer would I hide my talent and desire to write. Dr. Griggs's words reminded me to fulfill my destiny. The hands on the clock of my life warned that there was no more time to waste.

The semester I taught Life Management, I learned the importance of following my dream. Since July 1999, I've been a full-time writer, newspaper columnist, and radio host. Instead of regretting the years wasted, I focus on Dr. Griggs's advice to "choose wisely how I spend the time I have left." And I'm having the time of my life!

— Stephanie Welcher Thompson —

58

What I Deserve

One of the most beautiful qualities of true friendship is
to understand and to be understood.
~Seneca

"Is Rob coming?" one of my friends asked over the loud music pumping throughout the club. The whole group of girl-friends at our table turned and looked at me. They waited for my answer. In my heart, I knew he wasn't coming. But I found myself saying, "Maybe, maybe later."

My friend smiled sweetly and said, "Let's go dance."

I knew what they were all thinking, but no one said a word.

I'd been dating Rob for a few months. He was funny, cute and kind. He had so many great qualities, but nailing down a time to see him was nearly impossible. He'd say things like "My work is unpredictable." "I might have the kids this weekend." "I'm not sure, but I might be going out of town." He never really knew when he'd be free.

I wanted to believe him.

As the night went on, I grew increasingly more doubtful that he'd show. Finally, the dreaded text came.

"Sorry, can't make it tonight. The kids are coming over."

My heart sank. Again.

I found myself torn. He was a hard-working, single dad. It was one of my favorite things about him. He was there for his kids. His whole life was about his girls. How could I be mad at that?

I'd try to tell myself, *See him when you see him. Enjoy time with him when it comes. Go on with your own life. If he comes, he comes.*

But the truth is, it made me feel unimportant. If he really liked me, he'd make time. If he really cared, he'd find a way. If he wanted to see me, he would.

Each time I'd get that last-minute excuse, my heart would break a little more. Each cancelation was a little dig at my self-esteem.

I left the club feeling dejected. *I can't keep waiting for this guy.* My head knew it. I just couldn't convince my heart.

The following weekend was my girlfriend Lyndal's birthday. A few girls got together to surprise her with a weekend away. We rented a condo in Friday Harbor. It's a sleepy little town, but it's beautiful — the perfect place to go with friends for quality time. And it was a welcome distraction from my boy problems.

We got into town, went out to dinner, and returned to our condo, where we drank wine, played games, and danced around the living room to our favorite songs. One by one, our friends went to bed.

Finally, it was just Lyndal and me. She looked at me as if she were reading my mind. "What's up with Rob?" she said.

"I don't know. Nothing," I said.

"Do you want to know why I married Jason?" she said.

"Sure. Why?"

"He shows up," she said.

I wanted to cry.

She continued, "He shows up. When he says he's coming, he comes. When I need him, he's there. He shows up." She looked at me lovingly and said, "You deserve that, too."

I'll never forget the look on her face — the way she made me feel that night. The love and kindness of her words melted my heart. I got it. I got it so clearly. "You deserve a guy who shows up."

> "You deserve a guy who shows up."

She could have said Rob was a jerk. She could have said, "Don't put up with his wishy-washy crap." But instead she simply told me why she picked her husband: "He shows up."

It seems so obvious. But in the middle of it, I couldn't see clearly. I just felt confused. I felt my own self-esteem slipping away. But that's the thing about good friends—they won't let that happen.

When I got back to town, I ended things with Rob.

That night, a good friend taught me that I deserve someone who shows up. And now I know I will not settle for anything less.

—Diana Lynn—

59

You're Home Now

It is only with the heart that one can see rightly;
what is essential is invisible to the eye.
~Antoine de Saint-Exupéry, The Little Prince

didn't want to take Sasha back to the shelter. When she sat down on the river trail and gazed at me with her brown-sugar eyes, I understood that she didn't want to go back either. We had a bond, but I couldn't seriously keep this dog, could I?

"What do you think, girl?" I asked. "Are you my dog?"

Sasha and I had known each other for all of twenty minutes. We were taking a half-hour walk together from the Humane Society and back. I started volunteering with the dogs a few months before because I was living in a rental that didn't permit pets. I expected every dog to steal my heart, and I figured I would want to take them all home. But it turns out that dogs are like other people's children: I am happy they exist, and I want them to have loving homes, but I'm relieved that most of them are not mine.

Sasha was different, though. She was incredibly gentle, and she softened my resolve. She also displayed a submissive side, as if she'd been mistreated earlier in life. She needed a mellow home and someone to cuddle her more than she needed forty acres and a pack of playmates.

Now, I finally lived in a house that allowed pets. There were no logistical hurdles blocking me from adopting Sasha.

I walked her back to the Humane Society. "You're home now, girl," I said. I handed her leash to one of the kennel techs and left her there.

I drove home and reasoned with myself. My life was in no shape to care for another creature. Thirty years into life, I was finally taking care of myself. I was living on my own, had found an exceptional therapist, and landed a full-time job pursuing my passion. This was *my* time, and I wasn't going to give it up to another creature.

Or that's what I told myself. Obviously, I couldn't really let go of the thought of adopting Sasha because she came up first thing at my session that week. I offered my therapist all my logical explanations for not adopting Sasha. Then I expressed the emotions that are always percolating under our logical explanations.

"I'm also afraid I'm just putting off the hard work of owning a dog," I said finally. "I'm doing all this great work with myself, finding out who I am, and taking care of myself. If I get a dog, aren't I giving myself an excuse not to focus on me?"

I anticipated my therapist would do what therapists do — invite me to talk about what I'd just expressed, walk me deeper into the emotions, circle me around the underlying issues like a squirrel around a nut until finally I cracked into the truth.

Instead, she asked me one simple question: "What does your heart say?"

Her brevity startled me. "Say about what?" I asked.

"Do you want a dog?" she said. "What does your heart say to that?"

"Yes," I said. "Yes, I want a dog." And I meant it. My heart space had swelled when I presented it with that simple yes-or-no question, and I could only trust the response that made me feel free.

"There you go," she said. "You can trust your heart on these things."

I really could trust my heart, couldn't I? I had just felt it, physically, in my body. Her simple statement sounded like something I'd read on a hundred tea-bag tags. Those little sayings always sound nice, but they don't usually land. But this one — "You can trust your heart" — had an experiential component. I felt in my own chest what it was to trust my heart.

It was open and easy. There was no other way to live. I could listen to my heart. And my heart said I should go back to the shelter and see if Sasha was there.

That weekend, I made a beeline for Sasha's kennel. She was gone. Maybe she'd just moved. I asked one of the kennel techs about her. "She went home this week," he said.

My heart sighed. Dogs come into our lives for reasons. Sometimes, they come in to teach us about ourselves throughout a lifetime. Sometimes, they teach us valuable lessons on a thirty-minute walk. Sasha had come into my life for a reason, and then she found her home.

> *It was open and easy. There was no other way to live. I could listen to my heart.*

I walked a few dogs that day, and none of them spoke to my heart. I knew what it felt like to have my heart hum, though. I knew I didn't need to seek out a dog. My heart would tell me when I found the right one.

I tested that theory about a month later. I walked a dog named Wally. He was another chill dog, very gentle on the leash and comfortable with me. When I returned him to the shelter, I told the tech that Wally had done great on his walk.

"Wally did great?" the tech repeated.

"Oh, yeah. He was awesome," I said.

"Wally," he said. "Wally did great?"

"Totally." The tech's response baffled me, until I saw Wally in his kennel before I left. The shelter had clipped a sheet over his door to block his view because he was barking at everyone who walked by. He was throwing himself against the sides, miserable in his space. This was a different dog than the one I had just walked.

"Bye, sweet guy," I said. "Good luck finding your home soon."

And that was the end of that. Or so I thought. But Wally kept wiggling his way into my head that week. I'd find myself thinking about him while I was hiking to work and making dinner. He'd done well with me — me! — when he had not done well with anyone else in three weeks at the shelter.

I'd seen for myself how much living in a kennel stressed him. I'd also seen how relaxed he was while walking with me.

About mid-week, I finally heard my heart pounding against my ribs. It declared, in its outdoor voice, "Go walk that dog again."

I could trust my heart. Absolutely. The trick, though, was to actually listen to it. It had been sending me this message all week. My mind kept getting in the way, questioning my heart's decision-making abilities. But my heart knew what my mind could not comprehend. My heart knew love when it found it.

This time, when I returned to the shelter, my dog was still there. I took Wally for another walk, just to try out our connection one more time.

Then I walked him back to the Humane Society. "You're home now, bud," I said. I handed his leash to one of the kennel techs and added, "Wally's coming home with me today."

— Zach Hively —

60

The Chance to Follow My Dreams

The biggest adventure you can take is to
live the life of your dreams.
~Oprah Winfrey

I always wanted to be a writer. Some of my earliest memories are of Ma reading me stories and poems, and telling me about the lives of my favorite writers and poets like Robert Louis Stevenson, Tennyson, and Malory. I had my first story published when I was eight years old—a little piece about my Basset Hound named Milkbone—and I could not have been happier. I was always writing and telling stories to my friends, but to actually be "a writer" seemed impossible to me. Even though my friends and family were always very encouraging, I didn't think my work was anything special. I certainly didn't think of myself as a writer.

All through high school, I contributed pieces to the literary magazine, and I went on to college to learn how to be a writer. I wanted to study all the great works of literature and see how other writers told their stories. But the more I read, the more impossible it seemed that I could ever be one of them.

In the course of my studies, I found I had a talent for critical interpretation and public speaking. Before I even understood what was happening, I found I'd been turned into a scholar, not a writer. I went on to graduate school, taught entry-level composition courses, and then began a career as a college instructor. I loved the work in the classroom and enjoyed almost every minute working with my students. But at the back of my mind, I would sometimes catch a glimpse of the ghost of my former self — the little boy happily reading his story about his dog, who had wanted to be a writer.

I was offered a position with the University of Maryland's European Division, a program the school ran in conjunction with the Department of Defense to provide college courses for military personnel serving overseas. I had only been teaching a few years, and the offer was quite an honor. There was also the opportunity to travel in Europe. I was married by this time to my best friend, Betsy, and she was as excited about the whole adventure as I was. But even as I signed the contract, I felt this disappointment in the pit of my stomach as though I were signing away something I'd never wanted to lose.

Later, I was sitting outside my mother's house with my younger brother Jason, and we were talking about my new position and how I'd be leaving soon for Europe. Jason and I had always been close, and I knew I would miss him more than anyone once I left the United States. This feeling of loss brought to the surface those others of surrendering my early dreams for a comfortable career as a college instructor. I hadn't told anyone how I was feeling because it seemed so selfish and silly. What did I have to complain about? I was about to leave for a job that would take me to places I had always wanted to visit — a job I genuinely loved and was good at — and I felt ashamed to be feeling ungrateful for the opportunity.

Even so, that day when we were sitting out back together, I heard myself telling him what I was feeling about sacrificing what I'd always dreamed of because I didn't feel I could ever succeed at it. Writers were exceptional people, and I wasn't. I didn't see how I would ever be, but still I felt I had quit something important before I even allowed myself to begin.

Jason sat a moment and then said, "I think you're already a writer. You're the only one who doesn't. Sure, writers are special people, but so is everyone. What's a writer? Someone who writes. You want to write professionally? What's stopping you? You think a writer is 'somebody,' but you know what? You're somebody. You're somebody, too."

I thanked him for the advice, but I didn't really believe it. Maybe I could write, but I was no Hemingway. Betsy and I left for Europe, and I taught in Germany and then Greece and then Germany again. We traveled through Egypt, and went to Paris and plenty of other places. My job was even better than I'd imagined it would be, but I wasn't happy. I certainly did my best to enjoy and appreciate everything as much as I could, but at the end of an evening, when I was all alone, I had to admit to myself that this wasn't what I wanted to be doing with my life.

And that's when I remembered Jason's advice: "What's stopping you? You think a writer is 'somebody,' but you know what? You're somebody, too."

That night, I told Betsy I wanted to finish out the term I was teaching and then return home, get a simple nine-to-five job, and give myself the chance to become a writer. She supported me completely, much to her credit. And when the term ended, we went back to the United States. I got a job working in the basement of the County Office Building, and I wrote every day. I wrote in the morning before work, during breaks, and in the evenings after dinner. I kept a journal, I tried writing scripts, novels, short stories, poems, song lyrics and articles — working and working to learn the craft of writing. After a year, I had a handful of short pieces I felt were good enough to publish.

I think we give up on our dreams too often because we think they're impossible without ever giving ourselves the chance to find out. Once I started pitching stories for publication, I found markets for them within a month. I published a few articles afterwards and then some more stories. And when I was satisfied that I could call myself a writer, I returned to teaching at a local college.

I continued to write and publish. A few years later, I was contacted by Mr. Jan van der Crabben. He was starting up a history website and invited me to contribute. I've been writing for Ancient History Encyclopedia ever since and have published over 500 articles on that site alone, not to mention on other sites and in magazines. None of that would have happened if I hadn't given myself the chance to follow my dreams. But that chance was only possible because of the best advice I ever heard—when my little brother assured me that I was somebody, too.

—Joshua J. Mark—

61

Only If You Want To

*Life is a matter of choices, and every choice
you make makes you.*
~John C. Maxwell

"Would you like to play your fiddle with us on Friday?" my eighty-two-year-old friend, Leroy, asked as I was gathering up my things.

Was he crazy? Play with him? How could I do that? At fifty-seven, I had, for some reason, asked him to teach me to play fiddle. Now he had shown me two tunes that I enjoyed. He had made learning music fun for the first time in my life.

He had grown up with music, playing with his dad at dances since he was ten. Now he was a well-known, semi-professional musician.

My history with music was not good. I had always liked music, but it never seemed to work out well for me. I received subtle — and not-so-subtle — hints that I was not very musical. In regards to my short-lived piano lessons, I once heard my grandmother say worriedly to my grandfather, "Oh, dear! She should be doing much better by now." A couple of forced and poor piano performances were a disaster. Shyness and nervousness only escalated my feelings of inadequacy.

"I couldn't do that," I told Leroy in response to his question, thinking of my past.

I expected him to reassure me I'd do all right or that I'd get better with practise on stage. He didn't. He said, "Think about it. Only play if you want to."

I didn't know what to say. I made no reply except to tell him goodbye.

Little did I know then that the phrase "only play if you want to" would become an important guide for my entire life.

But at that moment, it made no sense to me. No one was forcing me to participate. I could play on stage at the town hall with this man and his family band or I could stay on the couch and watch a movie and eat popcorn to my heart's content.

And guess which one I chose? I didn't want to miss this opportunity. What a twist in thinking my life was taking. I had chosen the easier "popcorn route" too many times because I didn't realize what I really wanted… and didn't know there is always a choice for me.

> *Little did I know then that the phrase "only play if you want to" would become an important guide for my entire life.*

Suddenly, I felt fortunate to have this choice.

When I realized what I really wanted, it changed years of behavior. It helped me find my inner power and confidence, and I felt good about the risk.

I thought to myself, *This man is not only good in music, but he is a psychologist, too. He is like the music whisperer; he offered his trust and belief in me, and then gave me space to decide.*

It was clear that I wanted to play on stage with him and do the best I could. I started to practise more, in a focused and meaningful way.

And when the time came, I was there. I didn't lose all my nervousness, but enough to relax on stage and smile at Leroy before I began. I played my little fiddle tunes with a full band to back me up. What wonderful support. It was enough to make me laugh about how I had considered opting out. It went pretty well — not perfectly, but perfectly for me. I had made my first fiddle appearance as a lead player in a band, and it was enough for one night.

A short time later, my kind teacher and friend Leroy passed away. But his "only play if you want to" advice stayed. This advice has helped me not only in music, but in all aspects of life. When I honour the choice, I eliminate the fear. That makes more room for gratitude and joy in my life.

Today, I pick up my fiddle to practice, and smile. "Leroy, listen only if you want to."

— Glenice Wilson —

62

Go to MADD

Down in their hearts, wise men know this truth:
the only way to help yourself is to help others.
~Elbert Hubbard

The best advice that I ever received came from my brother as he waited to board a plane from Buffalo to Atlanta after attending my fourteen-year-old son's funeral. Mike was an Atlanta police officer, veteran patrolman, SWAT team member and coordinator of the Police Athletic League. He had a unique perspective on crime, the courts, victims and laws. He is fiercely protective of those he loves, and my son Andy was one of those people. He was frustrated that he couldn't make this horrible tragedy go away.

Andy was killed by a very drunk driver in front of our house as he was crossing the road on his three-wheeler to care for his horse.

Andy remained in a coma in the trauma center of a Buffalo hospital for three days, and then he was declared brain dead. I was hopeful he would miraculously wake up, until a doctor informed me that "brain dead means dead." Against every instinct, hope and fiber of my soul, I had to let Andy go. I had to find a way to cope with the fact that my son had been killed… by a drunk driver.

"Go to MADD, Luanne. They'll help you," my brother implored. "I've seen them in action."

He went on to explain that he had watched DWI trials in Atlanta when the presence of MADD (Mothers Against Drunk Driving) representatives had been a powerful influence. "I've heard the judge tell attorneys that he might discuss a plea bargain, but 'if MADD is there, all bets are off.'"

I thought about his advice, but I was far from ready for MADD. I was already busy every day, going through Andy's things, trying to sleep at night, fighting off nightmares, and boxing up the clothes and everyday things of his that were now precious and irreplaceable. And I wept. I was ambushed often by little things that intensified my grief — the school bus stopping in front of the house, his favorite TV show, finding his baseball glove in the back seat of the car. I cried myself to sleep every night.

I also battled guilt and regret. Why hadn't I been outside so I could have stopped him somehow? Why did we live on such a busy road? Why did we use a three-wheeler to take care of our animals? Why hadn't I allowed him to eat one of the cookies I had baked and was saving for a special event? Why, why, why? Most of all, why, oh why, was I still alive when he was dead? It's called survivor guilt, and it is devastating.

Eventually, my sorrow and heartache, guilt and depression were expanded by another very powerful emotion: blind, white-hot rage. I suddenly realized that the man who killed my precious son had made the choice to get behind the wheel of his van when he knew he was impaired. He chose to drive down my street, and he killed my son. I became driven by fury, and I wanted to scream, loudly and all day long.

So I followed my brother's advice: I went to MADD. As it turned out, there was no MADD chapter in our county, so with the help of another woman, Mary, whose son had also been killed by a drunk driver, I started one. I felt I had finally found a way to channel the gnawing anger, something that gave me the outlet I needed and an opportunity to do something to combat drunk driving, at least in my little community. We knew it wouldn't be easy for us to approach judges, prosecutors, and reporters; work with victims; get the word out about the dangers of DWI; and, most of all, fight to stop it. We were nervous, but we were also determined.

As it turned out, we had a lot of support — not just from state and national MADD sources, but in our own community. People who had lost loved ones in DWI crashes, and people who just wanted to help, joined Mary and me. We went from a tentative, inexperienced duo to a confident, savvy group of experts, bent on boosting public awareness of the dangers of drunk driving. We counseled victims of this appalling crime and organized public activities, including everything from decorating shopping mall Christmas trees with police tape and flashing red lights to monitoring court proceedings

We organized an annual police officer recognition event and we told our own stories whenever we were asked, at schools, community panels, and elsewhere. We learned to use every outlet we could, from the local media to civic and church groups, to get our message out. Most important, we supported and aided new victims of this heinous crime. Our local group even received a national award for our work. Although there is no way to prove it, I know in my heart that we made a difference.

There came a day when I could see the tangible evidence of that success. I made a call to a city official to voice MADD's disapproval of a plan he was pushing to organize a "bar hop" party that would shuttle drinkers from bar to bar, and then bring them back to where they began and leave them to drive themselves home. After learning of MADD's strong opposition to this reckless idea, the city council dropped it.

I'm grateful to my brother, Mike, who pointed me to MADD. He was right — MADD did help me. When I took his advice, I found a valuable way to honor Andy by working to help make my community, my neighborhood and my road a safer place for everyone. I think my son would be proud of me.

— Luanne Tovey Zuccari —

63

It's All about Passion

The most powerful weapon on earth
is the human soul on fire.
~Ferdinand Foch

I was studying chemistry at college because my family thought education was the key to success. One day, my professor took me aside and asked a very simple question, "Why are you in my class when it's obvious that you have little or no interest in chemistry?"

I stumbled through an explanation by blaming pressure from my dad, but he knew it was just a weak excuse. He gave me the following advice.

"Success can only be measured by oneself, and each of us is different. Your success will be different from mine and different from your neighbor's or your parents'. There is no secret formula, no examination you have to pass and no guarantee, but there is a secret ingredient. And that ingredient is passion. To be successful in life in the broadest sense, you must pursue your passion. Whether you are passionate about fixing cars or exploring the world, you must be passionate about your goal and set a path to satisfy it. Only then will you find true happiness."

At just nineteen years of age, that was pretty profound advice for me to absorb, but I knew instinctively that he was correct. I made a conscious self-examination of my short life to determine where my passion was hiding; it was so obvious that even my kid sister could have told me if I had asked her. My true passion was music. Music was in my genes. My father was a self-taught jazz pianist, and my mum could sing like a nightingale. I could play the piano by ear and had suffered through piano lessons for more than eight years, but had only considered music as a hobby.

Could I be a successful musician? Or a songwriter? Or a music critic? There was only one way to find out, so I took my professor's advice and switched to the university's music school, studied harmony and composition, learned how to play a clarinet and joined the symphony orchestra. I felt as though I was on top of the world, and that feeling has never left me.

> *"There is no secret formula, no examination you have to pass and no guarantee, but there is a secret ingredient."*

I'm now fifty-four years old, and a very happy and content man. As I look at the walls of my small office, I still get a thrill at seeing the records I made, the photos of the famous musicians I was lucky enough to play with, and the accolades from many of the finest instrumentalists in the world who I am honored to call my friends.

It was a long journey, and not an easy one, but I followed my passion and succeeded.

— Derek Hawkins —

64

When Things Are Good

Wherever you go, go with all your heart.
~Confucius

Many years ago, I was facing a decision. I had worked for a company for many years. I was good at my job, and yet I didn't feel fulfilled by it. I was struggling with my decision — to maintain the status quo, or take a risk and head in a new direction. I doubted my ability to make a wise decision.

Then one day I was hundreds of miles from home at a company conference. I was enjoying the training sessions and the company of my peers, and yet my mind still wandered.

A woman sat down next to me and struck up a conversation. She had noticed I was slightly detached from what was happening around me and recognized it as out of the norm. I confessed that I had been considering leaving the company for another opportunity, but was torn over the decision.

The woman smiled and asked simply, "On your best day, when everything is going right, do you still think of leaving?"

I thought a moment about her question and replied softly, "Yes."

She said she believed that the best time to make a big decision or change is not when we are in the throes of a difficult time. Instead, consider it when all the factors are working in our favor. When things are hard, it is much easier to throw in the towel and walk away. We can justify our exit or change of course because things are seemingly not working out. On the other hand, when we consider how we feel during the best of times, we have more clarity.

In my situation, things were going wonderfully and I was receiving bonus checks. But I wasn't happy. I wasn't celebrating my successes. Instead, my heart was being pulled in another direction.

> *"On your best day, when everything is going right, do you still think of leaving?"*

I left the company and entered into ministry service. My gifts and talents are no longer used to bring in profits, but to impact lives for the better. I feel more contentment and fulfillment in my everyday tasks because they contribute to the greater good versus the bottom line. I don't regret leaving and have never given it a second thought.

I'm thankful for the woman who imparted her wisdom to me that day. I've lived by those words ever since and share them with others who come to me for counsel.

— Gena B. McCown —

Good, Very Good, Best

It's never too late to start something new, to do all those
things that you've been longing to do.
~Dallas Clayton

High school was difficult for me in the mid-1950s. My high school counselor told me that college wasn't in my future. I would graduate in the middle of my class. And we were poor — my widowed mother often stretched a half-pound of hamburger to feed seven kids. He concluded our pre-graduation meeting with, "Benson, I believe the military would be a good fit for you."

I did well in the Army, and my electronics training was a foundation for later things. The counselor's advice was good, but it wasn't the *best* advice I've ever heard.

My work in the Army qualified me for a manufacturing job with a small company in Minnesota. It was a low-paying position, but any job to support my wife and three kids during a Midwest winter was a good job.

The agency I'd been with in the Army recruited me to return to Virginia for an unposted civilian job. The government salary wasn't significantly higher, but health benefits and other perks gave me the incentive to accept the offer. However, I still needed a part-time job to support my family once we settled in.

So I worked evenings and some weekends as a clerk at one of the stores in a rapidly expanding drugstore chain. After less than a year, I was recruited into the company's management program. Compensation in the training program was equal to government employment, so with the expectation of advancement, I changed jobs. Leadership skills I'd learned in the Army were a personal asset in my new occupation.

The day I was promoted from trainee to assistant manager, my district manager said, "You're moving up faster than most, but remember this — while climbing the ladder of success, you might have to climb back down someday. In other words, always treat those you supervise with respect and fairness." His advice was very good, but still not the *best* advice I've ever heard.

We were spending a summer afternoon with friends from church, and our conversation turned to our work and the future. Our friends were preparing to move back to their home state, where they were both certified to teach. My friend Lyle asked about my own work and what might be ahead for me.

I told Lyle that my previous boss, who had recruited and promoted me to manager, was moving up to the corporate office. He told me I was on the fast track for supervising one of the new districts. The increased pay and responsibility seemed like a good incentive to accept the position, but I lamented that the working hours and traveling time would increase.

When Lyle asked what I'd really like to do, I told him, "Teach." I explained that my favorite job had been teaching operation and field maintenance of communications equipment to U.S. embassy personnel when I was in the Army.

He asked if I had a teaching degree, and I told him I had taken only a few college classes. When he suggested that I could enroll and maybe transfer my previously earned credits, I said, "I'm nearly thirty-three, with house payments and a family to support. Do you know how old I'd be if I went to college now?"

He countered, "How old will you be if you don't go?"

That was the best advice I've ever heard.

Three years later, I graduated with a teaching degree and started a satisfying thirty-five-year career as an education professional. I retired from teaching with an advanced degree, and now I can afford hamburger.

My high school counselor's good advice was helpful. My district manager's very good advice was practical. But the best advice I've ever heard, my friend's question, was life-changing.

—John Morris Benson—

Awakening My Passion for Writing

People are capable, at any time in their lives,
of doing what they dream of.
~Paulo Coelho

My friend, Pamela, loved to write. Although she'd yet to publish a book, she'd finally made the decision to quit her day job and write full-time. We met for lunch, and she glowed as she told me about her latest story. I relayed to her how bored I was with my job, and how I'd dreamed of writing since I was a child.

"You should write a novel," she said.

"I think that would be fun, but I wouldn't know where to start. What would I write?" I asked.

"You should never give up on your dreams," she said. "Just start and see where it takes you. What do you have to lose?"

I returned to my office. *What the heck. I might as well try it,* I thought. I opened up a new document on my computer. I loved reading romances, so why not write the next bestselling romance novel? I typed away for the next four months whenever I had a spare moment. I loved it! I was surprised how often the words seemed to flow onto the page, the story and characters taking on a life of their own. Once that first, very rough draft was completed, I realized that I needed a lot of help to get my basic story into a form that anyone would want to actually buy. I started taking classes and reading books on the art of writing.

Pamela was right there to help and encourage me through every step. She invited me to her monthly writers' group. Although I was encouraged by other writers, I was also discouraged by their stories of how hard it was to actually sell a novel and how many rejections are involved before reaching any kind of success. Being a results-oriented person, I started to doubt that writing was for me. That's when, at my third group meeting, a published author recommended submitting stories to Chicken Soup for the Soul. I had always loved those books. I went home and found several well-worn copies in my grown daughters' former bedrooms. I smiled as I remembered how we read so many of those inspiring stories during their teenage years.

I got the books down and started reading. Maybe I could do this. I'd lived almost sixty years; surely I had some stories to tell. The next day, I went to the Chicken Soup for the Soul website and read through the possible book titles. I picked out two, sat down and wrote my stories. I uploaded them and pushed Submit. The instructions said that if they didn't decide to publish my story, I would not hear back from them. How disheartening.

Six months passed, and I all but forgot about my submissions. I continued to work on my first novel and realized that even if I didn't ever make a sale, I had truly found my passion in writing. Then came that fateful day in May, exactly a year after I'd started that first novel. I opened my inbox to see an e-mail from the Chicken Soup for the Soul associate publisher. My hands shook as I opened the e-mail. I could not believe my eyes when I read that my story had been selected as a finalist for *Chicken Soup for the Soul: From Lemons to Lemonade*. A month later, I received confirmation that my story would indeed appear in the book. Amazingly, a couple of months later, my second story was also accepted for publication, in *Chicken Soup for the Soul: It's Christmas!*

I was about to become a published author. I was so glad Pamela had encouraged me to write. My whole attitude toward life and my own value began to change. Maybe I could actually write for a living.

Since then, I have thoroughly enjoyed the process of writing. To date, I've written countless stories and submitted them. Obviously, not all have been chosen, but I now have stories in seven *Chicken Soup for the Soul* books. I've written and published eleven romance novels. Writing has taken me places I never thought I could go and introduced me to wonderful people. I know I have found a new love and a profession that will continue to give me joy throughout the rest of my life.

My friend, Pamela, changed my life with her advice. She continued to write and finished three novels, but as a perfectionist she did not believe any of them were polished enough to publish. Two years ago, she was diagnosed with a rare, fatal condition: Creutzfeldt-Jakob disease. The prognosis was less than a year. Her memory rapidly deteriorated. Within a couple of months, she could no longer write. I wanted to return the favor she'd given me.

"You need to publish one of your books," I told her. "I'll help you."

"Okay," she said. "I'd love to see one of my stories in print."

I try every day to pay it forward by encouraging those around me to follow their passion, whatever it might be.

With the help of a few other authors in our writing group, we were able to make a cover, and format and edit her book in less than two months. Her health continued to decline. A truly group effort allowed her book to be published. Her words — never give up on your dreams — kept echoing through my head.

We made her dream come true that day her book was published, and she could share it with her friends and family. Two months later, she passed away.

Pamela lives on in my mind. Her advice changed my life. I'm happy to say that I quit my day job and now write full-time. I am filled with a passion for what I do, which I thought I'd lost forever. I try every day to pay it forward by encouraging those around me to follow their passion, whatever it might be. Life is too short — sometimes shorter than we expect — to waste our time on mediocrity. Find what you love and follow that dream.

— Jill Haymaker —

Chapter
8

Take Care
of Yourself

Lisa Things

Solitude is where I place my chaos to
rest and awaken my inner peace.
~Nikki Rowe

By the time I was nearing my twentieth birthday, I had grown weary of the small tobacco-farming town where I grew up. I had to get out. Raised thirty minutes from Fort Bragg and having a father who was a career military man ensured that the Army was not a possibility. With not a penny in savings, the promise of life on the water, and its catchy slogan, "Join the Navy and See the World," I packed my bags and headed off for the open water.

Ironically, the only foreign soil I saw was Mexico, while stationed in San Diego, and the farthest I got away from my home was Hawaii. Four and a half years later, I returned to that no-stoplight town with two children and a divorce looming in my very near future.

Shortly after, I reconnected with my old college boyfriend and settled in for the long haul. A part-time job while obtaining my bachelor's degree in education, a husband, mortgage, and three more children that included a set of twins meant never having a free moment to spare or call my own. Five children under the age of seven ensured that my life did not belong to me anymore. A couple more fun-filled, completely chaotic years passed swiftly until a night came that shifted my world.

I sat in my living room... alone. My husband had gone out with his brother. I was supposed to have accompanied them. Arrangements for all five of the children were made for them to stay at different houses.

Take Care of Yourself | 207

My two oldest were staying at my best friend's house, and the three babies were staying at my parents' house for the night. So there I was, alone in a house that had been so completely filled for so many years, with no one to look after but myself. But what would I do?

My first thought was to hang out with my best friend, but she had a couple of my kids. If I were to go over there, it wouldn't be the escape night I had been hoping for. I thought about visiting my sister, but she had her own family. I could go visit my mom, but she had my other children. I sank back on my sofa and stared into the nothingness surrounding me. There was no one else to call, no one to hang out with who didn't have kids of their own and could get a sitter quickly. For the first time in seven years, I understood how dependent I had become on my family for defining my identity. Without them, I didn't know what to do with myself.

> "You know what? Just do Lisa things then."

I dialed my parents' house almost in tears, and my mother answered the phone. I explained to her that I hadn't been able to make the trip with my husband so I would come and pick up the babies from her. She asked me to hold on a second, and the voice on the other end was suddenly my father's. He assured me that the kids were all right, and he and my mother were handling things just fine. He nudged me to go out and enjoy my evening, and I started to cry.

"Lisa, just go take a shower and get dressed. Go out and have fun. Go see some of your friends and take the night off."

His voice, so strong and sincere, made me break down even more. I explained my current dilemma, and that none of my friends could get away on such short notice.

"Okay, fine, then just go out and do something." The military tone was starting to creep into his voice.

I didn't want to go out somewhere alone. The club scene hadn't interested me in years, and you never quite understand the meaning of feeling alone until you are surrounded by a packed house of strangers.

Then he said it, "You know what? Just do Lisa things then."

"Lisa things?" I muttered through the sniffles.

Chicken Soup for the Soul

Advice With
Which I Can Live

Almost everything will work again if you unplug it for
a few minutes, including you.
~Anne Lamott

tarted teaching high school science more years ago than I care
admit. It didn't take long for me to realize that teaching was
hat I was wired to do. Holding the bar high, I connected well
ith most of my students. It certainly wasn't the proverbial bed of
, but I liked almost everything — except the stress and the pay,
I thought was too low for what we do.

As many other teachers did — and still do — I worked side jobs
plement my income. For example, I worked as a night clerk at
MCA for six or seven years, and then I delivered newspapers. I
s had my ears open for other possibilities.

One spring, I saw an ad for an environmental awareness coordina-
local federal nature refuge. Perfect! I applied for the upcoming
er position and was called in for an interview.

flew to Atlanta for orientation and began my new job a week
was in charge of planning and implementing wildlife-centered
ts with twenty high school students from eight surrounding
es. There were two permanent staffers and me. Our program
eight weeks and included fairly strenuous physical work and
/classroom time in the afternoon.

"Yes! Lisa things: a hobby, a movie, an interest. Whatever you want to do, but don't have time for."

"But I don't know what that is anymore."

"Well, I guess you have tonight to figure that out." Ther[e] up. The Command Sergeant Major had given his order, and no refuting it.

I stood there a moment, dazed. "Just do Lisa things?"

A realization washed over me, practically drowning m[e] I had spent ten years taking care of other people, and neve[r] moment of my own had caused me to lose myself.

That night, I stayed in. Ultimately, I spent hours wi[th] paper making lists, pros and cons, journaling, and doodlin[g] margins. Through those pages of notes, I began to see a n[ew] a new path that I knew I needed to take. I would have to changes, and the first would be learning to ask for help.

When I awoke the next day, I made the rounds to children. My father met me at the door with a knowing across his face. "So what did you do last night?"

"Not a whole lot really," I answered in a noncomm[ittal]

"Well, did you find your thing?"

"I'm working on it."

Four years later, the first of many novellas was publish[ed] of my father's thumbprint hangs around my neck with t[he] do Lisa things" engraved on the back. I only wish that shared that moment with me, as it was his much-need[ed] guided me to pursue my own interests. His words of v[alue] me to understand that it was okay to be a person wi[th] interests, and still be a good mom, wife, and co-work[er].

— Lisa A. Malkiewicz —

Using questionnaires and data that the staff had collected during previous years, the students and I collaborated to decide what specific projects were crucial. Which ones, with our budget, could be completed and implemented in an eight-week period?

Our list was ambitious and included clearing duck blinds, building bird and duck houses, helping the resident biologist tag and monitor the local flock of Canada geese, and building a nature trail around one of the ponds.

My supervisor, Mr. Roberts, had been re-located from a busy people-centered park in Florida to one with a focus on wildlife and its habitat. He'd been transferred to a less stressful working environment after experiencing a cardiac event.

That summer, our area broke record-high temperatures. At times, the thermometer registered over 100 degrees! We did most of our physical work during the first part of the day and moved indoors for lunch and the afternoon classwork.

My main job was to prepare and deliver lessons and labs pertaining to the immediate environment, including water chemistry and quality, food chains and webs, and how migration affected the animals and plants on the refuge. The biologist was always available to answer questions and support our work.

Tim, the biologist, liked showing the students (at a safe distance) how he tagged alligators and studied their movements using sensors. They also helped tag the resident Canada goose flock, which "went off the map" during the Fourth of July weekend. Kathy suggested that they probably decided to go on a weekend vacation.

On the last day of our project, Mr. Roberts called me into his office at the end of the day.

"Pull up a chair," he said. I had no idea why he'd asked me to come in. Something was on his mind. What was it?

"Hold out your hands," he said. I was puzzled but complied. What was this about?

"Turn them over," he instructed. "Let me take a look at the tops of your hands… and your nails." What?

"What is it?" I asked.

"You bite your nails, don't you?"

I nodded my head.

"John, I've watched you work this summer, and you're pretty good with the kids, but you seem a bit stressed at times."

"I really haven't noticed that," I responded.

"I know. I didn't notice it either, and then I had a heart attack at the age of fifty-one."

"Yes, I think I recall you saying that once. I'm sorry, Mr. Roberts," I said.

"Call me Jim. I just want you to promise to try to be aware of your stress level and maybe sign up for some meditation or yoga."

I was surprised. Jim Roberts was a big man, over six feet tall, and he was as rugged as a lumberjack. For some reason, I had a hard time picturing him on a yoga mat or chanting a mantra.

"Tell me one more thing, and pardon me if I get too personal, but what are you planning to do when you get home today?"

"Well, I usually meet some schoolteacher buddies at a local pub, and we have a few drinks and then grab some food."

"And then what?"

"We might go out to a club and do some dancing. Or to someone's house for a movie or cards."

"Hmm, what do you really feel like doing today?"

"I'm beat," I admitted. "I'd love to take a long nap."

"Then that's what you should do. Go home and take a long overdue nap. When you wake up, see what you feel like. If you feel like staying in and watching some TV, do that. My advice to you, John, is to learn to take it easy, not to let things get to you, and relax. What is it that you young folks say? Chill?"

I smiled and said, "Yes, sir… chill."

The drive home that day was long, and I could see the thunderhead clouds building in the south. The lightning, although a long way from me, was fantastic.

When I got home, the rain had begun, and the thunder in the distance was soothing. The phone rang. It was my friend, Stuart, reminding me that they were all at the pub waiting on me to join them for Happy Hour.

"I'm not coming," I said.

"What? Did you just say that you're not coming?"

"Exactly," I said. "I need a nap."

"A nap? What has got into you?" I heard Stuart cover the mouthpiece and yell to my friends that something serious was wrong with me.

"Really, dude? You're gonna nap? Are you sick or something?"

"No, I feel like taking a nap. Had a long week, and I've been feeling stressed. So tell everybody that I'm okay… just need to stay in."

"So you're not coming out tonight either?"

"Don't think so. I'll catch you guys another time."

Stuart's concern made me chuckle. I made myself a grilled cheese sandwich, heated up some tomato soup, and curled up on the sofa for some TV time. The rain had tapered off into a slow, steady pace, great for staying in. Even after having a nap, I slept long and deep that night.

When school started a few weeks later, I started to become overwhelmed during the first week. I saw Jim Robert's face and remembered his advice to slow down and listen to what my body was trying to tell me.

Thirty-something years later, I still hear his words of wisdom, and I know that things will be okay.

—John Dorroh—

69

Put On Your Oxygen Mask First

Self-compassion is simply giving the same kindness to
ourselves that we would give to others.
~Christopher Germer

I sat in the parking lot of Rhode Island Hospital. Alone in the privacy of my car, I sobbed. It was 8:30 a.m., and I was already exhausted. I had gotten up at 5:00 a.m. and rushed out the door to drive a half-hour to get my father ready to go to dialysis, which was another forty minutes away. This was a typical morning for me. But this morning, in my haste, I had misjudged the threshold in the hospital lobby and had dumped my father out of his wheelchair in front of the elevator. I felt both helpless and hopeless.

As I sat crying, my cell phone rang. The number on the display indicated it was a newer friend whom I didn't know very well. Despite my hesitation, I decided to answer the phone. I tried to compose myself, but she could tell. "What's wrong?" she asked.

Perhaps because my new friend was a retired nurse, she knew people and could sense the strain in my voice. In response to her question, I began to sob again. "I just dumped my father like a sack of potatoes out in front of the elevators in the lobby of the hospital," I said.

"Well, at least you were in the right place for that," she said.

My tears changed to laughter.

"You know, Deb, you're lucky nothing worse happened," she said.

"What do you mean?" I asked.

"Well, you're running your family business, taking care of a family, taking care of a mother who has dementia, shuttling her and your father, who is in renal failure, back and forth from medical appointments, and managing their affairs and your own. Don't you think that's a lot?"

She was right. I was tired and felt like I was running on empty.

"And what are you doing for you?"

"There's no way I have time for me," I said.

"Deb, there's no way you *don't* have time for you. Think of yourself as being in a plane, and it's going down. You have a lot of people depending on you, but the one person who must come first to get you through all this is you. Put on your oxygen mask first, Deb, before you help others," she said.

"I guess I don't know how to do that," I said.

"What kind of help are you getting?" she asked.

"What do you mean?" I asked.

"Do you get homecare or have someone coming in to help make meals?"

"No, my parents would never go for that," I said.

"Since you have all the responsibility, you should be the decision-maker. Make it clear that if you go down, so will they, and they may then end up in the nursing home. So what kind of things are you doing for you?" she asked.

"I don't have time for that," I repeated.

"If you don't start building in a half-hour to an hour each day to either exercise or go have a coffee with friends or something fun, you're going to get sick. You must build that in," she said.

Slowly, I let her words sink in. Within the next few weeks, I put a plan into action that would allow me to take breaks. Even though it has been years since I've been in touch with this woman, I still remember her words as if they were just spoken. Even though my circumstances have changed, whenever I find myself or a friend running out of gas, I stop and say, "Put on your oxygen mask first."

— Deborah Henderson Roberts —

70

Accepting with Grace

Neither refuse to give help when it is needed…
nor refuse to accept it when it is offered.
~Lloyd Alexander

"**M**om, people want to help," admonished our daughter, Summer. "And they want to do it in meaningful ways."

My husband Gary was dying of cancer in the hospital bed in our living room. The women from our church had called to see if they could arrange meals. "Thank you so much, but it's not needed," I replied automatically. "It's just Summer and me, and we don't eat much."

Summer called them back because she knew these women. "We'd love to have meals. But, please, small portions, and every other day."

The daughter lecture series actually started about the time Gary's cancer picked up speed. Back then, a generous family member had offered to pay Gary's salary so he could quit his job. "Oh, wow, thank you, but we couldn't let you do that," we said, perhaps because it was too generous, or we were too proud, or it wasn't comfortable being on the receiving end of such a large gift.

I told Summer about it later, and she laughed. "Why did you just laugh?" I wanted to know because that had been my reaction, and I couldn't quite explain it.

"I don't know," she said. "Maybe because it's so absurd. I mean, who offers to pay someone's salary so they can quit work?"

Summer called back the next evening. Apparently, our adult

children and their spouses had taken a vote. It was unanimous. They decided we should accept the offer. Summer reminded us that we'd been praying for Gary to take an early retirement. "So, you get this offer, and you turn it down. Now what? You're going to keep praying that Dad can quit work, right?"

It was sort of like the guy who, when warned about an impending storm, prayed that God would deliver him. A policeman showed up at the man's front door to evacuate him. The water rose to the front porch, and a fire truck stopped by. The water reached the second floor, and someone in a boat rowed up to the window. Finally, the guy was on the roof of his house with a helicopter hovering overhead. He declined all offers of assistance, though, because he had great faith that God would rescue him. The man got swept into the flood and drowned. Standing before God, he was a bit annoyed that his prayers had gone unanswered. God looked puzzled. "What do you mean? I sent a policeman, a fire truck, a rowboat and a helicopter. I don't know what else I could have done for you."

And so we accepted this startling, over-the-top offer, which allowed Gary to resign his job and apply for disability.

"Not only do you need to *accept* help," the lectures from Summer continued, "but you need to *ask* for help."

A slow leak sprung in one of our tires. I was unable to leave Gary for very long because he was unsteady on his feet, so I sent out a request on Facebook: "Does anyone have time to take our car in for tire repair?" Before the end of the day, the vehicle had been picked up and returned with a repaired tire. And the girlfriend who did this seemed so pleased to be able to help.

Shortly after that, our toilet clogged. I tried using the plunger to no avail, and then e-mailed a handful of male friends who had said, "Let me know if I can help in any way." One friend and his wife arrived with more plumbing equipment than you'd think an amateur plumber would own. And just like that, our toilet was unclogged.

And then the Porch Fairy showed up. (A Porch Fairy is someone who leaves gifts on the front porch so as not to disturb the guy occupying the hospital bed.) She began leaving a steaming chai tea on our front porch every morning. When Summer arrived to stand watch with me, the Porch Fairy added Americano coffee to the daily delivery. Two steaming beverages in cheery red cups on our front porch. Even in snow and ice. Every morning at 7:30 for weeks.

Because of the Porch Fairy's whimsical initiative, our front porch saw quite a bit of activity: soup, scented candles, bouquets of flowers and fall leaves, pumpkin bread and pumpkin pie, socks, and bamboo knitting needles with soft yarn in warm autumn colors.

It was the season of graciously and humbly learning to say: "Yes, thank you." And with each generous gift, each acceptance of assistance, each ask for help, God was reminding me I couldn't carry this load alone. I needed this fiercely supportive team of friends, family, co-workers, and cancer community members.

Snow came early that year to central Oregon. A friend—who believes it's easier to ask for forgiveness than permission—showed up with her grandson to shovel our driveway and walkways when I was with Gary in Hospice House. She knew if she asked, I probably would have said, "Thank you. That's so sweet of you, but not necessary."

In addition to not asking for help, and not always accepting it when it was offered, I didn't always take care of myself.

There was the time I drove Gary to the emergency room at 5:00 a.m. with a fever and flu-like symptoms. After several hours of infusion with high-powered antibiotics, I brought him home, ran out to pick up his prescription, and hurried home to get him started on the meds. And then I reported to work—near tears and physically, mentally, and emotionally exhausted—because I didn't want to add to my co-worker's load. Looking back, I'm pretty sure my lovely co-worker would have been glad to take my load that day.

Throughout those last months of Gary's life, there were no small gifts. The sum total of the love that arrived at our doorstep — whether it made it past the front porch or not — was colossal.

And every gift carried this powerful message: "It grieves my heart to know your beloved is dying, and it brings me great joy to deliver this ray of sunshine."

After Gary's Celebration of Life service, Summer commented on how glad she was to be present with me as her dad was dying. "I saw community in action," she said. "And when you experience that, it changes you. You can't pay it back, but you can pay it forward."

Some of the best advice I ever received came from my extraordinarily wise daughter: "People want to be part of your story, Mom. They want to help in meaningful ways. You need to let them."

— Marlys Johnson —

71

Within Nautical Inches

The mind should be allowed some relaxation, that it
may return to its work all the better for the rest.
~Seneca

've heard it said, "Almost only counts in horseshoes and hand gre-
nades," but sometimes "almost" can scare the sass out of a fellow.

Not everyone can list almost wrecking an aircraft carrier on
his résumé. I had screwed up big time. Oh, I had help. It took
three of us to create the perfect storm, and I was the middleman in
this little at-sea episode.

We were steaming west, and as soon as we got to a certain point,
we needed to come left to a new course and overtake a supply ship so
we could come alongside her and take on essential supplies. A large
crew needs things like food, toilet paper, mail, duct tape and other
good stuff. It was my job to tell the officer of the deck when to change
course. There was, however, one small problem. An oil tanker would
pass between the supply ship and us at roughly the time we were to
change course.

When another ship was within a mile of us, it quit painting on our
radarscopes. This was to be expected; it did it every time. To overcome
this small difficulty, our computers were designed to create an image
that looked something like a real contact, yet clearly different. This
automatically happened when our radar operators updated the contact
three times. Once this radar-like blip was created, the only person on
planet earth who was authorized to eliminate it, before it disappeared

off the edge of the scope, was the commissioned officer in charge of that watch team. That night, I was that officer.

My radar operator didn't see the actual contact, so he hit Delete and wiped out my computer-generated blip. I looked at my empty radarscope and recommended coming left to the new course. In spite of my operator's error, I was supposed to remember small details like another ship within spitting distance of us. If the officer of the deck took my recommendation, we would be on a collision course with the oil tanker. The officer of the deck, who had eyes on the oil tanker, took my recommendation and ordered the course change. Fortunately, our Captain was on the bridge and ordered we come hard right, but it was a near miss.

The *USS Saratoga* (CVA-60) was almost as long as four football fields strung end-to-end. Turning a big girl like the *Sara* or a large oil tanker doesn't happen quickly. A mile for an ocean-going vessel is something on the order of maybe ten or twenty feet for an SUV going at highway speeds.

Yes, I realized my mistake almost immediately and radioed the bridge. Yet it would have been potentially too late if the Captain had not acted as quickly as he did.

As I finished my watch, the Ops Boss — a Commander who was in charge of the Combat Information Center — sat behind me without saying a word. He watched every move I made for the next two hours.

Long before the Commander showed up, I knew I was in line for a serious dressing-down. Had I not gotten the full dose of that well-deserved reprimand, I think I'd have been disappointed. At the height of my butt-chewing, the Commander's whole demeanor changed suddenly. He said, "This isn't like you. When was the last time you slept?"

I estimated as well as my terrified brain could. "About twenty-eight hours ago, Sir."

"How long did you sleep?"

"Maybe five hours."

"And before that, how long were you up?"

"I'm not sure, probably about twenty, twenty-one hours."

"What's so important that you're not sleeping?"

"I stood sixteen hours of watch, and the Chaplin and I have been trying to help one of my men with a serious problem that has been affecting his performance."

"And before that?"

"I observed and evaluated two naval exercises, plus wrote up the reports for the Pentagon. I also stood eight hours of watch."

By this point, the Commander sounded more like my father than a senior career naval officer dealing with a crisis. "A man can do phenomenal things if he eats regular, sleeps regular, and avoids worrying about everything." He continued, "The safety of this ship comes first, and your men come second. Let the Pentagon wait." He took a long pause as he searched my face to see if his remarks had registered. He continued, "Now I'm ordering you to hit the rack and sleep until you can't sleep any longer."

> "Now I'm ordering you to hit the rack and sleep until you can't sleep any longer."

I said, "I can't, Sir. I'm on the special sea and anchor detail to bring the ship into port two hours from now."

The Commander was emphatic. "I'm ordering you to go to bed. I'll find someone to replace you. When you wake up, go ashore, whether you're in the liberty section or not, and that too is an order."

I was finally beginning to catch on to what the Commander was telling me. To put it another way, he was saying, "You get your sleep because five thousand men are depending on you to keep them safe, and the taxpayers wouldn't be pleased if you caused them to replace eighty expensive aircraft and an aircraft carrier."

It wasn't just the sleeping bit that he was talking about. I tend to be a worrier. Just a few hours earlier, I'd been concerned about what some Admiral, whom I'd never meet, would think if my reports were late.

My Commander risked getting a letter of reprimand in his jacket for telling me, "Let the Pentagon wait." He did it anyway because the safety of his ship came first, and his men came second. If his bosses in Washington got all huffy about my reports, they could go twiddle their thumbs.

That was the night I had a first-class lesson in setting priorities. I learned people can do great things if they eat regular, sleep regular, and control that old worry machine. Yes, indeed, things can get a whole lot worse if we don't pay attention to the basics.

— Ed VanDeMark —

72

Snakes in a Bucket

All problems become smaller when you confront them
instead of dodging them.
~William F. Halsey

D ue to my mother's mental illness, I was raised mostly by my grandmother, who was as intimidating as anyone you could hope to meet. Imagine, if you will, a real-life version of Annie Oakley, a woman who had been born in the late 1800s, grew up in the Wild West and moved onto a Navajo reservation when she was young as part of a missionary family. Imagine a woman who spent the first five years of her adult life teaching Apache children in a reservation school. My grandmother could ride a horse, build furniture, shoot any type of gun and carry on with the best of them. Almost everything she said seemed so wise and practical, except for one saying she often directed at me: "Don't put too many snakes in your bucket." I was at a loss to figure out what she meant.

One day, I asked her about her experiences with those darn snakes, thinking that the saying had some literal meaning. And it did. She was the only teacher to a group of Apache children. And since it was so far from civilization, the teacher not only taught, but repaired the schoolhouse, slept in its loft, and basically served every function that was necessary to keep the school up and running. It was quite common to find various critters and rattlesnakes that had moved in to escape the bitter cold of a desert night. It was her duty to either kill or capture them before letting the children in for class. She developed the habit of selling some of what she caught to the local natives for food and leather. She sold others to the zoo or reptile botanical center in Phoenix so they could develop anti-venom for the rattlers' bites. After all, a young teacher made so little pay in those days that every extra dime helped. Hearing that, I figured that explained her strange phrase and let the matter drop.

But several years later, when I was a miserable teenager, my grandmother said it again: "Kamia, you're trying to stuff too many snakes in your bucket." What on earth? There were no snakes around and no bucket to be found.

It only took me a few more weeks to realize that she knew exactly what she was talking about. One day, she decided to illustrate her message while both of us were working at the truck farm my grandparents owned. This was a place carved out of the desert with grit and determination — a place that got its fair share of a wide variety of creatures. Since the farm was organic and committed to being environmentally sustainable, everything that was considered a "critter" had to be relocated. That meant carrying around various buckets and lids, catching whatever turned up, and putting whatever we caught into the buckets to be driven away or donated.

This particular day was immediately after one of the rare rains the desert got, and we found snakes everywhere we went. Most of them were harmless, but seeing one wiggle when we were getting ready to pick something was an inconvenience at best and heart-stopping at worst.

So my grandmother, being the old Western woman she was, began grabbing them and sticking them in the bucket, then plopping the lid back down. At first, it wasn't an issue. The snakes stayed dutifully in the bottom of the bucket. But as the day wore on, and more snakes got plopped in on top of each other, they began trying to get out in earnest. We could hear them striking against the lid time and again. And by the end of the day, there simply was no way to put another snake in the bucket. As soon as we tried to open the lid, heads peeked out all over. When we did finally take them someplace to relocate them and pried off the top of the bucket, it was like a snake explosion, with every one of them slithering off while we stood on a rock high above, making sure we got nowhere near the exodus.

"That's what I meant about you," she said as I watched this drama unfold. "There are all kinds of snakes that will come at you in your life — mean people who want to put you down; bullies who attack; misfortunes you didn't plan on facing; disappointments in life and love; illness, accidents and much more. Right now, you try to deal with how you're feeling about these events by stuffing them into a bucket and pretending they no longer exist. You're trying to present a face to the world that you're tough — too tough to let anything get to you. But that's just like putting these snakes in this bucket. You can push them down all you want, but only for so long. Eventually, if you fail to take them out and deal with them, they will all start pushing to get back out. Usually, your personal lid will blow when you least want it to — often in an inconvenient, embarrassing or even dangerous way.

"Instead of pushing those emotions, conflicts or confrontations away, it's much, much easier to deal with them completely as they come, one by one. Imagine how much easier it would have been to just take a single snake out into the desert and let it go. So, too, will be your life. Remember to stop putting too many snakes in your bucket. Deal with what bothers you as soon as it pushes up its ugly head. You'll be so much happier if you do."

You know what? She was right. I never forgot that graphic illustration, and I never again let my bucket get so full that the lid was pushed off.

— Kamia Taylor —

Talk Softly and Carry a Big Stick

*You teach people how to treat you by deciding what
you will and won't accept.*
~Anna Taylor

R osemary had attended the finest schools in Montgomery,
Alabama. She was elegance personified; a vision in smartly tai-
lored suits, fine silk blouses, and perfectly situated broaches.
In her eighties — her hands gnarled by arthritis — Rosemary's
rhythmic gait was punctuated by the tapping of an ivory-tipped
walking stick. Although necessary to support her fragile frame, in
Rosemary's hand it became a fashion statement.

We met while I was working at an institution of higher education
in Chicago. As Vice President for Development and Public Affairs, one
of my responsibilities was to maintain close relationships with our
major donors and board members. Each brought to the institution
vast financial resources and leadership skills. Rosemary was one of the
most respected and longest-serving members of the board. She was
also the only woman to have ever served as Chair.

I nervously anticipated our first private meeting; Rosemary was
easily fifty years my senior, and accomplished in both business and
philanthropy. Following her husband's death, Rosemary had taken over
managing his estate — substantial holdings from his life as a successful
Chicago businessman. Yet the respect she commanded did not spring

from wealth, but from her tremendous thirst and respect for knowledge.

We met in her beautifully appointed condo on Chicago's Outer Drive. There, we were seated upon chairs upholstered in the finest woven silk, sipping cups of Earl Grey tea while nibbling scrumptious petit fours. After discussions about the college, we began to share more intimate details of our personal histories. The hours flew by, culminating in a visit to her favorite room — a library filled with towering shelves of books on a vast number of subjects.

That was the first of many such visits over the six years of my employment, during which time we fell into a warm and loving friendship. Rosemary was my teacher and I her willing student. She was mentor and guide, providing me with insights about the organization we both served, and how she had successfully carved out a spot as an equal to the men who mostly ran it.

"What do you women find to talk about hour after hour?" my boss asked after one such marathon meeting at Rosemary's.

"Everything!" I responded.

The panoramic view from Rosemary's terrace overlooked a Lake Michigan beach, removing us from the frenetic energy, noise and intensity of both city life and the pressures of my office. Rosemary's place became my retreat, and I soon referred to her apartment as "the oasis." Whenever I felt as if I was losing sight of the importance of my work, I would call Rosemary, and grab a taxi to renew my purpose and refresh my soul.

Rosemary's propensity for "carrying a big stick" was not simply a fashion statement, but a necessity brought on by osteoporosis. As the years passed, she grew increasingly frail, no longer able to attend meetings at the college. The simplest motion was often sufficient to cause a bone within her spine to fracture as her skeleton collapsed in upon itself. Our private time together became increasingly precious to me, and our tête-à-têtes were finally moved to her bedroom, where she was more comfortable.

It was in that bedroom — her inner sanctum — that Rosemary would "hold court." Dressed in a powder-pink, silk dressing gown, propped up by large pillows, she would lie amidst a carefully organized file of correspondence with scholars from around the world, offset by whatever selection of books she happened to be reading at the time. We chattered away like high school girlfriends, me sitting on a chair beside her with my stocking feet stretched out upon her bed.

While most often our conversations were focused upon work, we would frequently divert our attention to matters of a more personal nature. Rosemary had an uncanny ability to "read" me, and one day in particular she stopped mid-sentence to ask why I was fidgeting so much.

Having inherited a familial medical predisposition, I confessed that I was having an unusually painful day. Chicago winters could be brutal for those suffering from arthritis, and I was becoming increasingly frustrated with the medical profession's inability to devise a way to provide me with some relief. Initially, I shied away from complaining about my problems, though. After all, Rosemary suffered with pain far greater than my own.

Despite my protestations, Rosemary pressed me to tell her everything. As I spoke, she frowned.

"Whenever I ask my doctor what can be done to alleviate the pain, he just shrugs his shoulders and dismisses it as 'arthritis,'" I said. "He's so dismissive that I end up dropping the subject and leave without any course of action being suggested. I'm just so frustrated by the whole thing!"

Rosemary gestured for me to pull my chair closer. "My dear," she said in that quiet yet powerful manner of hers, her words simply dripping southern magnolias, "a doctor sees you for fifteen minutes during an office visit. You live in your body twenty-four hours a day. You don't ask a doctor what's wrong with you. You *tell* a doctor what's wrong with you!"

Rosemary passed away a few years later, but I have never forgotten, nor failed to share with others, the wisdom of those words. Now, when I meet a new physician,

> *"You live in your body twenty-four hours a day. You don't ask a doctor what's wrong with you. You tell a doctor what is wrong with you!"*

I introduce myself by saying, "I understand many people view doctors as omnipotent; however, if you feel that to be true, you are the only one in this room who does. I invite you to join me as a partner in my healthcare. I will research and offer opinions of my own as we explore whatever is ailing me. If that is acceptable to you, we can form an alliance that will, hopefully, reap positive results. If that doesn't work for you, please let me know now so I can take my business elsewhere."

Unquestionably, it is the best advice I've ever been given — by one of the most magnificent women it has ever been my pleasure and honor to call "friend." Rosemary! The epitome of quiet strength who "talked softly and carried a big stick."

— Sue Ross —

74

First Day on the Job

My father didn't tell me how to live;
he lived, and let me watch him do it.
~Clarence B. Kelland

had just finished my first day on the job. It had not gone exactly to plan. I just hoped that I wouldn't be going to juvenile hall. The day had started out well, with my dad and I having breakfast together. I explained how I had applied for a paper route with the *Scottsdale Daily Progress.* I told him how my classmate James Hankins had recommended me for the job, and that I would be training with James after school.

I rode my Schwinn Stingray with high-rise handlebars and banana-shaped saddle to the newspaper drop station. I was the "newbie," and the other guys ribbed me about my bike. They all rode Schwinn Wasps — the best paperboy bike there was — and I was very jealous. In 1966, a heavy-duty Schwinn Wasp cost $59.95. This was a lot of money for a ten-year-old boy. As a paperboy, I earned ten cents a week from each customer and could keep all my tips. I might be able to earn $11 a week.

My first goal was to save up for a real paperboy bike. After that, I would put the money in my savings account at the First National Bank.

James showed me how to unpack, fold and band the papers, as well as how to pack the papers in canvas bags that hung on my handlebars. He gave me good advice on how to deal with customers, process billing and develop my delivery technique. I admired how professional he was and how easy he made it look. It took skill to ride, hold the bike steady, pull a newspaper out of the bag and throw it on the doormat of each home. Most of the time, it was best to ride up the driveway and short-toss the paper to the front door. Once in a while, I got a chance to throw long and imagine I was Bart Starr throwing for a touchdown against the Dallas Cowboys.

"Consistent delivery time, accurate placement, good manners and a clean polo shirt on collection day — they're all important to earning good tips," James advised.

We finished in an hour and a half and returned to the station to clean up. Just as we started to leave, we were confronted by a tall, thick-framed boy, well over two hundred pounds.

"Rich Kopf," James said in a low voice, "the neighborhood bully."

"Hankins, I need some money now, or someone is going to get roughed up," he threatened.

"I don't have any money," James replied.

Rich blocked the bike and grabbed the handlebars, twisting the bike to the ground and spilling James with it.

"Knock it off, Rich!" James yelled.

James was shoved backwards into a brick wall, and the bully hovered over him.

"You need to stop. Now!" I said.

He turned and looked down at me, laughing as he swung his meaty fist toward my head. I ducked under his arm. I didn't have time to think. I just reacted. It was over quickly. We rode home on our bikes and stopped at the corner of my street.

"Thanks for helping me out with Rich. He's been bullying us for a while," James said.

"I need to figure out how to explain this to my parents," I said guiltily. "I didn't exactly turn the other cheek back there with Rich. My dad will want an explanation."

"Your dad will understand," James said.

He was right. My dad did always seem to understand. It was as if he watched every episode of *Leave It to Beaver* before it even appeared on our black-and-white TV. He didn't spout the platitudes of Ward

Cleaver; he simply provided a quiet, humble example. Just like the Cleaver family, our dinner tradition was to say a blessing, and then go around the table and share our intentions for others. Then we would talk about the events of our day as we ate our meal.

That night, we were seated at the dining room table, and I was thinking of how to explain my first day of work, when the knock came at the front door. My younger brother stood and went to answer the front door.

"Dad, a Mr. Kopf and Police Officer Gallagher are here to see you," my brother announced.

"Please come in, gentlemen. My father will be right here," my brother told them.

My dad got up from the dining room table and walked to the foyer.

"Gentlemen," he said, reaching to shake their hands, "what can I do for you?"

"Mr. Kopf has a son who is alleging your son assaulted him," Officer Gallagher explained.

"I see. May I have a moment to talk to my son? Please make yourself comfortable," he replied.

He walked into the dining room, paused for a moment, and looked over at me.

"Is it true that you assaulted his son?" he asked.

"Yes, sir. I was defending my friend James and myself," I said, shaking my head in affirmation and lowering my eyes in guilt. "I used a hold and throw… and a punch… or two."

"Come out to meet Mr. Kopf and Officer Gallagher. Let's see if we can resolve this," he said calmly.

Officer Gallagher looked friendly and reached out to shake my hand. Mr. Kopf glared down at me, not in anger but in shock.

"*This* is your son?" he asked my father in amazement.

"Excuse me just a minute," he said and walked out the front door, returning with Rich in tow.

"*This* is the boy that beat you up?" he shouted at his son, pointing at me.

"Are we done here, Mr. Kopf?" Officer Gallagher asked.

"Yes, we are, and I want to apologize," he said, glaring at his son.

"A lot to learn at their age," my father responded. "Good evening, gentlemen."

My father put his hand on my shoulder and gave it a gentle squeeze as we walked back to the dining room. We sat down at the dinner table, said our blessing, and went around the table to state our intentions. When it was my turn, I looked across the table at my father. His hands were folded, and his eyes looked to me with a quiet nod of support.

"For Rich and his dad," I said.

Sometimes, the best advice we get in life isn't through words at all, but through quiet example.

— Greg Shea —

75

Learning My Limits

Saying no can be the ultimate self-care.
~Claudia Black

Somewhere in my mom's vast collection of photographs is a picture that is forever imprinted in my memory. It shows me with Dad, Grandpa, and my four sisters standing arm in arm and grinning for the camera. Looming in the background is the Magnum XL-200, the world's tallest roller coaster at the time. The picture is almost thirty years old, but the memory it contains is timeless.

When I think of this photo, all the details of that summer day at the amusement park rush back. The heavy smell of popcorn and fried food in the air. The morning sun, already fierce, on my arms and shoulders. The way we huddled in a family clump to decide if we should ride their newest roller coaster, which boasted a height of 205 feet and speeds up to seventy miles per hour. The surprise I felt when Grandpa raised his hand. The pre-ride photograph. The sticky feel of the metal guardrail beneath my fingers as we inched our way up the line.

What no one knew was that I was secretly terrified of strapping myself in and riding the roller coaster. I was afraid of heights, the very thing that gave the Magnum its claim to fame. But most of my family was going to ride it. I didn't want to be the only one to stay behind with Mom and Grandma. I looked over at my little sister, who barely met the height requirement, standing fearlessly in line. If she wasn't afraid, how could I admit that I was?

I swallowed my fear and stood resolute. *You can do this, you can do this,* I repeated to myself throughout the long, hot wait. I kept a wary eye on the line, which zigzagged up a slight incline until it reached a platform at the top. With every forward step, a sense of unease grew in my chest. I kept hoping it would disappear, or that a miracle would take place and my nerves would be replaced by the same excitement everyone around me seemed to be feeling.

From my place in line, I had a clear view of what scared me the most: the first hill. I had plenty of time to see how long it took the cars to reach the top, and it seemed like an eternity. This would be the most difficult part of the ride for me, as the anticipation of the first steep drop would be drawn out.

All too soon, we reached the end of the line. Our turn was next. The cars rolled up and clicked to a stop, and the gate swung open. It was time to step into the waiting seat and pull the safety bar over my lap, but no miracle had occurred. My body was stiff with fear, and in that moment I knew: I just couldn't do it. I could not ride the Magnum, and nothing would make me change my mind.

I looked at the attendant and said, "I don't want to go." I must have expected her to scold me for wasting her time because I was surprised when she simply waved me toward an exit ramp and instructed me on how to find my way down. Too embarrassed to face my family, I simply called over my shoulder to Dad that I was leaving. There wasn't time for him to say anything, and I didn't look back. I walked slowly down the exit ramp on shaky but relieved legs. Whatever disappointment or ridicule I would face for chickening out was a small price to pay for skipping that ride.

Halfway down the exit ramp, I stopped to watch the roller coaster that carried my family chug sluggishly up the first incline. When it crested down and out of sight, a brief feeling of regret washed through me. They had done it, made it through the worst part, and I wondered if I should have stuck it out. I found Mom and Grandma chatting on a bench in the shade and sat down next to them to wait for the others.

It wasn't long before they showed up. To my surprise, no one looked very thrilled about what they had just experienced. Grandpa had wrenched his neck on the first turn and was in pain the rest of the day. My youngest sister sobbed openly, her face red with outrage over how the ride had scared her. Another sister simply shrugged and said, "It was okay." I began to feel somewhat reassured that I had made the right decision when I looked up and met Dad's eyes.

"So what happened to you up there?" he asked.

Shame flushed my face. "I don't know. I guess I was just too chicken. Sorry."

What Dad said next completely surprised me. "Don't ever apologize for knowing your limits," he said. "And don't ever let someone make you do something you're not comfortable with. I'm proud of you for the choice you made."

This was the exact opposite of what I expected him to say. For a few stunned seconds, I let his words wash over me and sink in so that I would never forget them. And I haven't. I have remembered his advice, and it has served me well through the difficult high-school years, through college, in the workplace, and in my role as parent and advocate for my seven children.

> *"Don't ever apologize for knowing your limits,"* he said.

Not too long ago, I realized I have passed this advice on to my children. My oldest had just gotten his learner's permit for driving. On the way home from the DMV, I pulled the car over to a side road, unbuckled my seat belt, and traded places with him. "Okay," I said. "I want you to drive home."

Sitting behind the wheel, his body looked tense and uncomfortable, his knuckles white on the wheel. "Mom," he said quietly, "I can't do this. I'm not ready."

"It's okay," I said. "You're never going to feel ready. At some point, you just have to go for it."

He took a deep breath and echoed my father's words to me. "No, I'm really not ready. I don't feel comfortable right now, and you always say I shouldn't let anyone make me do something I'm not comfortable with."

For a brief moment, time froze. I was thirteen years old again and trying so hard to be brave. In that instant, I understood exactly how he felt. If driving the car made him feel the same way riding the Magnum felt to me, I knew he was absolutely right. I couldn't make him do it.

I saw that old photograph once again in my mind's eye. I think it will always be there when I need to remember this: Knowing my limits isn't an indication of weakness. It's actually a sign of strength.

— Debra Mayhew —

Be Still

God not only sends special angels into our lives,
but sometimes He even sends them back again
if we forget to take notes the first time!
~Eileen Elias Freeman

have heard these two words distinctly several times in my life: "Be still." Spoken with what sounds like a man's voice, they have been calming and reassuring, gentle and persuasive. On other occasions, the words have also been urgent and authoritative, demanding attention.

The first time I heard those words, I was a small child living in Brussels, Belgium. I had foolishly run across a busy four-lane roadway where I was struck by a trolley car. I was about to be run over by another trolley as I lay stunned between the steel tracks in the road, but a strong pair of arms picked me up and held me safely as the trolley cars passed one another. The words were clear, yet gentle and comforting. I heard the words distinctly in my ear as those arms cradled me.

I wrote about that life-altering encounter with what I believe was an angel, and it was published in *Chicken Soup for the Soul: Angels and Miracles*. But throughout my life, I have heard the same words spoken by that very same voice seven times.

The second time I heard those words, I was about ten years old, so it was around 1956. After moving from Belgium because of my father's work, we lived in England, but many summers were spent back home in Newport, Rhode Island, and that particular summer was no exception.

On that one day in early July, we met up with the Fobergs. My mother's life-long friend, Lillian Foberg, suggested that we all drive up to the ferry and go to Martha's Vineyard for a picnic on the beach. With Charlie Foberg at the wheel, we headed out of little Rhode Island and arrived at our destination a few hours later. It was a gloriously bright and beautiful day in southern New England, and the warmth from the sun felt wonderful on my face as I looked up toward the heavens.

Not one to sit around for very long, I had to do some exploring amongst the endless sand dunes, so off I ran along a sandy path. A few moments later, however, and well out of sight of my parents and the Fobergs, that small voice in my ear repeated the now-familiar words to me, "Be still… Be still." The words this time were urgent and pressing, demanding immediate attention.

I did what the voice said and stopped running amongst the sand dunes, standing very still, not knowing what to expect but doing what I then knew to do: to be very still. And just then I heard the warning sound. A very large diamondback rattlesnake, its tail twitching vigorously, was lying in wait along the same sandy path I had been running. Had I blindly taken a couple more steps, had I not stopped running when that sweet voice told me to "Be still," that rattlesnake would have struck.

I backed away slowly while watching that large snake coiled up ready to strike until the sounds of it could no longer be heard. Then I walked back to where my parents and the Fobergs were sitting on a blanket on the beach sharing a laugh about something.

I never told them what happened that day. I've never told anyone. As a matter of fact, this is the very first time I have even thought of mentioning anything about what happened on that warm summer's day all those years ago.

Many years later, I learned that a strike from one of those snakes carries enough venom to kill five or six adult men within minutes, never mind the fact that I was just a small boy. And its strike is almost impossible to avoid as it hits at around 175 miles per hour.

The incident with the trolley car was the first, and the encounter with that awful snake in the sand dunes of Martha's Vineyard was the second. But throughout my life, I can clearly recall five more times when I heard that now-familiar voice. The words have always been the same, "Be still," and are always repeated twice. And, oddly enough, for some strange reason, I have heard them distinctly in my right ear.

I've tried to place an accent with the voice — Middle Eastern, European, something — but a country of origin escapes me completely. Instead, it is somehow familiar, reassuring and calming. But, no matter the circumstance, it's a voice that cannot be ignored. And it has somehow instilled in me a keen sense of awareness, an appreciation of my surroundings, and I will be forever grateful. The seven times I heard those words, I had no other options but to listen carefully and pay close attention. In so doing, I fully acknowledge that it has saved me from what, in all likelihood, would be unthinkable tragedy.

One of the last times I heard that voice was in the late summer of 1985, and I had been running for my life for nearly eight full hours. The men with the guns were getting closer, and the dogs that had my scent were urging them on, ever nearer to where I had just fallen face-down in the tall grass, with my nose touching the dark brown dirt beneath me.

I was a member of the Special Operations Group, an adjunct of the CIA and the U.S. Department of State, and this latest assignment took me to the rugged land of northern Colombia and into the stronghold of a notorious drug cartel leader. The assignment didn't go as planned, however, and upon my discovery I had but two options. I had to either run for my life or be killed by the cartel's henchmen, the ones who were now a mere hundred meters or so behind where I was lying in the tall grass.

I could hear their shouts and the barking of the dogs. They were getting closer quickly, and I knew I was about to die. My lot in life at that moment was to either get up and try to run some more, knowing I would be seen and shot in the back, or to turn and face the men with the guns, in all likelihood being shot in the chest and face. Either way, I was done for. They were on to me, now no more than fifty or sixty feet away, with the dogs straining at their leashes.

I said a prayer — an imperceptibly short plea for mercy, no more than a half-second in length, barely uttered with my last breath. Just then, with my face pressed to the ground, believing I was finished, I witnessed the strangest thing I have ever seen in my life. Just two or three inches from my left eye, an insect with the body of a ladybug, no bigger and just as round, was slowly crawling toward what looked like a tiny morsel of food on the ground. And I heard the two words that resonated clearly in my ear, "Be still." The words were repeated once more, "Be still."

That ladybug, for lack of a better description, had stopped at the morsel of food and was spreading its tiny wings. I was mesmerized by what I was seeing, unable to move, barely able to breathe. Just then, seven or eight miniature versions of the ladybug came out from beneath those wings and quickly surrounded that bit of food on the ground. I couldn't pry my eyes away from that magnificently beautiful and unfolding scene taking place just an inch or so away from my face.

The "baby" ladybugs, for I'm assuming that is what they were, consumed the entire morsel of food, but it must have taken them all of three or four minutes to do so. Finished, they walked hurriedly back to their mother, who once again spread her little wings, and they climbed on board. She closed her wings around them and continued to walk along until I could no longer see her at all. From beginning to end, that extraordinarily incredible episode took no more than perhaps five to seven minutes of time, but it was to me an earth-shattering and life-changing event.

When I raised my head to look around cautiously, the men and their dogs were nowhere to be seen. Apparently, they had walked right over the top of me, never realizing I was there. Somehow, the dogs had mysteriously and completely lost my scent. I was stunned, initially confused and astounded all at once. I got to my feet quietly and bent over in a silly posture, as if that would stop me from being spotted by the cartel henchmen.

Four days later, I was on a commercial flight out of Bogota toward Miami, staring out the window toward the Caribbean Sea so many thousands of feet below, with my heart beating faster and faster as I thought back to the events that took place just a short while before. The words came back into my heart, "Be still. Be still." When I returned home to Rhode Island following a quick meeting in Washington, D.C., one of the first places I visited was the little church that sat on the edge of the reservoir adjacent to Easton's Beach in my hometown of Newport.

—John Elliott—

How to
Be Happy

77

Like Daughter, Like Mother

*One woman filled with self-love and self-acceptance is
a model more super than any cover girl.*
~Amy Leigh Mercree

She was unlike anyone I had ever seen. I watched her while lying on the beach in Hollywood, Florida. And I didn't know what illuminated her more — her wind-blown, tightly spiraled curls or her radiant happiness.

But what struck me — even more than her presence — was the fact that I was able to conflate the two.

Some background: I was thirty-three years old, and I literally had no idea how to style or maintain my natural hair. I had spent my life trying desperately to make my curly hair something it wasn't, and I worshipped my flatiron like it was my religion.

I would sooner gouge out my eye with the nearest blunt object than be seen in public with my hair in its natural state. But there I was, mesmerized by a complete stranger with the kind of hair I had previously despised.

I wanted to talk to her.

Looking back, I now see that my desire to approach her was driven less by curiosity and more by a primal need for understanding.

When the man she was sitting with rose from his Adirondack chair and walked off, I made my way to her and asked blatantly, "How do you wear your hair like that?"

As soon as the words escaped my lips, I cringed. I knew she didn't do anything to her hair — my question wasn't literal, no. What I really wanted to know was how she was able to experience such apparent joy in the wake of vulnerability. I likened wearing my hair curly in real life to one of those bad dreams when you're inexplicably walking down the street naked and embarrassed, and everyone's laughing at you.

But, somehow, she had deciphered my intended context. She chuckled and responded, "How do I *not* wear my hair like this? These curls are mine. And I love them. How can I deny who I am?"

I heard her words, but I still didn't understand. I unleashed on her my feelings about hair, identity, and unrealistic beauty ideals — topics better suited for a therapist's couch. Again, I asked, "But how do you do it?"

"Oh, honey, you just do!" the woman said, laughing. She was so carefree. "Embrace your curls. Don't think about it. Just do it. It's a heck of a lot easier than you think. One day, it will be clear, and you will understand," she said.

That was in September 2010.

Fast-forward to a Saturday in November 2015.

Despite my best intentions to evade the massive raincloud looming over the parking lot, an all-out monsoon had broken out by the time I had exited the market with my two small kids in tow. (Scotty was four then, and Kennedy was two.) I sprinted to my minivan, soaking my hair and nearly pulling a hamstring in the process. Then I drove home as fast as I legally could and immediately commenced flatironing my hair in my bathroom. Only after I had finished did I realize that I had neglected to put the kids' frozen treats — a hard-earned reward for good behavior — in the freezer.

The bag was a pile of mush on the kitchen counter.

Frustration and shame washed over me.

I couldn't function like this anymore.

One might dismiss my mishap as simply what women do in the name of beauty. But the lengths I have gone to — to make my curly hair straight — are no laughing matter.

There is nothing funny about spending my entire life shunning my natural hair texture. And there's certainly nothing pleasurable about enduring scalp burns — and the subsequent scabbing — that result from the use of chemical hair straighteners, which I had put up with for years.

To be clear, straight hair isn't the enemy; it's lovely, in fact.

The problem, though, is when the pursuit of straight hair rules your life. There is a difference between straightening your hair because you want to, and doing it because you feel it's mandatory or, worse yet, you know no alternative.

From the time I was knee-high to a grasshopper, Sunday afternoons were spent sitting still as my mother blow-dried and then braided my hair. When I hit the teenage years, I wanted my hair even straighter, so she used a hot pressing comb, too. And, before long, that didn't get my hair straight enough — enter chemical relaxers.

As the late poet Maya Angelou stated so beautifully, "When you know better, do better." But there were few alternatives back then. In the eighties and nineties, drugstores didn't have entire aisles dedicated to serving the natural-hair community — there *was* no natural-hair community. YouTube didn't exist, and no one had any idea what a hair tutorial vlog was.

But the birth of my daughter sparked a change in direction for me.

Kennedy was born with thick, dark, perfectly clumped spiral curls, and from day one I instilled in her that her curls were beautiful. And she agreed. I prided myself in caring for — and never straightening — her curls, despite my need to straighten mine incessantly.

> **"These curls are mine. And I love them. How can I deny who I am?"**

And herein lies the problem.

When I straightened my strands during my lengthy blowout sessions, I noticed how Kennedy studied my every move. I could see the wheels in her head beginning to churn: *If you think my curls are so pretty, why do you straighten yours?* The day Kennedy would call me hypocritical was heading toward me like a freight train.

The image of the gorgeous woman on the beach began appearing in my head more frequently, poking my conscience; her words were more poignant than ever.

I decided, at age thirty-eight, that I would stop straightening my hair.

But imagine the horror I experienced when I washed my hair… and it wouldn't curl.

Come to find, all the years of applying excessive direct heat in the form of blow dryers and flatirons had permanently altered my curl pattern.

Instead of "big chopping" — cutting off all my hair at once — I chose to trim my hair over the course of several months until the last of my damaged ends were cut off on my fortieth birthday.

Although I've been on this journey for nearly three years now, I feel in some ways that I've only just begun. But, make no mistake, the woman on the beach was right: That day had come, it is now clear, and I do understand.

Here's what I've since learned: I should have done this sooner, and that chance encounter on a Florida beach many years ago was a clarion call.

And here's what I'm most grateful for: In an effort to teach my young daughter to love her wildly curly hair, I've finally learned to do the same.

— Courtney Conover —

78

Be the Duck

Rule number one is, don't sweat the small stuff.
Rule number two is, it's all small stuff.
~Robert Eliot

"You should never play poker," said my friend Anna Marie, stepping through my front door.

"Poker?" I asked. "What brought that to mind?"

Anna Marie plopped herself down on the couch. "Your face shows too much emotion. You couldn't bluff your way out of a paper bag."

Attempting to change the subject, I asked, "Would you like some coffee?"

"Sure thing," she replied. "And then we're going to talk about that beaten-dog look in your eyes."

I went to the kitchen, poured two cups, and returned to the living room. I set one cup down on the coffee table in front of her. "Hey, look," I said cheerfully, "we're actually using the coffee table for coffee!"

"Nice try," said Anna Marie, "but you're not getting out of it that easily." She cocked an eyebrow. "So, what's up?"

I sighed. Anna Marie had been my friend my entire life. We'd grown up together, gone to college together, and now lived in homes just walking distance apart. She knew me better than anyone on the planet.

"Honestly, I don't know where to begin." I shrugged my shoulders and avoided her gaze. "Everything seems to be coming at me all at once.

It's like I can't do anything right at work. I'm feeling overwhelmed, and the pressure just makes me want to scream."

"Hmm." She took a sip of coffee. "Is any of it your fault?"

"My fault?"

"Is there anything specific you can do about the situations or the pressures you're experiencing?"

I thought for a moment, and then shook my head slowly. "Well… No… It's pretty much all out of my control."

"Then be the duck," said Anna Marie matter-of-factly.

"The duck?"

"The duck," she repeated. "Ducks don't worry about adverse weather. They just let the rain roll right off their backs. If you approach your problems like a duck approaches the weather, you'll let them roll off your back, too."

"You think it's that simple?" I asked skeptically.

> *"If you approach your problems like a duck approaches the weather, you'll let them roll off your back, too."*

"Be the duck," she replied with a knowing nod. "Don't let your feathers get ruffled; just let it roll right off your back."

Then, changing the subject abruptly, she asked to see my new cell phone. "It's smarter than I am," I said as I handed it to her.

Anna Marie, a whiz at keeping up with technology, quickly pushed a few buttons on it and handed it back to me. "Nice."

I eyed her suspiciously. "What did you just do?"

She smiled, perhaps a bit too broadly. "I just set it to remind you to 'be the duck.'"

"Oh, but I don't know how to retrieve my notes or reminders yet," I admitted.

"Don't worry," she said, setting down her empty coffee cup and starting for the door. "It's not that type of reminder."

I didn't understand what she meant, but I refrained from asking any more dumb-sounding questions. I bid her goodbye, gathered our coffee cups, and headed for the kitchen.

"Quack! Quack! Quack! Quack!"

What in the world?! Stopping in my tracks, I turned to see where all the quacking was coming from and burst out laughing.

Anna Marie had changed my ringtone to that of a quacking duck. I picked up the phone, slid the arrow across, and answered without hesitation, "You come right back here and fix it this instant!"

"Be the duck!" she exclaimed joyfully. "And now you'll be reminded every time your phone rings — at least until you figure out how to change the ringtone to something else."

I growled something about how I'd eventually get even with Miss Smarty Pants and hung up. That was three years ago. My ringtone, although I now know how to change it, remains the same.

— Jan Bono —

79

Sweet Summer Savior

Out of every crisis comes the chance to be reborn.
~Nena O'Neill

I raced to Fred's house to escape the wrath of my father once again. Pedal to the metal, my heart pounded.

Like the rest of the homes in Upper St. Clair, Fred's house was more like a mansion. Fred and his rich friends seemed to live without worry. I was in my early twenties and felt the weight of the world pressing on my shoulders. I relished the opportunity to flee from my troubles and bask in the lifestyle of the rich.

When I got to Fred's, I was surprised to see a strange car in the driveway.

Since we were like brothers, I never knocked. I walked into the game room. Across the room, Fred was talking with the most beautiful girl I had ever seen.

When he saw me, he turned and smiled. "Larry, this is Julia. She just got home from college for the summer."

Wow! She took my breath away. Long brunette hair. Big blue eyes. Radiant smile. I was mesmerized.

I managed to gather my wits enough to shake her hand. "Pleased to meet you," I stammered.

For the rest of the evening, we all played pool, laughed, and celebrated life.

Before she left, Julia said, "My sister Stephanie's coming home from college tomorrow. We're having a party. Would you please come?

Fred will be there. Please tell me you'll come."

"That would be great. Thanks."

I knew Fred would be there because he dated Julia's identical twin sister, Stephanie.

I went to the party. Julia's house was even more spectacular than Fred's. I made a lot of new friends. Julia stole my heart.

One thing led to another. I mustered up the courage to ask her out. Love came fast.

I couldn't get enough of Julia. We spent our evenings cruising the back roads of western Pennsylvania and West Virginia. I couldn't wait to get home from work so I could see Julia. She was my soul mate. She was my escape.

What fun Fred and I had double-dating the twins. We were the Four Amigos.

Things were still rough at home. My family teetered on the brink of losing our house.

Mom was the family breadwinner. Dad was unemployed. To fill his days, he watched TV. To fill his nights, he drank. He didn't bother looking for a job. Mom struggled to keep the house. She had eight kids to care for.

Alcohol was dad's drug of choice. It fueled his rage.

Being the oldest, he took his frustrations out on me. I was his easy target.

Night after night, I fled to Julia for comfort and understanding.

She did her best to calm me, wrap me in her arms, and whisper comforting thoughts. Julia never failed me. She was always there. She let me wallow in my horrors and complain about Dad. My affection grew.

Our beautiful summer romance deepened. We celebrated the Bicentennial 4th of July at Buck Run Farm with hundreds of other fun-loving Americans. The summer continued with parties, cruising, and love.

When I wasn't with Julia, I dreamed about her... whisked away in a perfect fantasy.

In late July, the Four Amigos went on vacation in the great North Woods on the border of Pennsylvania and New York. We camped, hiked, laughed, and fell more in love. At night, we cozied up to the campfire and told stories.

The lake, forests, and enchanted mountains were the perfect backdrop for our romance. I wrote poems. I shared dreams. I griped about my father.

The closer we got to the end of summer, the heavier my heart grew. It was only a matter of time before Julia would be going back to school.

One Tuesday evening, after a fight with my dad, I sped over to Julia's.

The second she opened the door, I knew something was wrong. She stood in the archway. Her arms were crossed. She gazed at the floor. She sniffed back tears.

The world stood still.

Then she announced, "Larry, I can't see you anymore."

"Wh-why?" My knees buckled.

"I'd rather not say now. I'm going back to school. It just won't work. Please understand." She burst into tears and closed the door.

My thoughts spun out of control. I stumbled back to the car, not knowing where to go. I cruised around the back roads, trying to make sense of it all. *We didn't fight. What happened? Did she fall out of love with me?*

I tortured myself for answers. None came.

On Saturday, I met Fred for a hike.

"Bro, I can't sleep. I can't eat. I'm confused. Do you know why Julia left me? What in the world happened? Did she say anything? Man, I miss her."

"She'd kill me if she knew I told you," Fred answered.

"Fred, we're amigos. Tell me, please."

"Okay. Promise you won't go running to her after I tell you. Julia told Stephanie she was tired of you being miserable. She thinks you complain too much."

"But my life *is* miserable. I have it tough," I answered.

"Your choice. That's what she said."

I was crushed. I had every right to complain. She knew that.

Fred knew that.

I replayed his words over and over. *Does Fred feel the same way? Does he think I complain too much, too?*

Later that week, I drove to Al's Cafe to drown my sorrows.

I ran into my friend Mike. I couldn't wait to unload my sorrow and pain.

"I'm so bummed. Julia broke my heart. My dad just had another tantrum and…" I stopped. The bells went off. Oh, my heavens, Julia was right. Fred was right.

I brightened and smiled, "Actually, everything is good. I have a great job. I live in a great house. I have great friends. Cheers!" I raised my glass.

That was my turning point.

There is endless good in this magnificent world of ours.

Julia led me to the greatest gift life can bring — the ability to appreciate the joy in what we have instead of what we have not. True love of life.

I never saw Julia after those glorious days, but I'll always be grateful for the incredible life-changing lessons she imbedded into my soul.

Later, I came across the words of Doris Day: "Gratitude is riches. Complaint is poverty."

Present day: I shared this story with an old friend. She said, "I've never heard you complain."

How different my world would be without having experienced that heartbreak so many years ago.

— Larry Schardt —

80

Out of the Blue

Be happy when God answers your prayer but be
happier when you are an answer to others' prayers.
~Author Unknown

My friend Patty once shared the story of how she got over a bad case of "the blahs," and within her account was the best advice I have ever received. It was a simple bit of wisdom, casually conveyed, but has since become a precept I try to live by every day.

Her tale began on a gray afternoon in late February, when winter's drab skies, barren trees and numbing cold had left Patty feeling forlorn.

"I was down in the dumps and just couldn't perk up," she recalled. "I tried giving myself a manicure, watching a bunch of sappy rom-coms, making double-fudge brownies — nothing helped; I was stuck in the doldrums."

Desperate to overcome the gloom, Patty decided to try "retail therapy," but even an impromptu shopping trip left her hollow. Weary and defeated, she retreated into the comfort of her favorite coffee shop for a caffeine boost.

As Patty sat sipping a double cappuccino, she noticed an older woman walk into the café, struggling with a half-dozen overstuffed grocery bags. The lady looked to be about sixty, well dressed but slightly disheveled, and something about her was vaguely familiar. Patty kept glancing over, trying to place her, and it seemed the woman was doing likewise. After a few minutes, the stranger came up to Patty's table.

"Excuse me," she said timidly. "I hate to bother you, but I think I've seen you at church…"

Of course, that was it! Patty recognized her as one of the ladies who sang in the Sunday choir. The woman introduced herself and they chatted briefly before she asked for a favor.

"My car is in the shop, but I really needed to get to the store today so I walked," she explained, setting her bags down on the table. "Now it looks like it's going to rain any minute. If it isn't too much trouble, would you mind giving me a ride home? It's not too far from here."

Patty told her it wouldn't be a problem, and the two headed out to the van. Before they left the shopping center, Patty asked if there was anywhere else she needed to go, and the woman admitted she had hoped to get a few more errands done that afternoon. In the end, their trip included a visit to the pharmacy and a stop at the dry cleaner's to pick up her husband's shirts.

And sure enough, just as they pulled into the woman's driveway, an icy sleet began drizzling down. If the woman had walked home, she would have been caught in the storm long before reaching her house. The two joked about the timing of the wicked weather, and then Patty helped carry the thankful woman's parcels inside.

"I had so much to do today. I was praying God would help me make it through," she told Patty as the two were saying goodbye. "You were the answer to that prayer."

Patty smiled, hugged her and returned to the van, feeling better than she had in months. The blues were gone, replaced by a deep and dynamic jubilance. She turned on the radio and sang along with the music, her mood a complete contrast to the dismal day around her.

"I felt wonderful!" Patty exclaimed, relating the story to me. "All the while, I had been trying to cheer myself up and nothing worked because I was going about it all wrong. That day, I realized that the way to feel better is to be someone else's blessing."

Be someone else's blessing.

Over the years, that simple, straightforward concept has become a goal I try to meet every day. And whenever I've been fortunate enough to accomplish it, I find that helping others not only gives me a sense

> *"That day, I realized that the way to feel better is to be someone else's blessing."*

of purpose, but also reminds me of the many, many things I have to be thankful for in my life.

There are always plenty of ways to be someone else's blessing. Some are big opportunities like volunteering at the local soup kitchen or leaving a huge tip for the server who looks exhausted and overwhelmed. Others are small gestures that can have a big impact, such as letting the frustrated driver cut into the lane, or offering kind words to the mom whose toddler is having a meltdown. Oftentimes, these actions begin a ripple effect, with one good deed setting off a chain reaction of kindness, until it's hard to tell exactly where the blessings began and knowing they may never end.

— Miriam Van Scott —

81

Thrice As Nice

When we focus on our gratitude, the tide of
disappointment goes out and the tide of love rushes in.
~Kirstin Armstrong

Blah, blah, blah. I could barely stand to hear my own words anymore. How could anyone else tolerate them? Yet more and more, I found myself repeating my litany of woes to anyone I could corner. The loss of my childhood home, my Dad's terminal illness and the passing of my brother as well as two close friends in a little over a year's span had put me in a state beyond grief. I felt like one of those carnival game moles who pops out of a hole only to get hit over the head, pop up again, get hit and pop up again. Only now I couldn't pop out of my hole anymore.

I was battered, broken and lost — and I couldn't stop talking about it. I'd walk away from each of these conversations vowing not to speak of my tragedy, yet invariably the subject always found its way into each discussion I had.

In order to curb my behavior, I found myself avoiding social situations. Friends had been supportive initially. After all, that's what friends are for. However, it was starting to become apparent to me by the strained looks on their faces and the uncomfortable body language of my captive audiences that both their patience and tolerance was wearing thin. So, I withdrew.

Many years earlier, during another difficult period in my life, it was suggested to me that I keep a journal. At that time, I found it helpful to recount the day's happenings and my corresponding thoughts. I started to enjoy these few minutes each evening alone with those blank pieces of paper so much that I never gave up the habit. Now, however, it was on these same pages where I recounted my litany of sadness and woe. Over and over again.

Day after day, every entry sounded the same: sad, bitter, angry. I knew journaling wasn't helping me this time, but at least I wasn't burdening someone else with my troubles. At least now I was keeping them to myself. Pleased with what I perceived as progress, I decided to venture back out into the world and signed up for an Adult Education class in numerology. Having worked with numbers my whole life, I found the idea of what they could reveal interesting and entertaining. Besides, it might get my mind off my troubles for an hour or two.

At first, all went well. The instructor walked us through calculations based on our names to determine our personality types, likes and dislikes. Then she walked us through calculations based on our birthdates to determine what "number" year we previously had, what "number" year we were in and what we could expect for the coming year. Then she went from student to student asking if the results rang true. When my turn came, the floodgates opened.

Though I was able to contain myself from rambling, I did state in no uncertain terms that I had had a horrible year, was continuing in a horrible year and didn't expect much from the coming year either. The instructor stopped dead in her tracks. She leveled her index finger at me. "You need to change your thinking," she asserted with such passion it left me speechless.

Stunned by her admonition, I approached the instructor after class. "You say I need to change your thinking. But, how?"

"Start by practicing gratitude."

"Gratitude?" I scoffed. "I don't have much to be grateful about."

"Oh, yes you do," she asserted again. "Go home tonight and write down three things you're grateful for. Do that every night and see how quickly your outlook changes."

The whole drive home, I racked my brain for three things I could count with gratitude. When I arrived, I grabbed my journal and began to write my list. Boosted by the adrenaline of the evening's happenings, the first three items were easy to come by. Other nights, I could barely eke out one or two entries. Yet, I stuck with the practice. Soon, I noticed I began seeking out even the smallest parts of my day to mark with gratitude: the good weather, a tasty meal, a moment of laughter. And soon I noticed a shift in my attitude. I started to feel lighter and less burdened. I caught myself smiling more, feeling more hopeful. More importantly, friends no longer seemed pained during our conversations. My life had turned around — like those entries — slowly at first, but steady all the same. And in time, I realized that though much had been taken from me, much more remained — with even more to look forward to.

I still journal daily, with one addition — a minimum of three gratitude items per entry. I like to think of it as "maintenance." I never want to get knocked down that dark hole again. It's much better out here where I am now.

— Monica A. Andermann —

82

Don't Drink the Poison

To forgive is to set a prisoner free
and discover that the prisoner was you.
~Louis B. Smedes

t had been a busy morning at the Health Services Center where I worked as the nursing supervisor when I got a life-changing phone call. A disembodied voice said, "Mrs. Panko, your son has been in a fight, and you need to come to the principal's office to get him."

I prayed as I raced to the parking lot, got in my car, and drove the eight blocks to the high school.

Finding my way to the principal's office, I encountered my son sitting in a straight chair, being verbally pummeled with questions from an agitated man whom I assumed was the principal. Something was off. The man seemed oblivious to Tim's disorientation.

Even without my nursing assessment skills, I could tell he was hurt. He was bruised about his head and face. Both eyes were bloodshot, and his pupils were unequal. Alarm bells went off in my head. While the overbearing principal droned on about the rules about fighting in school, I asked Tim to tell me how many fingers I was holding up. He couldn't get it right and was confused about the day, date, and time. Finally, I held up my hand to the annoying man in charge. "Quiet! He's hurt. I'm taking him to see a doctor, and I'm calling the police."

I led my son from the room. Tim just kept asking over and over, "Mom, did I eat lunch?" I felt like I was going to throw up.

Arriving at the offices of the large medical/surgical group for which I worked, I led Tim in through the back door and was greeted by one of the nurses I knew. I quickly gave her the rundown of his condition, and she led us into a suite where Tim could be assessed. Soon, the room was crowded with medical personnel, all of whom were my friends and co-workers. One took Tim's blood pressure; another got oxygen on him; another performed neurological checks while conveying information to someone on the phone. He turned to me and said, "We're calling an ambulance to take him to the hospital. Tim has a concussion, maybe even a brain contusion, and we don't have a pediatric neurologist in town. Nancy, we may have to Life Flight him to the trauma center."

I looked up at my friend, Olivia, and said, "Liv, get me a paper bag." I sagged to the floor while still holding onto my son's hand hanging limply at his side. Tim was in and out of consciousness even though we continued to beg him to "stay with us." Liv handed me the bag into which I breathed in and out, trying to slow my hysterical, rapid breathing.

The ambulance delivered Tim to the hospital, and my husband, George, met us there. The next thing we knew, our only son was lifting off in a helicopter from the hospital landing pad and being flown sixty-five miles away to the trauma center. We had to drive while the chopper was in the air. The only comfort we had was that Tim was accompanied by a trauma doctor and nurse.

When we arrived at the cubicle in which Tim was being evaluated, we couldn't believe our eyes. He was sitting up eating a Popsicle!

The doctor standing at his side explained, "His neuro signs are much better. He definitely has a brain contusion, but there's no bleeding. He has some amnesia, which may or may not clear up. You can take him home, but he's got to rest with absolutely no exertion for a few days."

We rushed to Tim, hugging him gently from both sides. "Thank God!"

"Can you tell us what happened, honey?"

He proceeded to tell us a story of a guy who saw his girlfriend talking to Tim at lunch. He became so enraged that he and his friends ambushed Tim outside the cafeteria, pummeling his head until he was semi-conscious. Finding him bleeding and crumpled in the hall, a friend took him to the nurse's office. Tim knew his assailant. That name became embedded in my consciousness as the embodiment of evil.

Tim recovered with the exception of the amnesia. However, I began having headaches and recurrent nightmares about this faceless young man beating my son. I'd wake up in a cold sweat.

Two years later, while working at the health services center on campus, I grabbed the sign-in sheet to attend to the next student. I couldn't believe my eyes — it was the name emblazoned on my brain, the kid who had assaulted my son and got off with only a year's probation. I put down the clipboard and turned to another nurse, telling her, "Donna, you'll have to take care of this one. I just can't." I went to the lounge and sat with my head in my hands, shaking.

Donna came to get me when the young man had left the building.

"He's here at the university. I can't believe he came to the infirmary."

Donna replied, "Maybe he didn't know you worked in Health Services."

"Oh, yes, he did. His father teaches on campus, and he knows where I work."

At our staff meeting the next morning, I asked all my co-workers for solutions to this situation. My friend Anne offered, "Maybe he won't come again."

Anne pondered the problem and offered some wise words. "Nancy, you've lived with this agony for two years. It's as if *you* have taken a poison and expected *him* to die. The only solution is to forgive him for what he did to Tim. It would be giving a gift to yourself."

> "It's as if you have taken a poison and expected him to die."

I thought about Anne's words for weeks. It finally hit me during Lent. Could I give up my hatred toward someone for an evil act against my family? It was time.

I had been asked to speak at one of the fraternities on campus one evening. During my talk, I choked on my own saliva. I signaled for someone to get me a drink. A young man jumped up before anyone else had a chance to move, ran out of the room and came back with a bottle of cold water. Our eyes met. It was him. I said, "Thank you." He said, "You're welcome." Something in me softened.

The next day, I sat down with pen in hand and wrote a note to the young man telling him I was giving a gift to myself—a gift of forgiveness to someone who had hurt my family. It was not to excuse or condone the act. It was simply to say, "I forgive you." Putting a stamp on it, I sent it out. I felt like a huge weight had been lifted off my heart. I was done drinking the poison.

— Nancy Emmick Panko —

83

Snap Out of It!

*In the depth of winter I finally learned that there was
in me an invincible summer.*
~Albert Camus

E ver since I was a kid, I had wanted to work at NBC. In New
York. In my scrapbook, I still have little business cards I made
for myself using the NBC logo from the *TV Guide* when I was
eleven.

I didn't just want to work in entertainment. Or television. It had to
be NBC. In New York City. I can be a little single-minded sometimes.

My single-mindedness came in handy when my goal was something no one in my small town in Indiana considered possible. I was
a journalism and musical theatre major. I knew I wasn't headed to
Broadway, so the journalism degree was my "serious" degree. I was
told that I needed an internship to land a job. I knew where I wanted
that internship. I sent letters to four networks: ABC, CBS, FOX, and
NBC. In New York City.

I was granted interviews at all four (partly because I was applying
from somewhere other than the tri-state area). Television internships
are unpaid, so travel for interviews or jobs wasn't covered either. Bless
my parents for believing in me and sending me out there over spring
break. I was offered all four internships, but there was no question
which one I would accept. I happily commuted two hours each way
into New York City from my cousin's house for my summer internship
at NBC in Rockefeller Center.

While there, I found out about the NBC Page Program. It dates back to the early days of radio and is extremely competitive and well respected. Again, I became focused on getting that job after graduation. I was so focused that, when a family flight was canceled at JFK, I convinced my parents to let me use the time to take the train into the city and plead with the NBC HR manager for an interview. I got one, and I got the job.

I moved to New York City and worked my way from being a Page to working on shows like *Dateline, NBC Nightly News*, and *Weekend Today*. Eventually, I landed an opportunity to work on a new talk show. Working on television shows is a little scary. There's very little job security. Shows can be canceled at any moment. Staff members are routinely cleaned out when new executives come in.

I had mostly worked in the news industry, so entertainment was a bit new. In news, people can be cutthroat. It's all about getting the story. If it bleeds, it leads. I'm not really a cutthroat kind of gal, but I was holding my own. I chose to leave after the Oklahoma City bombing, however. I was the one who had to choose the clips people saw during *Dateline, Today, NBC Nightly News*... But I saw everything. I'm tearing up just writing that sentence. It was traumatic.

A daily talk show hosted by a comedian sounded like the perfect place to me. Free of traumatic news.

So I made the jump. If I thought talk-show people were any less cutthroat than news folk, I was sorely mistaken. It may have been even worse — a different kind of worse. The way people treated each other was shocking. I hated being talked to like I was an idiot. I wanted to scream, "I'm a member of Mensa! I'm not *stupid*!"

Three years later, the show was extremely successful. We'd won numerous Emmy Awards. I'd moved up a bit. I was in charge of interns and placing NBC Pages in positions, which was fun for me. I granted Make-a-Wish dreams and worked with the audience a lot. I liked what I was doing, but knew I was capable of so much more.

And, very unconsciously, I changed. I became impatient and sarcastic. I snapped at interns and co-workers. I was grouchy with friends. Without realizing it, I was becoming quite mean. I was miserable.

One day, my best friend from college, who had moved to New York City a year after me, stopped me in the middle of a stroll in Times Square. I don't even remember what I said, but it was something heartless about a vagrant who was begging for cash. My friend grabbed my arm and said, "Who *are* you?" She let me know, in no uncertain terms, that she was done with the new me. I wasn't fun, nice, or pleasant. And frankly, I'd moved on to being horrible. She wasn't going to hang out with me until I did some soul searching and changed. "Snap out of it!" she yelled, as she walked away.

Needless to say, I did not take her words or advice kindly. I was in a bad place, and I lashed out and stormed off. But it takes a very special friend to be able to hold up a mirror, say something like that, and let you blow off the steam before letting her meaning sink in. And that's what happened.

At work, I caught myself using not only the tone, but the very words that, when spoken to me, had crushed my soul. I caught myself being impatient, nasty, and cruel. I never smiled. I never laughed. And it broke my heart.

After the suggested soul-searching, crying, and option weighing, I decided that I needed to leave the show. In doing so, I basically cut off contacts that would lead to more jobs in the industry. But I wasn't sure I should be there at all. It had been my dream. I'd made it happen. But I didn't belong there.

I went back to graduate school and made a complete career change. In doing so, I rediscovered myself — the nice, kind self who was buried under years of professional abuse. And that friend? She was right there, waiting for me. I appreciate the guts it took for her to say what she did to me. That moment in Times Square changed my life. It brought me back to me, and I appreciate it so much.

Sometimes, we get so deeply entrenched in misery that we forget we are capable of changing things. Sometimes, it takes a really good friend to yell, "Snap out of it!"

— Kristin Ingersoll —

84

Straight Talk from Mom

Happiness is not defined by any circumstance,
condition, or person. You need not tie your happiness
to anything. The choice to be happy is always
yours to make.
~Dr. Anil Kumar Sinha

t was November 25th, the day before Thanksgiving, and I
unloaded my senior year angst in a heartfelt letter to the universe, detailing my unhappiness and how everyone in my family
thought I was a grouch.

"I'm never happy anymore," I bemoaned. "Basically, that's the
whole problem. All my happiness is temporary. I can be happy for
one day or so — maybe I've had an elevating talk with someone or a
really fine weekend with my boyfriend — but the feeling just doesn't
last. In fact, within a short time I can hardly even remember being
happy and feeling good."

For all its highs, my final year of high school was extremely
conflicted. Excitement at the thought of leaving home mixed with a
fear of failure and intense sadness at the thought of leaving my safe
and loving family, possibly forever.

After dumping my conflicted thoughts in blue ink on lined school
paper, I folded the missive, shoved it out of sight under my dresser,
and got back on the treadmill of schoolwork, piano and organ lessons,
a part-time job, and endless college applications.

Thanksgiving came and went, followed by Christmas and New

Year's, as my forgotten letter gathered dust under my dresser. Then, one January day, I came home from school to find my letter lying in full view on top of my dresser. Pulse racing, I unfolded it and an additional sheet of lined paper folded around my one-page missive. My page was written in blue ink. But my mother had added her own words in flowing red pencil, completing the front and back of my sheet of paper and extending onto a second sheet.

Mom started out by assuring me that no one in my family viewed me as harshly as I viewed myself, and added that we all have occasional periods of grouchiness. But Mom's amazing outlook on the subject of happiness was what really caught my attention.

"Happiness isn't something you can grasp. It is mostly anticipation of a future event or recollection of a past one. Sometimes, present happiness is found in many small ways every day — the joy of feeling needed, the pleasure of helping someone, the gratification of creating something, the satisfaction of a job well done — fleeting moments to be sure, but woven together they blend into a state of happiness that is more constant and longer lasting than a highly elated happiness of shorter length.

"Wendy, everyone learns to recognize all the forms of happiness as they go along in life if they only look around them and outside of themselves. Even then, there will be a few November 25ths to reckon with. Keep the faith!"

No doubt worried that I might interpret her discovery and subsequent outreach as a breach of the Teenager's Bedroom Privacy Act, Mom added a whimsical P.S. that made me smile then and still makes me smile today.

"Dressers need to be dusted under every so often, even by me."

I don't remember what I said to my mother after reading her uplifting response, but I know we discussed the subject in greater detail. And in the many years since, I've found her sage advice to be spot on. Happiness — that precious fuel that drives our daily lives — isn't something tangible that is handed out to us. It's a purposeful choice we make when we decide to seek and find happiness every day in the crazy world around us. As Mom so kindly and clearly pointed out, happiness abounds in the small things, whether past treasures, present moments, or anticipated futures. The key is to learn to recognize happiness in its many forms, to watch for it continually, savor it fully, and remember it always.

My mother gave me a piece of advice that resonates as surely and purely today as it did back then. Woven together, a lifetime of happy moments creates a tapestry of contentment, peace and joy that swaddles us like a cozy blanket when times are tough. Happiness is out there waiting for us even on our darkest days if we only leave our hearts open… and keep the faith.

—Wendy Hobday Haugh—

85

Just Burn It

Cherish your yesterdays, dream your tomorrows
and live your todays.
~Author Unknown

"Why don't you just burn the stupid candle?" My best friend, Wynter, and I were thirteen years old and had a close enough friendship that she could provide little gems of unsolicited advice like this without making me feel too annoyed or offended.

On this particular day, we were in my bedroom trying to decide what to do for the next couple of hours until her parents came to pick her up. She had wandered over to my dresser to examine my rather impressive candle collection. I had a candle shaped like a cup of coffee, one that looked like an ice-cream sundae, one that looked like a fishbowl, and various other oddities.

Wynter picked up a large, round, dark blue candle. Unlike most of my other candles, it wasn't shaped like any particular object. A subtle swirl of colors reminded me of a sky at twilight. The candle had tiny holes poked into the side so that, when lit, it would presumably cast a luminescent glow. I say "presumably" because I had never actually tried it.

"It's part of my candle collection," I explained. "If I burn my candle collection, then I won't have a collection anymore!"

Wynter was undeterred. "But it's a candle! It's meant to be burned! Let's just see what it looks like when it's lit. I bet it's really pretty."

"Maybe someday."

Wynter rolled her eyes at me, but I would not be persuaded. The candle remained unlit that day — and for years afterward until, at some point, my mom cleaned out my old room and got rid of most of the junk cluttering it up, including the candle collection that had been too precious to burn.

My friend didn't realize it that day, but she had provided me with a piece of advice that I've continued to follow years later: "Burn the stupid candle."

As an adult, this phrase has popped into my head many times and in various situations. Debating whether to use my "fancy lotion" or save it for later because I don't want it to run out? *Burn the stupid candle.* Wondering whether I should get out the china my grandmother gave me as a wedding present or keep it shelved until a more impressive occasion comes along? *Burn the stupid candle.* Considering whether to use a restaurant gift card to surprise my husband with an impromptu date or hang onto it until we have something meaningful to celebrate? *Burn the stupid candle.* It's such a simple piece of advice, but I think that's the reason it's meant so much to me. It's something I've been able to joyfully put into practice over and over again.

> **"But it's a candle! It's meant to be burned!"**

After all, restaurant gift cards get lost; china gets broken; fancy lotion gets poured onto the carpet by the three-year-old. And candle collections get unceremoniously dumped in the trash when we go off to college. None of the material things matter, but memories do.

Life is short, and "someday" is today. Now I burn all the stupid candles — and relish every luminous moment.

— Jayna Richardson —

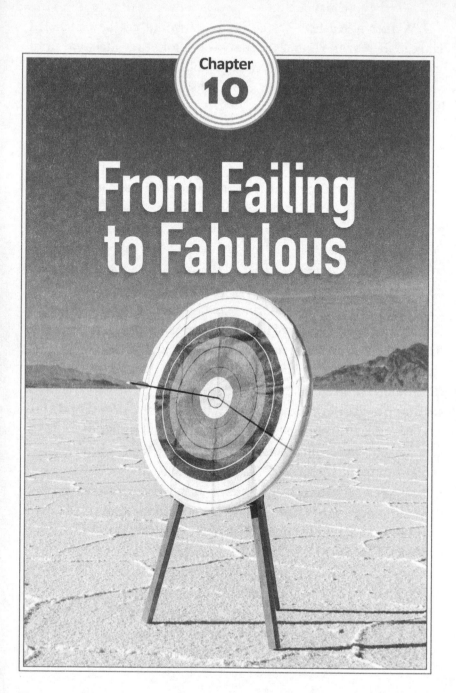

Chapter
10

From Failing to Fabulous

86

The Crutch

A teacher affects eternity; he can never tell
where his influence stops.
~Henry Adams

When I was in sixth grade, I was diagnosed with a learning disability. And with that I discovered that all I had to do was say the magic words — "I'm dyslexic" — and I would receive sympathy from teachers, easier work, and the same grades as everyone else.

Those magic words worked really well — until I moved to Arkansas for seventh grade and was placed in a class called Study Skills. My teacher's name was Mrs. White, which I found hilarious considering she was African-American. Mrs. White gave lessons the same way a Pentecostal preacher would give sermons — with lots of drama and emotion.

Unfortunately, all the passion in the world wasn't enough to combat my learning disability.

One particular day, we had a spelling test — and I failed it. The words were too hard. I needed something easier. At the end of class, I approached Mrs. White and said, "I don't know if they told you, but I have a learning disability. I'm dyslexic."

I could already imagine what her response would be. "Oh, you poor thing. Here, let me give you some less challenging assignments. And don't worry about the spelling test. I won't record the grade. Would an additional study aide be helpful?"

Imagine my shock when I heard, "Are you going to use that as a crutch the rest of your life, boy?" I stared at her, dumbfounded. She continued, "I've had dyslexic students who have been top of their class." She proceeded to tell me that I would need to work twice as hard as everyone else.

I left that classroom angry. I had a learning disability. Didn't she understand that? When I went home and told my mom, she was just as upset as I was. "It's not your fault you have a learning disability," she said. "You need easier work!"

But Mrs. White had struck something within me. Now I had something to prove.

I studied and studied and studied. And on the top of my next spelling test was the biggest A I had ever seen. Mrs. White shook my hand and said, "Well done."

What Mrs. White said about using my disability as a crutch my whole life really got to me. I had never thought about the rest of my life before. But as I grew and entered high school, I never forgot. Easier classes were offered to me, but I always refused. I knew that out in the real world they wouldn't give me easier work just because I had a disability. I decided that I wouldn't accept easier coursework unless I had already put all my effort into the regular assignments.

> "Are you going to use that as a crutch the rest of your life, boy?"

This was how I handled college too. When I first entered college, I had to redo my first math class three times. It was discouraging and disheartening. I began looking at the majors that had the fewest math requirements. That was until I found my true love: economics. I loved everything about it, and I worked hard, pushing my way through many advanced math courses before finally graduating with my bachelor's degree. I never told my professors I had dyslexia. I didn't want special treatment.

I didn't stop there. I couldn't. I loved learning too much not to continue. I studied hard and took the GRE test for grad school. The time limits were very difficult for me and I struggled with reading the questions fast enough. But I did well enough to be accepted into every master's program I applied to, including at Johns Hopkins University.

Ultimately, I decided to attend Utah State University and graduated with a Master's of Economics and Statistics. And now? I am currently enrolled in a Doctorate of Economic Development program at New Mexico State University.

What Mrs. White told me all those years ago was very true. I still need to work twice as hard as everyone else. The heavy reading assignments are very taxing on both my mental stamina as well as my patience. I have my wife proofread all of my papers because I still struggle with spelling, although I've improved greatly over the years.

Disabilities are real. They are difficult to overcome. But no one will ever be able to say that I used mine as a crutch. And I thank Mrs. White for that.

— Kyle Eagar —

Closed Doors

Life is funny… we never know what's in store for us
and time brings on what is meant to be.
~April Mae Monterrosa

M y job teaching in a secular school had become increasingly stressful, and I was having migraines and anxiety attacks. The demands of the job left me very little time to spend with my husband and family, and now a favorite co-teacher was retiring.

There was a Christian school downtown located inside an old, beautiful church. I imagined the children would be sweeter, the parents in agreement with school policies, and the curriculum gentler. The more I thought about working at a Christian school, the more I realized this was my dream job.

It felt like a sign when a position was advertised for an early-childhood teacher in that very church, right when I needed it. I updated my résumé, arranged strong references, and studied the instruction methods that the faith-based school preferred. Within a couple of weeks, the principal called to schedule an interview. She said I was exactly what she was looking for in her program. I went shopping and bought the perfect interview outfit — a long floral skirt and a pink sweater that implied "sweet lady, good with kids."

I wasn't required to attend the church where the school was located, but the principal wanted a reference from my minister confirming my commitment to the faith. I met with my priest and explained my career plans to him. I was over the top with enthusiasm. My life had a new purpose: I would not only be a teacher, but in a Christian school. I could say the blessing over the kids' sandwiches each day. Life would be good, carefree. Father Dan agreed to give me a fine recommendation, but then he paused for a few seconds and furrowed his brow.

"Be grateful for closed doors," he said.

Closed doors? This was troubling. How could he say such a thing when I was so hopeful and excited? I wouldn't need to worry about closed doors. I was going to get the job! I was praying; he was praying. There would be no closed doors. This was my calling.

A few days later, the principal of the Christian school left a message canceling my interview. More time passed, and she did not return my calls. I sent her a lovely card with a hopeful yellow sunflower on the front asking to reschedule our meeting, but she didn't respond to that either.

I was hurt. She'd never even checked my references and hadn't confirmed my faith with the priest. I'd spent so much time practicing interview questions and studying new teaching methods. I'd bought a cute outfit!

My priest was right, except this door wasn't just closed; it was slammed. I was not grateful. I was angry, and I stewed over it for months. It didn't make sense. I needed to know why, but there didn't seem to be an answer.

The next year, I decided to leave the teaching profession altogether. I was sad, but it had become too stressful for me. I was anxious all the time and exhausted from being on my feet all day. I missed my teacher friend. And I was still deeply disappointed over the job at the Christian school; it felt like a personal rejection or some black mark on my character.

In an effort to better manage my own mental health, I found a job at a behavioral guidance clinic. It was a surprisingly easy change. I had time and energy left to spend with my husband and family. I could sit down during the day. There was an actual lunch break, and my new co-workers were fun people. I was still able to use my teaching skills, but now I was working with vulnerable adults on healthy coping strategies and self-care. I appreciated their gritty, off-color humor. My own anxiety stabilized, and it was no longer a struggle to get through each day. There was a natural fit at the clinic that I had never felt in the classroom.

One morning, while on a home visit to check on a client, I drove by the beautiful old church where I had so desperately wanted to teach school. There was construction going on around the building and a sign on the entrance that read, "KEEP DOOR CLOSED."

Suddenly, I remembered my priest's words: *Be grateful for closed doors.* I had forgotten it until that moment. Not getting that job had been the best thing that could have happened to me. If I had simply changed schools, I would have had the same stress in a different place. My health would have continued to suffer; I would have been miserable. Because of that closed door, I now had a happier life — a life that was satisfying in ways that I couldn't have imagined before.

In the years since, I've had many closed doors and chances to appreciate the priest's advice. When something I hope for doesn't work out, I'm disappointed, of course. But now I recognize the loss for what it is: protection. And I know that something much better is coming.

— Carrie Malinowski —

88

Making Change

Change your thoughts and you change your world.
~Norman Vincent Peale

I was lying in bed attempting to fall asleep, and my mind was all over the place. It had been another day full of struggle, sadness, and defeat. I had been struggling with an eating disorder and depression for years. These days had become the norm, and I was forever wishing they would change. I had been through therapy and rehab centers, but lasting happiness never seemed to stick. I honestly believed my life was doomed to be this way forever.

I met a friend at work who struggled as I did, and she told me something that forever changed my pattern of thinking. I cannot remember exactly what I was telling her about, but I can assume it had something to do with how horrible my life was. In reply, she said, "Nothing changes if nothing changes."

Fireworks didn't immediately explode after hearing this saying, but a few days later when I processed what that string of words meant, a light bulb went off, and everything seemed to make sense.

> *"Nothing changes if nothing changes."*

I was spending my days hoping things would miraculously get better. Yet I was doing this without taking any serious action or personal responsibility for my recovery. Yes, I had been through different treatment programs, but looking back I think I carried the subconscious thought that one day I would simply wake up to a better life.

Finding wellness was not something that was going to *just happen*. I realized I needed to actively make changes in my day-to-day life if I was ever to feel the peace I was consistently longing for. If I changed nothing, I could not expect to get better.

With this new epiphany, I began to look at small things in my routine that I could begin to alter. I took action to stop isolating myself instead of waiting for the time when I would "feel" like being social. If I continued to wait, there was a chance the time I felt like doing things would never come. I looked for the solution to my problems instead of focusing on how awful I felt. I took necessary steps to resolve my issues rather than wishing them away.

Today, things are not perfect, but they are getting better. I have learned to take personal responsibility and understand the importance of action when it comes to reaching a place of wellness away from my eating disorder and depression. I know that if I sit back without placing my whole heart into the remedy of my illnesses, nothing will ever get better.

To this friend who changed my life with a simple phrase, thank you. I am filled with gratitude for what you have done for me. Nothing changes if nothing changes. I'm out there now, fighting for the life I want.

— Grace Jean —

89

Just Sit Down

More and more, when I single out the person who
inspired me most, I go back to my grandfather.
~James Earl Jones

awoke to the sound of heavy boots hitting the floor as Dave walked across the roughhewn pine floor to the fireplace. He squatted on the hearth and coaxed the embers back to life. In minutes, Dave had a lively blaze going, and the whole cabin suddenly felt warm.

It was 5:30 in the morning on a cold January day, deep in the mountains of central Pennsylvania. I was here with my grandfather and four other men on an annual deer-hunting trip. This trip was my reward for getting good grades.

Dave looked up and saw me watching him from the security of my blanket. He smiled. "Mornin' sport. How 'bout you tend to the other end of the cabin and get a fire started in the cook stove, maybe get some coffee going?" With the eagerness of a twelve-year-old boy yearning to prove his worthiness for membership in this male club, I hopped out of my bunk, put on my boots, and headed for the cook stove.

My maternal grandfather was a man's man — short, stocky, and generally formidable. Grandpa was a self-made businessman in the construction business. Above all, though, he was an avid sportsman. The rug in his bedroom was made from the hide of a bear that he shot in these same mountains. And Grandpa smoked cigars — White Owls. My cross to bear, as part of the hunting-trip privilege, was riding the hundred miles to that cabin with Grandpa in his old pickup truck with all of the windows rolled up and him puffing on a White Owl. The memory still brings tears to my eyes — stinging tears.

After breakfast, we left the warmth and security of the cabin and headed out into the dark, snowy morning. It was unlawful in Pennsylvania to hunt before sunrise or after sunset, but hunters were allowed to be "in transit" before sunrise. As I trudged along beside my grandfather, plowing through the knee-deep snow, I secretly wished I were back in that cabin, sitting in front of the fire.

We walked for what seemed like miles, up one side of a mountain, down the other side, and across frozen streams. My grandfather admonished me to be mindful of where we had been and where we were headed. I tried to keep track of our route, but after about an hour I had no earthly idea. Occasionally, he asked me if I thought I knew how to get back to the cabin; I always lied and said "yes."

About mid-afternoon, we made our way down the side of a mountain to the creek bed below. Grandpa told me to head to the top of the next mountain, walk along the ridge for a few hundred feet, and then come back down. If there were any deer on that part of the mountain, I would essentially be herding them down to the bottom where my grandfather waited. So, off I went, the human Border Collie.

It took me twenty minutes of climbing and plowing through snowdrifts to get to the top. I walked dutifully along the ridge, or what I believed to be the ridge, and then headed back down. I didn't realize that I had inadvertently crossed over the top and had started back down the other side of the mountain. The Allegheny Mountains of Pennsylvania are very old and worn, with ridges that are indistinct, sometimes hardly discernible. When I got to the creek bed at the bottom, I turned right and headed in what was the wrong direction. After walking for about thirty minutes, I realized that something wasn't right. I should have already been back to where my grandfather was. I walked faster. After another fifteen minutes, an awful reality began to sink in. I was lost, and it was getting late in the day.

Then I remembered what my grandfather had told me on the way to the cabin the previous morning. We were in that pickup truck, with Grandpa puffing on his White Owl. He used that three-hour, smoky ride to the cabin to lecture me on what to do if I ever got lost in these hills.

"The instant you sense that you might be lost, sit down. Just sit down! You need to sit down and put to work the most powerful tool that God gave you—your brain. You need to sort through what you know, and you need to form a plan. In Pennsylvania, it gets dark early in January. What will you do if you're still out there, and it gets dark? You need to have a plan for that, because it doesn't have to be a terrible thing. There are worse things than spending a January night in the woods in Pennsylvania. Plan for where and how you'll spend the night. Plan for a fire—how to build it and how to keep it going all night—and plan for a place to sleep. Don't ever try to find your way out of the mountains after dark. Just sit down and plan for a long, but safe, night where you are. We'll find you in the morning. There is no need to panic.

"If there is still enough daylight to attempt to find your way back, then begin by getting your bearings. If you can see the sun, use that as a guide to keep you moving in a straight line. If you're on a mountainside, go down, always down. Find the bottom and head downstream. Be aware of all that's around you, not just the three-square-foot zone that you're walking in. Listen carefully; you might be surprised at how close you are to a town, road, hunting camp, or something. Then, if you're still lost, fire your rifle three times in rapid succession, and sit back down. Chances are you're not very far from the last person you were with. Wait ten minutes and fire three more shots. You have a dozen rounds, so don't use them all."

So, I sat down and thought about all of that. I looked at my watch. It was 4:00. I probably had another hour of usable light—barely. I looked up at the sun, noted its position and headed downstream. After trudging alone in dimming light for twenty minutes, I could wait no longer. I fired three shots, sat back down, and waited. Almost immediately, I heard three answering shots, and I was pretty sure which direction they had come from. But, once again, I remembered Grandpa's words, "Stay put. It's a lot easier to find a lost person who's sitting still." About five minutes later, I heard Dave calling my name. He had been about a half-mile away when he heard my shots. I was found.

Grandpa was pretty easy on me and never said all that much about the episode. We certainly never mentioned it to my mother. I guess we were both just glad that he had given me that lecture on the way to the cabin. I never forgot it. Sometimes, you need to "just sit down."

— Richard Knowles —

90

The Card

*A moment's insight is sometimes worth
a life's experience.*
~Oliver Wendell Holmes

hurried to my classroom, feeling grown-up in my new high-heeled shoes. It was my first day as a first-grade teacher. Brimming with confidence, I hung up my jacket and sat at my desk. I could not wait for my students to arrive.

Everything had fallen into place so perfectly that it felt scripted. During my senior year of college, I had been placed at a lovely local elementary school to begin student teaching. I was assigned to a seasoned kindergarten teacher with a crisp and professional manner. Mrs. Kathleen Buckley ran an efficient classroom that was organized and highly structured. Although I admired her abilities greatly, I couldn't help thinking that someday, when I had my own classroom, I would be more relaxed in my approach. I wouldn't make the children adhere to such a strict routine.

As the weeks progressed, Mrs. Buckley allowed me to take on greater responsibilities. A strong rapport developed between us, and I could tell, despite her business-like manner, that she found me capable. At the end of my time at the school, a first-grade teacher unexpectedly announced her retirement. Mrs. Buckley actively campaigned for me to get the position. I was so grateful to have a position waiting for me directly after graduation. I would now be working alongside Mrs. Buckley and would teach many of the students from her kindergarten class. Unlike many of my colleagues, I would begin my career in a familiar place.

The morning of my first day, I sat at my desk, taking in all the brightly colored posters that decorated my classroom. Then I spied a

> "Beginnings are difficult."

small white envelope propped up against a red apple. Immediately recognizing Mrs. Buckley's precise handwriting, I tore it open, thinking how kind she was to leave me a card. The inscription caught me by surprise. It simply read: "Dear Elizabeth, Beginnings are difficult. Love, Kathleen." How strange, I thought, since I had expected a card with an inspiring quote from a famous educator or at least some words of encouragement.

I tossed the card in a desk drawer and decided not to think about it. Nothing was going to dampen my enthusiasm.

When the morning bell rang, I opened the door to twenty-four smiling and eager faces. I was determined to give them a classroom environment that was more relaxed and less scheduled than last year.

My instincts that day proved to be disastrous, as I quickly lost control of my little charges. Giving them a choice of where to sit turned into mass confusion and several teary episodes as feelings were hurt and school supplies became mixed up.

Jenny raised her hand to use the bathroom, which resulted in a parade of students who suddenly had to go. Marcus asked to go to the nurse, which resulted in a chorus of requests. We arrived late at the first-day-of-school assembly, and my students entered in a rush, like a mob of commuters searching for a seat on a train.

After the children were dismissed, I fell into my desk chair in a heap. What had started as a promising day had ended as a disorganized mess, like the crumpled pieces of brightly colored construction paper that now littered the classroom floor. I opened my desk to clean up and there was that note from Mrs. Buckley. She was right about my beginning — it was difficult — and she was right about the many tips and tricks she had taught me along the way.

Mrs. Buckley's card, with its simple inscription, has served me well for over thirty years. She reminded me that when we attempt something new, we will not be a master. Skills take time to develop, and when we fall, we must wipe ourselves off and keep going. Falling is part of the journey to greatness.

I have used her words many times when I have encouraged struggling students, reassuring them that reading might be difficult to learn at first, but the reward is awesome. When teaching my own children how to ride a bike or to tie their shoes, I would remind them that no one is born knowing how. Each new adventure or major achievement usually begins with shaky steps and false starts. Michelangelo once said, "I am still learning." Even he had a beginning.

My first day of teaching was indeed "difficult" and very far from perfect, but in that moment I knew I was only at the beginning of my journey, and tomorrow was a new day.

— Elizabeth Rose Reardon Farella —

91

Let Me Tell You about Shorty

We know nothing of tomorrow; our business is to be
good and happy today.
~Sydney Smith

When I was a young boy, I got a lot of advice from my parents, aunts, uncles, cousins and teachers. I ignored almost all of it.

The only person I ever really listened to was Shorty. Everyone called him Shorty because, well, he was short, but somehow he never seemed small. His smile, voice, laugh and personality were king-sized.

My parents disapproved of almost everything about Shorty, which of course made me like him even more. He was my hero. Shorty earned a precarious living doing odd jobs. My mother called him a derelict, which seemed to put him in the same category as pirates, gypsies and other free spirits. He rarely had more than five dollars on him, and his standard of living was "barely surviving."

"I'm temporarily broke," he'd say, "but other people are temporarily rich. Everything is temporary."

Shorty considered all of his troubles to be temporary. No matter how bleak things might seem, he'd smile and say, "This too shall pass. Everything good in life is temporary; everything bad in life is temporary. Life itself is temporary. Endure the hard times and enjoy the good times."

No one ever knew if Shorty had a family or if he'd ever been married, and no one knew his real name. He was just "Shorty." He lived alone in an old cabin in the woods. He had horses, goats and a variety of animals that seemed to come and go.

In his younger days, he'd ridden broncos in the rodeo, and he'd been an extra in Western movies. Shorty was usually the stagecoach driver in the movies because he had a magic touch with horses.

Sometimes, one of his old movies would be on television, and we'd watch it together. He'd get so excited when the outlaws were chasing the stagecoach he was driving that he'd jump up and down in his chair. I could see in his mind and heart that he was that twenty-five-year-old cowboy again. In half the movies, the outlaws shot him, and he fell off the stage and rolled in the dust.

It seemed like Shorty had been everywhere and done everything. My parents said he "sailed a little close to the wind," which meant he didn't exactly break the law, but he came awfully close sometimes. I personally didn't believe Shorty could do anything dishonest.

I never saw Shorty when he wasn't smiling, and simple things made him happy: fried chicken and gravy, hot coffee, a new pair of work gloves, thunderstorms, sunsets, the first snow in winter, and any kind of pie.

On Saturdays, I'd walk a mile to his cabin to see what new adventure he was planning. Shorty had a thousand stories, and I knew half of them weren't true, but I was never sure which half were true and which half were tall tales.

When kids at school teased me because I was shy, quiet and skinny, he'd tell me to endure the hard times, and that they would evaporate faster than the morning fog. It helped to believe the school bullies would disappear like morning fog, and I would outlast them. Shorty made being an outsider seem fearless and exciting—something to be envied.

When something good happened at school, Shorty was the first person I told. When something bad happened, he was the first person I told. He always listened but never judged. And no matter how bad things seemed, he could make me laugh.

Instead of feeling overwhelmed and powerless at school, I began dividing things into two categories. Things I couldn't change — like bullies, algebra class with Mrs. Hoffman, and being too small to play football — were to be endured. Getting good grades in all my classes (except algebra) and sitting next to pretty Sonya Evans in English class were to be enjoyed.

In the fall, Shorty and I would watch wild geese flying overhead, and I'd get tears in my eyes because they were so beautiful, magnificent and free.

He'd smile and nod. He understood about my heart leaping at the sight and sound of wild geese, and he acted like he didn't notice my tears. We stomped through piles of autumn leaves in October. We waded through snowdrifts up to our waist in December. We went fishing in July. I was a kid, but he treated me like I was his equal.

Shorty didn't promise me life would be perfect or fair. He told me there would be good times and bad times, but they all would pass, and to enjoy and appreciate all the things that made life good. He said to endure the bad times, and I liked the word "endure" because it had power in it. Endure: to outlast, to rise above, to live on.

I vowed that I would endure every disappointment or hardship I faced in life, and I would endure it with dignity. I would choose to be happy. I would smile. I would laugh, and I would enjoy the good things.

I knew Shorty and I would be friends forever.

Then, Shorty packed up and left. He told me he was going to Arizona to look for a lost gold mine, and when he found it, he'd give me half the gold.

I believed him. I got one postcard from Shorty. It had a picture of a big cactus on it, and he just signed it, "Your friend, Shorty." That's all there was; nothing else.

I never saw him again. I kept hoping he'd come back someday. At first, I felt sad because I thought we'd always be friends. When I got older, I realized it didn't matter where he was or whether he was dead or alive — we would always be friends. He influenced me more than anyone else in my life. He helped make me who I am.

I wish he'd stayed longer so I could have learned more, but I did learn to smile, laugh, endure and enjoy. I learned that everything is temporary — and this too shall pass. I guess Shorty did give me half of his gold.

I'm a man now. I still watch for wild geese flying overhead, and I still walk in the woods in autumn and wade in the snow in December.

Sometimes, a colleague or a client will have a problem and ask me for advice.

I smile. "Pull up a chair and get comfortable. I'll share the best advice I ever heard. It was from a man named Shorty…."

— Aaron Stafford —

92

A Lesson in Failure

*Most of the important things in the world have been
accomplished by people who have kept on trying when
there seemed to be no hope at all.*
~Dale Carnegie

The text said *I think I made a mistake in coming here.* My twenty-year-old son Aaron is a biology/pre-med major at Morehouse College in Atlanta and at the time of the text was a rising junior. But the "here" referenced in his text wasn't Morehouse; it was Case Western Reserve University in Cleveland, Ohio. He was there for a ten-week summer internship.

Why? What's wrong? I texted back.

I'm frustrated… I'm wasting my time here.

I wrote back. *Let's talk about it.*

But he responded, *It's gonna have to wait till later.*

I remember how helpless I felt as I ended the exchange. *Okay. Keep the faith, son. Things happen for a reason.*

From previous conversations, I fully understood his angst. Aaron's experiments exploring the connection between fructose and hypertension weren't going well. He couldn't figure out what he was doing wrong. His repeated requests for in-house assistance left him feeling incompetent and further confused. His feelings of isolation and his inability to bond with the other research students compounded the already precarious state of his emotions.

Plus, I suspected a recent encounter at a science conference had chipped away at my son's self-esteem. A couple of attendees implied that students from historically black colleges and universities (HBCSs), like my son, were not as intellectually gifted as those who attended other institutions of higher learning. The emotion I heard in Aaron's voice every time he mentioned the incident suggested the instigators had succeeded in making him doubt his ability and his academic choices.

When my son finally called, I did my best to encourage and reassure him. I reminded him of his proven capabilities and past achievements. He'd scored in the 95th percentile on the ACT. He'd been named a National Achievement Finalist. He'd been offered scholarships at a variety of colleges and universities. He was at Morehouse College on a full academic scholarship. The Case research coordinators wouldn't have selected him if they thought he was incapable of doing the work.

I even offered suggestions for coping with the situation — meet privately with the professor in charge, do the same with the administrator who recommended you to the program, solicit advice from friends with research experience at other programs, stay hydrated, get plenty of sleep, and try to exercise.

But what I didn't do was suggest he leave the program. Instead, I said, "You know you can't quit, don't you?" His silence indicated that wasn't what he wanted to hear. Nonetheless, I continued, "Because if you do, you'll always wonder what might have happened had you stayed. Besides, sometimes it's better to be dismissed than to give up on yourself."

Later, while second-guessing my response, I gave in and said he could leave the program if the situation didn't improve. But when I spoke with my seventy-five-year-old mother about her grandson's struggles, she instructed sternly, "Do not let him come home!" Furthermore, she said as soon as our phone call ended, she was contacting her morning walking partner so they could go into full prayer-warrior mode. She vowed to do the same with the ladies in her Christian fellowship group.

As amused as I was by my mother's impassioned church-lady response, I, too, am a firm believer in the power of prayer. My husband and I both sent up daily prayers on our only child's behalf, but with the understanding that the outcome — good or bad — was one we would have to accept.

In Aaron's case, not only did his experiments continue to fail, but a series of additional bad breaks and setbacks transpired. One morning, while making breakfast, he inadvertently set off the fire alarm, which drew the fire department and led to his dorm's evacuation. His plans to shadow a local emergency room doctor vanished in a never-ending shuffle of administrative paperwork. A black male medical student from whom he'd hope to seek advice all but ignored him. And just when we all thought it couldn't get any worse, Aaron's efforts to relax and stay fit led to him hyper-extending his knee during a pickup game of basketball.

It pained me, not only to watch my child fail, but to witness him do so in such a devastating and spectacular fashion. Deep down, though, I knew learning how to gracefully accept a catastrophic outcome was an experience he needed. Any attempt by me to assist in his rescue would only impede his growth and maturity. His life wasn't in any real danger, I reminded myself repeatedly. He wasn't being harassed or discriminated against. And the internship, not to mention his suffering, would be over by summer's end.

Aaron informed us that his lack of lab results meant he would have no research findings to exhibit on presentation day. He would also likely have to forfeit the program's final paycheck. Resigned to such an outcome, I began focusing on how to help my son manage his disappointment and care for his bruised ego upon his return home. So imagine my shock and disbelief when I received a text message on July 13th — accompanied by several crying emojis — that read: *THE EXPERIMENT WORKED!!!*

It turned out that my son's failures in the lab were due, in large part, to a bad chemical reagent. Once the error was discovered and corrected, everything took a turn for the better. Not only did he present his findings at Case upon his return to Morehouse in the fall, but my son and another Morehouse student were selected to present their research projects at Icahn School of Medicine at Mount Sinai in New York City. More recently, the same summer research landed him an invite to the Annual Biomedical Research Conference for Minority

Students (ABRCMS 2017) that was held in Phoenix, Arizona. Last but not least, there's been talk that the work might be published in a science-related academic journal.

In the end, my son experienced a victory that no one privy to his situation could have ever predicted. It was a victory that, in my opinion, can best be described as miraculous. What I most hope he takes away from the experience is a greater appreciation for the power of patience, persistence and prayer. I think what my son and I both learned is that sometimes, just on the other side of what you're convinced is a total and complete failure, is actually a win so stunning and bright that you have no choice but to bow your head in acknowledgement and appreciation.

—Lori D. Johnson—

93

Failure Is Not the End

When patterns are broken, new worlds emerge.
~Tuli Kupferberg

f you had asked me in high school, I would have told you that college was going to be great. But instead, at age twenty, I was in a panic. I hated the entire environment of my school, and I felt like I was drowning in the academic work.

How on earth was I going to tell my parents that I needed to leave school and figure out something else? I was already locked into an apartment for the next year.

When I confessed my failures to my parents, I was surprised to find an incredible amount of support. "You'll figure it out," my mom told me. "So this program and school weren't for you. It's okay." But still, in spite of her reassurances that they weren't disappointed in me and that it would work out, I felt miserable.

Then one day, while I was sitting on the couch, my dad sat down on the other end. He turned to me and said, "I want to tell you about what happened to me in college and how I had to switch schools." I nodded reluctantly and struggled to hold back my tears. "I started school at Johns Hopkins," my father continued. "You know that, right? But I couldn't pass a couple of classes I needed there for my pre-med requisite. It was too hard for me there, and I couldn't do it. So I switched to Binghamton."

He told me it hadn't been an easy transition but that it all worked out in the end. "Had I not switched schools, I would have gone to a different medical school, and then had a different internship and residency at a different hospital," he continued. "And, as you know, that hospital is where I met your mother." He turned to me and said, "Think about it. If I hadn't failed at Johns Hopkins and been forced to switch, nothing would have happened the way it was supposed to, and you might never have been born! So maybe this will work out for the best for you, too."

I rolled my eyes and giggled at his conclusion. He told me to think about it and reminded me I'd be okay. What he didn't realize was how much his words and his story impacted how I began to view my situation. Yes, my school hadn't worked out. And it was too late to apply to another one for this year. But maybe things would work out the way they were meant to. Maybe I'd still find success in life despite failing out of college. After all, my dad still managed to become a successful doctor with a loving family in spite of his failures. Maybe the plan I had made had gone off track, but it didn't mean that I couldn't figure out something else.

At the end of the summer, I returned to my apartment, but not my school. Over the next few years, I found myself doing and experiencing new things that helped me grow into the person I was becoming—a person I was pleased to become. "Life experience instead of college experience," one friend called it. I volunteered on ambulances, worked in a daycare facility with babies, and then worked as a nanny. I found independence. I met unique people and formed amazing friendships. I found a home in a place I love, where I feel like I belong.

Eventually, I decided to try school again. I found an online program that suited my needs and interested me. I found confidence again in my intellect.

My parents had been right: It worked out, and I was okay.

— Ally Abraham —

Chapter 11

Positive Parenting

94

Parentology

Calmness is the cradle of power.
~Josiah Gilbert Holland

The letter had just come. Our twelve-year-old son, Andrew, had been accepted into a competitive junior high. My husband John and I had chosen the school because it was strong in sports *and* academics, and we thought it would be a good fit for Andrew, and eventually, his two younger brothers.

Andrew had been a little hesitant about leaving his friends behind, but after we assured him those friendships could continue, he had agreed to go if he got in. If I'd had any inkling as to what his reaction would be when he came home from school that afternoon, I would never have flung open the door, announcing that I had wonderful news as I waved the letter over my head.

After studying its contents for a long moment, Andrew's excited smile turned into open-mouthed horror as he started crying out, "I'm not going, I'm not going," ultimately blurring into one never-ending "I'mnotgoing…" Since he didn't normally throw tantrums, I thought it seemed reasonable to let him get it out of his system. Yet, after an hour and a half with no sign of his slowing down, my nerves were frayed and my patience gone.

"Enough is enough," I finally said, a bit louder than I'd intended. I stood at the counter, aggressively chopping onions to go with the chicken and vegetables I was making for that night's dinner. Our other boys, Matthew and Bobby, had long since fled upstairs. John hadn't come home yet. I was the only one suffering through Andrew's meltdown.

When I was his age, my mother would never have tolerated a tirade like the one that was playing out in our kitchen. A few precise words from her would have stifled any outpouring from me as effectively as a cork in a bottle. All she had to do was say something like, "If you don't wrap up this performance by the time I count to three, you can forget about that sleepover at Susan's house on Friday." And even if nothing was imminent, I knew she had a long memory.

It wasn't that I was critical of my parents' child-rearing style; I'd had a happy childhood. And as an adult, I was close to my father — and even closer to my mother. Nevertheless, John and I were determined to do things our way. I read the latest parenting books and briefed him as if I were a consulting child psychologist. When it came to children, I figured I could teach my mother a thing or two.

I was giving myself a silent pep talk when the phone rang at 6:05 p.m., the same time my mother called every evening after the rates went down. She lived in Manhattan and I, having married a Canadian, lived in Ottawa, Canada.

I reached for the phone on the wall and said, "Hello."

"I can barely hear you," she said, "what's that terrible yelling?"

"Oh, that's your grandson," I replied, covering my free ear with the hand that wasn't clutching the phone. "He just found out he got into the new school and he doesn't want to go. It's been like this since he got home, and…"

Interrupting me, my mother said, "Tell him 'fine, he doesn't have to go.'"

"What? Are you kidding?" I hissed into the phone, taking my hand away from my ear and cupping the mouthpiece.

"Trust me on this," she said.

"Trust you…" I repeated, too shocked to challenge her recklessness, perhaps because she sounded so confident.

"Do. It. Now," said my mother, spitting out each word.

Maybe it was merely to prove her wrong that I turned to my son, raised my voice, and said, "Fine, you don't have to go."

Instantly, the yelling stopped. All that remained was for me to thank my mother for sabotaging her beloved grandchild's education. But before I could utter a single sarcastic syllable, Andrew called out, "Okay, I'll go." It was the reluctant tone he sometimes used when doing a favor for one of his brothers. Still, it was good enough for me.

But not for my mother. Having also heard Andrew's grudging surrender, her response was swift: "Tell him it's too late."

"I won't!" I snapped back.

"You must!" she insisted, in a tone that could still make me obey.

This is craziness, I thought, as I wet my lips and took a deep breath before diving back in: "It's too late," I said, sounding as if I really meant it. Anyone listening might have thought I was the one who was calling the shots.

"Mom, please…" mumbled Andrew, his words trailing off.

"We'll talk about this later," I told him.

Through the receiver, I heard my mother's voice warning me to wait at least two hours before giving in.

"Hey, what just happened?" I asked, "How did you do that?"

Ignoring my questions, she laughed and said, "So, how was your day?"

"Don't try to change the subject," I whispered, "How did you know that old-fashioned reverse psychology nonsense would work on him?"

"Because," she began, a trace of laughter still in her voice, "it always worked on you."

Later that evening, when I finally told Andrew that "yes" he could go to the new school, he was so grateful that I almost felt guilty.

— Hanna Kelly —

95

The Men They Will Become

If there is a measure of good parenthood, it could be
when our children exceed our own achievements.
~Tom Haggai

had become a father, and I had no idea what I was doing. As the nurse prepared our newborn son, David, to go home with us, I said, "I can't believe you're so irresponsible as to send this defenseless baby home with us."

She laughed. "You'll be fine. Besides, he knows how to tell you what he needs."

It was the beginning of a lifelong journey that, two years later, would include a sidekick when David's little brother, Mark, joined the mix.

I remember wondering if I was up to my new role and how I could raise the boys to become great men — not men of stature or prominence, but men of character, integrity and positive influence. At six pounds, thirteen ounces, David was, in effect, like a lump of clay — clay that Karen and I could, to some degree, shape. There was only one problem: Instructions were not included.

A few years later, when our sons were toddlers, I stumbled across a piece of advice that served as a guiding principle to help us raise them. It was a simple yet powerful twelve-word adage: "Always treat your children like the adults they are capable of becoming." As the father of two sons, I modified it to: "Always treat your sons like the men they are capable of becoming."

This advice spoke volumes to Karen and me about what really matters in life and about being intentional in the way we raised David and Mark. We asked ourselves: "Do we have a plan to build values into their lives instead of assuming it will happen through osmosis? What are the most important values to teach them?" So, in addition to our church life, we began having daily devotionals and used biblical role models in addition to positive sports figures.

> *Always treat your sons like the men they are capable of becoming.*

As the boys grew, we strived to have meaningful daily dialogue with them. On warm summer nights, we walked around the neighborhood on what we called, "Night Walks, Night Talks." We talked about everything on their young minds. And the darkness served a purpose. It was a calming catalyst that encouraged discussion, eliminated distractions and created teachable moments to bond us.

We also wanted our home to be a place for their friends to gather. So, Grandpa Larson built a sandbox and bolted a basketball hoop to an old oak tree in the back yard. In just a few days, my grass had been turned into a dirt court by running, jumping feet. Dirt patches and tree stumps marked the bases for our baseball diamond while the north end zone of our football field was just beyond the willow tree. The south end zone was past the evergreen near the chain-link fence. In one corner was the swing set, a place for the plastic pool, and space for a tent or to build a fort. Our yard served as the "go-to" playground for the neighborhood kids for nearly a decade.

One night, when I was reading my sons a bedtime story, I realized something: Just as the story reached the climax, I glanced at the expression on their faces. I saw wonder in their eyes and awe on their faces. I realized I often missed those expressions by reading to them.

I stopped reading stories to them. Instead, I started telling them stories I created so I could watch their faces. I made up my own recurring characters with a good boy and bad boy facing a moral dilemma. Near the end of each story, I asked, "Now, what would you do?" Then we discussed the right thing to do before I revealed how the character handled the situation.

This full-eye-contact storytelling kept them fully engaged in the story and kept me fully engaged in them. It's astonishing what you see, and how connected you feel, when you gaze into your child's eyes.

There is perhaps no better way to reach and teach kids than to literally climb into their world. David and Mark lived in the world of sports, particularly football. So, I joined them there as we played backyard football every summer and fall.

I played steady quarterback and pitted my sons against each other on offense and defense. Thus, one son would win the game, and the other would lose. They hated losing, particularly Mark. When he was ten and lost to his older brother, he shed a few tears. I wondered how to teach him a life lesson through loss. After the game, when he regained his composure, we sat on the floor in my bedroom, our backs leaning against the wall. With a Cherry Coke and a chocolate-covered strawberry in hand, we talked.

I learned Mark was upset about more than his loss; he was disappointed with his attitude toward losing.

"Dad, I hate losing — and the way I act when I lose," he confided.

"I know, Mark. What can you do about that?" I asked, sipping my Coke.

"I need a better attitude, I guess."

"Yeah? So, how can you develop a better attitude?"

"I don't know." He took a bite of his chocolate-covered strawberry.

"We all love to win, Mark. But sometimes we need to care more about others than ourselves. When you're angry about losing, you steal your brother's joy of winning. Why not be happy for him?"

The light went on. It was a moving moment to see him willing to celebrate his brother's victory — at his expense. When you climb into your kid's world, it's remarkable what you'll witness.

Many years later, I was playing golf with my co-workers. My sons were away at college. On the tenth green, two colleagues approached me with a question I didn't see coming.

"Jim, what is your greatest achievement?" Lisa asked.

I paused. "You mean greatest career achievement?"

Michelle clarified. "No, what is your greatest achievement in life?"

I thought for a moment. "My greatest achievement in life is that my sons embrace the values Karen and I hold most dear."

For me, this encounter was another precious moment. It was the moment I realized that the random advice I had stumbled upon years ago, and practiced so often, paid big dividends.

Looking back, Karen and I attempted to treat our young sons like the men they were capable of becoming. Today, at thirty-four and thirty-two, we believe our sons became those great men. And then some.

—James C. Magruder—

96

Invisible Love?

Children will not remember you for the material things
you provided but for the feeling
that you cherished them.
~Richard L. Evans

My children were sitting at the kitchen table, playing a game. They had taken a stack of index cards and written a secret word on each one. Without looking at the word on the card, they had to tape the card to their foreheads. Then they took turns asking yes-or-no questions until they were able to guess the secret word on their card.

"Is my secret word 'fork'?" Jordan asked.

"Yes! You got it! You won!" both of his sisters yelled.

"Okay, I know my word is an animal," said Lea. "So does it fly?"

The other two nodded. I smiled and said, "It sounds like Lea is getting close."

"I think I'll figure it out in just a few more turns," she said.

I nodded. "I'm sure you will, honey."

"Mommy, mine is really hard," my youngest daughter Julia said. I nodded sympathetically. The poor girl didn't stand a chance. Her siblings had to guess the words "fork" and "hawk." The card on Julia's forehead read "love."

She'd already asked more than a dozen questions, and each answer seemed to confuse her even more. I was just about to suggest that Julia choose a new card when she asked another question. "Is it invisible?"

Lea and Jordan looked at one another, unsure of how to answer. They whispered for a few minutes and then deferred to me. "Mom, what do you think? Is the word on Julia's card invisible?"

I paused. Is love invisible? For the sake of the game, it obviously was. "Well, guys, yes, the word on Julia's card is invisible," I said. "We can't see it in the same way we can see a concrete object like a fork or a bird."

"That doesn't make sense," Julia said.

I tried to explain. "In the game, the word on your card is invisible. But in real life, it shouldn't be."

Poor Julia shook her head. "I still don't get it."

I looked at Jordan and Lea. "Can I help her? She's never going to guess her word if I don't help her."

They agreed, and I said, "Julia, when I want to show you your word, I bake chocolate chip cookies or make your favorite dinner."

Julia thought for a minute. "Is my word 'hungry'?"

I smiled. "No, but that was a good try. If I wanted to show you your word, I might also play a game with you or maybe even buy you a present."

"Ooh, is my word 'birthday'?"

"Another good try. If you wanted to show me your word, you would give me a hug or a kiss."

Julia's eyes lit up. "Mommy, my word is 'love'!"

I nodded, and the kids clapped. Julia grinned and took a mock bow. Then Lea guessed her word, and all three of them chose new cards.

But later, when the kids were finished with the game, Julia came to me looking troubled. "Mommy, why did you say that love is invisible?"

"Well, because it's not an actual object that we can see."

"But love isn't invisible," she said. "In fact, I don't think invisible love is love at all." She folded her arms and added, "Love should never be invisible."

I smiled and stroked her hair. "You're right, honey. Love should never be invisible."

Over the next few days, Julia's words ran through my head over and over again: *Love should never be invisible.*

I thought about my day and how I spent my time. Had I shown my love that day, or had it been invisible?

More often than I'd like to admit, I am too busy cooking and cleaning to show any actual love. Surely the kids knew that I was doing those things for them. But did young children appreciate mopped floors and freshly laundered sheets? My kids didn't even notice those things, let alone feel loved by them.

> Had I shown my love that day, or had it been invisible?

I decided to make some changes. I gathered the kids together and said, "You guys know that I love you, right?"

The kids looked at me strangely and then nodded.

"So someone," I said, and grinned at Julia, "reminded me that love should always be visible, so I am looking for more ways to show you guys that I love you." When no one said anything, I said, "I'm taking suggestions." I held up a pen and a notebook to show them that I was serious.

"Bake more brownies!" someone said.

"Have a water balloon fight!" another said.

"Play *Monopoly* every single day!" someone else called out.

Soon, I had a list of more than a dozen suggestions. Some were completely doable, and others, like the *Monopoly* thing, would take some tweaking. But I definitely had a starting point. I titled the list "Ways to Make Love Visible." I hung the list on the fridge, determined to make good use of it.

Over the next few weeks, the kids and I pulled several suggestions from the list. I made more cookies and played more games. I read books and kicked soccer balls. It was a great time.

One afternoon, Julia came into the kitchen and smiled at me. "You're doing a good job, you know."

"Um, well, thank you, but I'm not sure what you mean."

"I'm seeing your love," she said simply. "I mean, I always knew it was there, but now, I can really see it."

I smiled, beyond pleased with her words. "Really? That means a lot to me, honey."

I thought about the changes over the last few weeks. There'd been more playing and less cleaning. There'd been more smiles and deeper conversations. I'd given them more of my time, and what I'd gotten in return was so very worth it.

Now, when I'm tempted to put a clean house ahead of happy kids, I remember my little Julia's wise words: Real love should never be invisible.

— Diane Stark —

97

A Little Dot of Truth

Mothers and children are in a category all their own.
There's no bond so strong in the entire world.
No love so instantaneous and forgiving.
~Gail Tsukiyama

When my niece, Kellie, was four years old, she was wise beyond her young years. She knew that she could win people over simply by batting her big, brown eyes at them. She loved to debate with her mother and was certain that she could outsmart her parents. So my sister, Chris, had to get creative as she tried to find a way to teach Kellie to always tell the truth. She decided to tell Kellie that whenever she lied, a black dot would appear on her tongue that only her mom and dad could see.

The first few times that Chris tested her trick was when she knew that Kellie was lying to her. Kellie was quickly convinced that her mom was right — a black dot would surely form on her tongue when she lied. Soon after, when Chris felt that Kellie was trying to deceive her parents, they would say, "Stick out your tongue." And, sure enough, Kellie would either proudly stick out her tongue, or she would hesitate and merely stick out the tip of her tongue. On other occasions, she would clench her mouth shut and shake her head no.

As the years went by, the black-dot trick became an old family story. That is, until Kellie became a mom. I was babysitting her boys, Landen and Gavin, when an argument broke out between the two of them over who knocked over the bowl of popcorn that spilled across the living-room rug. Her four-year-old son, Gavin, looked up at me with those same big, brown eyes and stated, "It wasn't me, Aunt Char. I'm not lying. See!" He stuck out his tongue and said, "There's no black dot on my tongue." I couldn't help but laugh. The story of the black tongue was back.

— Charlotte Hopkins —

98

Move Through the Mess

Some of us think holding on makes us strong;
but sometimes it is letting go.
~Hermann Hesse

The lasagna is baking in the oven. The cheese plate is on the table, and the red wine sits next to the wine glasses. There are still a couple of stray dog hairs on the rug in the living room that I must have missed while vacuuming. There are two red LEGOs in the corner of the living room.

The guests are about to arrive at our house for a dinner party. But instead of a second round of cleaning, I take a deep breath and move through the mess.

"Move through the mess" is a mantra my therapist created for me after my first child was born. My stress and anxiety about the cleanliness of a house started during childhood. I grew up in a clean house. It was immaculate. There's a quote from *Ferris Bueller's Day Off* that best describes my parents' house: "The place is like a museum. It's very beautiful and very cold, and you're not allowed to touch anything."

My father spent a lot of time cleaning. The hum of the vacuum was the soundtrack to my evenings and weekends growing up. When I had sleepovers at my house, I would cringe at the sound of it at seven in the morning.

I became well versed in how to keep a place immaculate. I felt that the cleanliness of a house represented success, drive, and achievement. My personal life could be chaotic, but if my bedroom was pristine, everything was under control.

When I lived on my own, I spent a lot of time keeping my apartment spotless. If work was stressful, I vacuumed. If my boyfriend was a jerk, I scrubbed the bathtub. If the subway commute was a nightmare, I cleaned the sink with a toothbrush.

When I was pregnant, my cleaning regime amplified. Any particle of dirt or dog hair on the floor was a reason to bring out the vacuum. I started to vacuum every day. The anxiety of returning to our messy studio apartment after giving birth haunted my pregnancy.

Then, I had my son, and my once immaculate apartment turned into a dirty daycare crammed with toys and baby gadgets. I found myself cleaning to manage my postpartum stress and depression. But no matter how many times I mopped the kitchen floor, the anxiety of motherhood remained. I became overwhelmed with my new responsibilities as a mom and the pressure I placed on myself to have a clean apartment. Rocking my baby, I would bawl while thinking of the chores I needed to do. I was never present — because I was always thinking about what I had to clean.

Finally, I had a breakdown. I had to choose. Either my house was going to be clean and my baby neglected, or I would just have to deal with the mess. As much as it pained me, I had to accept the chaos that went along with the new addition to my world. It was a struggle. I had to give myself little pep talks, and I started therapy. My therapist created the mantra, "Move through the mess."

At home, I had to tell myself that even though the apartment felt dirty, I was going to be okay. I started to focus on my breath and my baby when I wanted to clean.

"Move through the mess" drew me out of my studio apartment, and I started to have mini adventures with my baby. We would go on hikes with our dogs, listen to music on long car rides, take classes with other moms, and have picnics in the park. At home, I would try to do different activities with my little one so I could divert my focus away from dirty dishes or the dog hair on the rug.

Even though I fell behind on my chores, I began to feel my self-confidence build as a mother. I managed to take the stress from a messy apartment and transform it into feeling empowered in overcoming an obsession.

It's been almost five years since I started to "move through the mess." I still find myself wanting to clean obsessively when my life feels out of control, but I also have developed the self-control to stop myself and recognize the compulsion. My cleaning obsession has not disappeared, but I now acknowledge it and try to move past it. Talking about it with friends, family, and my husband helps a great deal.

Now, we have two children, and we have moved from a studio apartment to a house. With two little ones running around, there's a lot of space and grime that could fuel my cleaning obsession. I have to remind myself continually that life is a little messy, so my house can be messy, too. When I find myself reaching for the vacuum the minute I see dog hair on the carpet or scattered LEGOs on the floor, I breathe, close my eyes, and move through the mess.

— Deana Morton —

Chinese Food

Great things happen to those who don't stop believing,
trying, learning, and being grateful.
~Roy T. Bennett, The Light in the Heart

W hen I held Andrea for the first time, she weighed only ten pounds and was nearly a year old. Patrick and I gladly accepted her regardless of whatever health issues she had. We thanked our lawyer and brought her back to the Romanian apartment we lived in until the rest of the adoption paperwork was completed.

On that first night with Andrea we introduced her to a new life outside of the orphanage. We gave her a bath, clean clothes, toys, and a bottle of warm formula, but she wasn't receptive to any of it. We imagined it would take her a while to adjust. We planned to give her ample time and patience, but I was very concerned that she wasn't eating.

After a few weeks, we brought her home to meet her sister, Juliana. In the comfort and safety of our home, I believed Andrea would adapt, but she continued to refuse food. A barrage of therapists invaded our home in an attempt to help Andrea overcome her delays. She needed physical, occupational, and behavioral therapy. Andrea progressed by leaps and bounds in every aspect of her life, except with the oral/motor speech therapist who was helping her eat. Because Andrea was only fed a bottle of cold chamomile tea each day in the orphanage, she developed an abnormal sensitivity to food. Kirsten, the speech therapist, was working with her to overcome that. "I guarantee that Andrea will eat Chinese food someday," she said. She took my hand in hers and squeezed it gently. "Trust me."

I fought back tears as I thought about how Andrea was overcoming obstacles every day. "She's a tough kid," I said timidly.

"Yes, she is," Kirsten said. "Give her time. She will eat."

Andrea looked miserable in her highchair. It was the last place on earth she wanted to be. Juliana stood next to her, eating the food off her tray. "Yummy!" Juliana said to her sister. "This tastes good," she said as she continued stuffing her mouth with the Cheerios strewn across Andrea's tray. Juliana held out a tiny bit of cereal on her finger to Andrea. "You eat," she said.

Andrea took the food, put it in her mouth, grimaced, and then swallowed. We cheered wildly as she smiled and reached for another Cheerio. Kirsten praised her the loudest. She turned to me, smiled, and winked. "I told you she would eat."

When I put more cereal on Andrea's tray, she turned her head away and cried. Our smiles faded.

"She's had enough," Kirsten said, taking Andrea out of the highchair. She continued to praise her to bring back Andrea's smile.

"She only ate two Cheerios," I cried.

"I know," Kirsten cooed. "Remember that she's a baby, and she will improve with baby steps." She cleared her throat and spoke in a hushed tone. "Be patient and celebrate the victories, no matter how small they are. They are still victories. Someday, she will ask you for Chinese food, and she will enjoy eating it. Have faith."

> "Remember that she's a baby, and she will improve with baby steps."

My head bobbed while Kirsten's advices reverberated in my head: *Celebrate the victories, no matter how small they are, and have faith.* That became the motto I lived by.

By the time Andrea's speech services were terminated, she was enjoying mealtime and incorporating a larger assortment of fruits and vegetables into her food repertoire. She even had a few favorites: cheese doodles, baby carrots, and chocolate chip cookies. Andrea was able to attend school without the need for any special services whatsoever. There were days of regression—like the times she had surgeries or illnesses—but with much faith, coaching, love, and understanding, she bounced back with gusto.

Kirsten was right. Everything had turned out okay. Both Andrea and Juliana tried new foods happily, and they encouraged each other when their bravery faltered. We used tablecloths and dined with candlelight almost every evening. At holidays, when the girls piled food on their plates, I offered a silent prayer of thanks to Kirsten, who enabled our family to reach that level of achievement by celebrating the small victories and maintaining faith.

We dined more frequently at restaurants when Andrea and Juliana were teenagers. One day we were waiting for our order to arrive at our favorite Chinese restaurant, and I recalled Kirsten's prediction that Andrea would one day eat Chinese food. I smiled at the thought. Then I noticed a familiar face at a table nearby. It was Kirsten!

No one else in the restaurant understood the significance of the moment. As we embraced, Kirsten said, "I told you Andrea would eat Chinese food someday!"

— Barbara S. Canale —

Motivation

Every child comes with the message that God
is not yet discouraged of man.
~Rabindranath Tagore

I couldn't quit smoking, even though I had developed a chronic cough. I had tried many times, but nothing worked. And then I asked my youngest child what she wanted for her ninth birthday. She looked down at the ground and said that she didn't think I could give her what she wanted.

I implored her to tell me anyway, thinking to myself that it was probably something very expensive. What would an eight-year-old want that I couldn't provide?

With her eyes tearing up, she told me that she wanted me to quit smoking for her birthday because she didn't want me to die. I was stunned at first, and we sat together in silence. Then I picked her up and held her tight, closing my eyes as I sought an answer for her. Suddenly, the answer became quite obvious to me.

Of course, I would, I told her. Of course, I would stop smoking for her as her birthday present. I had finally found the motivation I needed to rid myself of a terrible habit, and I haven't smoked since that day more than seventeen years ago.

— Barry Girolamo —

Let Him Find His Way

The most interesting people you'll find are ones that
don't fit into your average cardboard box. They'll make
what they need, they'll make their own boxes.
~Dr. Temple Grandin

Our son was diagnosed with autism spectrum disorder when he was four-and-a-half years old. I have to admit, I grieved for the loss of what he might never experience. Would he ever play soccer or football? Would he ever develop a close friendship with a best buddy? Would he ever have a girlfriend or get married? Would he ever live outside our home or even get a job? It was hard to imagine what the future held for our beautiful, sweet boy.

The first couple of days were difficult, as I couldn't imagine he would be happy or feel successful in his life without experiencing those rites of passage. Then I received two key pieces of advice: one from my brother, and one from my husband. My older brother Gerry told me, "You know, you don't have to treat him any differently. He's the same boy he was yesterday, but now you have access to more tools and resources. Having a diagnosis like this doesn't change who he was, who he is, or who he will become. It will just allow you to understand why."

That was so reassuring to me. This diagnosis wasn't a great weight I had to carry around; it was the opposite. It was freeing, because now I understood *why* he behaved differently. Now I had access to services and people who could help me better mother my child.

My husband Brian also told me something that helped me feel better about the future for our son. He said, "Best friends, football and girlfriends… those are all things that society tells us will make him happy. Maybe he'll participate in those experiences, and maybe he won't. Why don't we allow *him* to find what makes him happy, and we can support and encourage him through the experiences he chooses." It sounds so simple, really, but I needed to hear it. I needed someone to tell me that our child would be happy if we would just allow him to be.

> *I needed someone to tell me that our child would be happy if we would just allow him to be.*

I have taken these pearls of wisdom and paid it forward by sharing them with the parents of other newly diagnosed children. I have heard on many occasions, "Thank you. I needed to hear that." And I completely understand because I'll never forget the time when I needed to hear those words, too.

— Bridget Shanahan Ferrara —

Meet Our Contributors

Originally from New Mexico, **Allison Abraham** moved to Tucson, AZ when she was eleven years old. Allison has always been an avid reader of books, which ultimately inspired her love of writing. These days she lives with her adorable dog and continues to work on her writing.

Monica A. Andermann lives and writes on Long Island where she shares a home with her husband Bill and their very playful tabby, Samson. Her work has been included in such publications as *Sasee*, *Guideposts*, and *Ocean* as well as several *Chicken Soup for the Soul* books.

David-Matthew Barnes is a best-selling author, playwright, poet, and screenwriter. He is a member of the Dramatists Guild of America, International Thriller Writers, and the Society of Children's Book Writers and Illustrators. He earned an MFA in Creative Writing at Queens University of Charlotte in North Carolina.

John Morris Benson graduated high school in Alexandria, MN, and spent nearly ten years in the Army. While teaching in Kelso, WA, he earned his M.S. degree. He authored *An Odyssey of Illusions* in 2012 and *Nescient Decoy* in 2018. He and his wife of nearly sixty years live in Vancouver, WA.

Mary Ann Blair is a stay-at-home mom living in the Pacific Northwest with her two little gentlemen and husband. Her work has been featured on *Her View From Home*, *Perfection Pending*, *That's Inappropriate*, *Pregnant*

Chicken, and *Red Tricycle*. She can be found at miraclesinthemess.com and on Facebook at Miracles In The Mess.

Jan Bono writes a cozy mystery series set on the Southwest Washington coast. She's also published five collections of humorous personal experience, two poetry chapbooks, nine one-act plays, a dinner theater play, and has written for magazines ranging from *Guideposts* to *Woman's World*. Learn more at www.JanBonoBooks.com.

Betsy Burnett and her husband Adam live in rural Illinois and have four children. Betsy works as a church administrator and volunteers with Operation Christmas Child and a local youth center. In addition to writing and doing anything creative, Betsy enjoys reading and bike riding.

Jill Burns lives in the mountains of West Virginia with her wonderful family. She's a retired piano teacher and performer. She enjoys writing, music, gardening, nature, and spending time with her grandchildren.

Award-winning author **Barbara S. Canale** has three devotional books from Liguori including: *Prayers, Papers, and Play* for college students (2013), *To Have and to Hold* for married couples (2014) and *Hope and a Whole Lotta Prayer* for parents of teenagers (2015). She is a frequent contributor to the *Chicken Soup for the Soul* series.

Danny Carpenter enjoys his family, his church, golf, and the ukulele. Since reading *The Winter of Our Discontent* in 8th grade, he has been fascinated with the power of the written story.

Jacqueline Chovan is a mother of three and a military wife currently residing in Germany and drawing inspiration for her first novel from the fairytale-like surroundings. This is the second time she has been published in the *Chicken Soup for the Soul* series. Aside from writing, she enjoys adventures and traveling with her family.

Courtney Conover is a writer, YouTube content creator, and yoga teacher who resides in Michigan with her former NFL player husband, Scott, and their two young children. After abusing her hair with a flat iron for nearly thirty-eight years, she has finally learned to love her natural curls — sometimes even more than chocolate.

Laurie Davies is a twenty-five-year journalist and marketing professional whose passion is to inspire readers to see that their best days are ahead. When she's not writing for the corporate world, she blogs (and can be reached) at lauriedavies.life. She lives in Mesa, AZ with her husband, son and two very spoiled Puggles.

John Dorroh taught high school science for thirty years. He facilitated the use of writing and reading strategies in his lessons. His passion for writing poetry is reflected in the fact that he's had about fifty poems accepted this year in digital and print journals. He likes to travel, cook, and play tennis.

Sarafina Drake is a determined writer and mother who refuses to cram her star-shaped spangly self into a beige round hole. She believes there are no limits to what you can do and the only boundaries to success that exist are the ones you create in your own mind. E-mail her at sarafinadrake@gmail.com.

Kyle Eagar is currently working toward his Doctorate in Economic Development at New Mexico State University. He enjoys martial arts, strategy games, and listening to podcasts. Kyle would like to thank his wife, Heather, for helping write and share his story, as well as for all the years of proofreading his papers.

Shawnelle Eliasen and her husband Lonny live in an old Victorian in a small Illinois town on the Mississippi River. They have five sons, and Shawnelle home teaches the youngest two. She blogs, writes inspirational stories for publication, and hopes to begin a book soon.

John Elliott is a forty-four-year law enforcement veteran in the United States, and worked with Interpol in Lyon, France. He has earned a Bachelor of Science degree in business, an MBA, and a Juris Doctorate degree. He is fluent in English, Gaelic, Hebrew, and Hungarian, and can also converse in both French and Italian.

Michelle Emery lives in a small village in the north of England. She works for the National Health Service and writes in the evening. She graduated with a First Class Honours degree in English, and she has always had an interest in the written word.

A teacher's unexpected whisper, "You've got writing talent," ignited **Sara Etgen-Baker's** writing desire. Sara ignored that whisper and pursued a different career; she later rediscovered her inner writer and began writing. Her work has been published in *Guideposts*, *Wisdom Has a Voice*, *The Santa Claus Project*, and the *Chicken Soup for the Soul* series.

Martha M. Everett is a Midwest-based freelance writer who has lived on both coasts, covering everything from Washington politics to the Westminster Kennel Club Dog Show. She holds a master's degree from the University of Missouri School of Journalism and enjoys traveling, biking and dogs.

Elizabeth Rose Reardon Farella received her bachelor's degree in Elementary Education from Molloy College and her Masters of Science in Literacy from Adelphi University. She is a first grade teacher in Syosset, NY. She enjoys reading, writing inspirational stories, and traveling with her husband and three daughters.

Bridget Shanahan Ferrara is wife to a homicide detective, and mother to a ten-year-old boy with autism and ADHD and a busy twelve-year-old girl. She is also currently the PTA President at her son's school, so to say her life stays hectic and interesting would be an understatement. She also enjoys traveling, cooking, movies, reading and writing.

Josephine Fitzpatrick is a retired attorney. She has been married for fifty-six years, is the mother of three and grandmother of six, and loves to write. She facilitates a memoir-writing class for senior citizens at Cal State Long Beach.

Sharon Frame Gay grew up a child of the highway, playing by the side of the road. She has been internationally published in many anthologies and literary journals. She lives in the Seattle area with her miniature Dachshund, Henry Goodheart.

Sandy McPherson Carrubba Geary lives with her husband and old dog in the house built for her maternal grandparents. She enjoys gardening, theater events, and encouraging other writers.

Pamela A. Gilsenan still grows, shares and eats vegetables… except lima beans. She is the mother of five adult children and the grandmother of assorted grandchildren.

Barry Girolamo received the inspiration for his stories while raising his family. He has three children, and enjoys reflecting on and sharing his life experiences.

Freelance writer **Wendy Hobday Haugh** has had hundreds of articles, stories, and poems for adults and children published in more than three dozen national and regional publications. Mother to three grown sons and grandmother to two spunky kids, Wendy lives with her husband Chuck and their two eccentric, elderly cats.

Derek Hawkins is the author of several suspense novels and two collections of short stories. Learn more at writerofnote.com.

Jill Haymaker writes Western contemporary romances centered in small towns in the Colorado Rocky Mountains. She lived most of her life in Colorado, but now resides in East Texas. When not writing, she enjoys gardening, sports, and walks with her Toy Australian Shepherd, Merlin. E-mail her at jillhaymaker@aol.com.

Rebecca Hill's favorite yoga teacher is Wendy Hartley. Rebecca is grateful for Wendy's grace, intelligence, wisdom and spiritual insights. The greatest lessons Rebecca learned from Wendy are how to "get comfortable in an uncomfortable position" and how to live life to its fullest through "strength and surrender." Blessings!

Zach Hively writes nonfiction, poetry, and *Fool's Gold: The Column*. He dances and teaches Argentine tango, and he plays guitar and harmonica in the duo Oxygen on Embers. Dogs love him. He thrives in the desert, wears fine hats, and once changed his own tire.

Charlotte Hopkins is a freelance writer and literary agent from Pittsburgh. She enjoys photography and history (especially the Civil War era). She is currently working on several projects, including a book of short stories and a series titled *365 Days*. She is also writing *Listology* with her daughter, Megan Lewis.

David Hull is a retired teacher who enjoys reading and gardening. He tries to write something every day and spends way too much time watching *Star Trek* reruns. E-mail him at Davidhull59@aol.com.

Kristin Ingersoll, MS Ed, is an Instructional Designer based in Indianapolis, IN. She has two cats, Daisy Serendipity, who was featured in *Chicken Soup for the Soul: The Cat Really Did That?* and Inigo Montoya, who was very jealous about that. They hate each other, but Kristin loves them both. E-mail her at ID4hire@hotmail.com.

Ellen Javernick grew up in New Jersey, attended DePauw University in Indiana, and now lives in Colorado. She enjoys a dual career as a kindergarten teacher and a writer. She's proud of the success of her children's books. Her most recent is *What If Everybody Said That?* but she's proudest of her ten grandchildren.

Grace Jean received her Bachelor of Arts in dance from Western Michigan University in 2013. She currently works as a dance teacher and mental health blogger in the Midwest. Grace hopes to one day become a dance movement therapist and work with others who have been affected by mental illness.

Lori D. Johnson has an M.A. in Urban Anthropology from The University of Memphis. Her work has appeared in a variety of publications, including *Chapter 16*, *Mississippi Folklife*, *The Root*, *Memphis* magazine, and *Obsidian II: Black Literature In Review*.

A speaker and blogger, **Marlys Johnson** took an early retirement from the St. Charles Cancer Center in Bend, OR to write and speak full-time. She loves getting outdoors and has a passion for helping people navigate life's challenges, having negotiated a few herself. Learn more at www.RenewRepurpose.com.

Elaine Jolly grew up in Savannah, GA. Currently she lives in Birmingham, AL, where she raised her two sons, Alex and Nick. In her spare time she enjoys writing and is currently working on her first fiction novel.

Hanna Kelly studied English Literature at Boston University and worked as a corporate librarian for a New York City law firm. She moved to Canada after marrying in 1985. She enjoys travelling, reading and writing. She has been published in *The Globe and Mail*. Hanna has three adult sons and resides with her husband in Ottawa.

Nancy B. Kennedy is the author of seven books, including four titles in the *Miracles & Moments of Grace* series, a collection of inspiring true-life stories. Her eighth book will tell the dramatic story of the American women suffragists. To learn more about her writing, visit her website at www.nancybkennedy.com.

Vicki Kitchner is a retired educator who taught Exceptional Student Education for thirty years. She divides her time between North Carolina and Florida. She and her husband love to travel, hike, garden, and entertain friends and family.

Richard Knowles grew up in western Pennsylvania, near the edge of the Appalachian Mountains. Lessons learned from his grandfather on the many hunting and fishing trips into those mountains formed much of the foundation of his character. He now lives on a small island off the coast of North Carolina with his wife Jill.

Gregory A. Kompes (MFA, MS Education) has authored fifteen books and contributed to a dozen anthologies, including *Chicken Soup for the Soul*. He teaches writing in Las Vegas and Henderson, NV. Walking the 1000-km Via de La Plata Camino de Santiago has proved to be one of the great inspirations of his life. Learn more at Kompes.com.

Cindy K. Krall hails from the prairies of South Dakota. She's grateful for Doc, her high school honey and husband of thirty-one years, and their three grown children. Cindy writes (and speaks) about life, faith and everything in between. To learn more, visit CindyKrall.com. Follow her on Facebook at CindyKKrall or Instagram cindy_krall.

Since 2001, **Tom Krause's** reputation has continued to grow on the motivational speaking circuit. Tom has presented to thousands of educators nationwide and overseas. Standing ovations are the norm as audiences spontaneously react to Tom's motivational/inspirational presentations. Learn more at www.coachkrause.com.

Brooke Adams Law has been a writer since she could first hold a pencil. She has written numerous essays and articles and is currently creating her second novel. She makes her living as a copywriter and marketing strategist at Soul Aligned Marketing. Learn more at www. brookeadamslaw.com.

Lisa Loosigian has a B.A. in English. Her writing background includes greeting card verses, news headlines, ad copy, essays, reviews, interviews, and fiction. She works with her husband and has one handsome son. She enjoys needlepoint, bonsai, antiquing, time spent at the ocean, and of course… writing.

Diana Lynn is a freelance writer and business owner from Washington State. She loves kickboxing, dancing and writing. This is her ninth story in a *Chicken Soup for the Soul* book. Her goal is double digits! Find her on Facebook at Pieces of Me: Life of a Recovering Dysfunctional.

Kelley Lynn is a writer, comedian, TEDx speaker, grief coach, and involuntary widow. Her new book, *My Husband Is Not a Rainbow*, arrived as a bestseller online in June of 2018. She hopes to soon move out of her parents' basement, help others heal from loss, and change the world.

James C. Magruder has been published in *Writer's Digest*, *HomeLife*, *Christian Communicator*, and seven *Chicken Soup for the Soul* books. He blogs about the writing life at www.thewritersrefuge.wordpress. com. He and his wife Karen have two adult sons who remain their pride and joy.

Carrie Malinowski is the author of *Tattletale: A Teacher's Memoir*, *Hand-Me-Down Bear*, and is a frequent contributor to the *Chicken Soup for the Soul* series. Carrie enjoys working with anxiety sufferers in behavioral health and lives in Arizona with her husband and her dog, Chester. Learn more at carriemalinowski.com.

Lisa A. Malkiewicz writes from a little plot of country, tucked away in the North Carolina Sandhills. She acquired her B.A. in Education after serving in the Navy for some years and teaches full-time online. To relax, she hikes, paints, sews, and of course writes.

Joshua J. Mark is an editor/director and writer for the online history site Ancient History Encyclopedia. His nonfiction has also appeared in *Timeless Travels* and *History Ireland* and his short fiction in *Litro* and

Writes for All among others. He lives with his daughter Emily and the spirit of his late wife, Betsy, in New York.

Debra Mayhew is a pastor's wife, mom to seven, teacher, editor and writer. She loves small town living, stormy weather, good books and family time. Learn more at www.debramayhew.com.

Gena B. McCown is an author and speaker, born and raised in South Florida. She and her husband of twenty years, Justin, have three daughters: Casey, Shelby, and Naomi. Founder of the Women's Ministry Council, Gena has a calling to build up leaders in their local churches and communities.

Kate Tanis McKinnie grew up in Roanoke, VA and attended college at Appalachian State University. She now lives in Nashville, TN and has built a career in the nonprofit sector doing fundraising and event planning. She is married to Ryan, has two stepchildren, Savannah and Ryland, and a dog named Archie.

Marya Morin is a freelance writer. Her stories have appeared in publications such as *Woman's World* and Hallmark. Marya also penned a weekly humorous column for an online newsletter, and writes custom poetry on request. She lives in the country with her husband. E-mail her at Akushla514@hotmail.com.

Deana Morton is a freelance writer and radio DJ in Colorado. She has two kids and a Beagle named Shasta. Deana enjoys running, Parmesan cheese on her pasta, and impromptu dance parties. She is currently working on her first YA novel.

Alice H. Murray is a Florida adoption attorney by profession and a writer by passion. Alice writes a weekly blog, has had three pieces published in the compilation work *Short and Sweet* book series, and is a staff writer for www.adoption.com. In her spare time she volunteer teaches ESL.

Alice Muschany writes about everyday life with a touch of humor. Her grandchildren make wonderful subjects. Her essays have appeared in numerous anthologies, magazines and newspapers. When she's not busy writing, you can find her hiking, swimming or taking pictures. E-mail her at aliceandroland@gmail.com.

Nell Musolf is a lifelong Midwesterner. She has two adult children, three cats and an extremely spoiled Labrador Retriever. Nell enjoys thrifting with her husband, reading, watching classic movies and cooking. She writes creative nonfiction along with cozy mysteries.

Sandy Newman received her BFA in Graphic Design from Auburn University in 1986. She works as a graphic designer in Lower Alabama. Sandy enjoys reading, learning, creating, travel, living life, and supporting the Auburn Tigers. War Eagle! This is her first published writing.

Nancy Emmick Panko is a retired pediatric nurse and nine-time contributor to the *Chicken Soup for the Soul* series. She authored the award-winning novel, *Guiding Missal: Fifty Years. Three Generations of Military Men. One Spirited Prayer Book.* Nancy is a member of the Cary Writing Circle and Military Writers Society of America.

Jenny Pavlovic, Ph.D. is the author of *8 State Hurricane Kate*, *The Not Without My Dog Resource & Record Book*, and many published stories. She lives in Wisconsin with dogs Chase and Cayenne and cat, Junipurr. She loves to walk dogs, swim, kayak, garden and (yes!) ride horses. Learn more at www.8statekate.net.

Colleen Perisutti is a college graduate with an associate's degree in early childhood education. She currently works as a library page. Colleen has enjoyed writing since first grade and her biggest dream is to have her poetry and personal essays published. She also enjoys music, gardening and creating art.

Diane C. Perrone is a Christian mother of seven, teacher, public speaker to/about "seasoned citizens," skin care consultant, private pilot, "Grandma Di" to fifteen, and great-grandmother of one (so far). "Between babies," she writes from Phoenix, AZ. E-mail her at Grandma1Di@AOL.com.

Lori Phillips has a B.A. in communications/journalism and an M.A. in education. She enjoys writing both nonfiction and children's nonfiction, gardening, learning languages, trying new recipes for her family, and visiting all types of museums. She lives in Southern California with her family.

Mary C. M. Phillips is a caffeinated wife, working mother, and writer. Her work has been published in numerous national best-selling anthologies. She blogs at www.CaffeineEpiphanies.com. Visit her on Twitter @MaryCMPhil.

MJ Plaster is a former international flight attendant and veteran freelance writer, author, and magazine editor. She resides in Nashville, TN, and when she's not writing or editing, you can find her in the kitchen or the garden.

T. Powell Pryce lives in St. Louis, MO and has written for several *Chicken Soup for the Soul* books as well as other publications. She credits Chicken Soup for the Soul's uplifting philosophy for helping her through some hard times, and she is making agonizingly slow progress on a book.

Jayna Richardson graduated from the University of Central Arkansas with a double major in English and Writing. She loves reading, writing, and exploring the world with her husband and kids.

Deborah Henderson Roberts enjoys writing humorous and inspirational pieces that draw on real-life experiences. She recently completed a historical fiction novel and she has begun work on the sequel. Deborah makes her home in Florida.

Kimberly Ross, M.Div. is a spiritual teacher and writer living in the Kansas City, MO metro area. She is the mother of three wonderful adults and grandmother to two feisty grandchildren. "Three Choices" is her fourth essay to be published in the *Chicken Soup for the Soul* series.

It is rumored that the first word **Sue Ross** uttered gave her such satisfaction that she said it twice. "Author! Author!" Finding stories in everything she does, Sue revels in language that lifts and inspires. With a B.A. in English, she is editing her first novel, *Golanski's Treasures.* E-mail her at kidangel@me.com.

Larry Schardt, Ph.D., is an author, speaker, and creator of "Success That Rocks." He encourages people to live with passion, lead with heart, and explore the world with a sense of gratitude and wonder. He is a professor at Penn State. Larry loves blogging, reading, writing, walking, music, and the outdoors. Learn more at LarrySchardt.com.

Mannat Sharma received her J.D. from the New York University School of Law in 2018. She enjoys traveling, yoga and reading. Mannat would like to dedicate this story to her family and fifth grade teacher. Contact her at linkedin.com/mannatsharma.

Greg Shea is retired and living in Long Beach, CA. He rediscovered his love of writing during a nonfiction writing class given by the Osher Life Long Learning Institute at California State University, Long Beach. He writes a monthly column for *Long Beach Living* magazine.

Billie Holladay Skelley received her bachelor's and master's degrees from the University of Wisconsin–Madison. A retired clinical nurse specialist, she is the mother of four and grandmother of two. Billie enjoys writing, and her work crosses several genres. She spends her non-writing time reading, gardening, and traveling.

Connie Cameron Smith is an international speaker and has authored three books, eight stories in the *Chicken Soup for the Soul* series, and hundred of articles. She enjoys prison ministry and missionary work in Africa. Widowed in 2015, she is now married to Pastor Rocky, and happily learning to "love each other unconditionally." Learn more at www.conniecameron.com or e-mail her at conniecameron@sbcglobal.net.

Aaron Stafford was born in Alaska and has degrees from Hawaii and Arkansas. He is a Realtor in Seattle and has written three books in different genres (Mystery, SF and Suspense) each featuring a Realtor as the hero. He seeks a literary agent and a publisher. E-mail him at aaronts@hotmail.com.

Diane Stark is a wife, mother of five, and freelance writer. Her work has been published in *Guideposts, Focus on the Family*, and *Woman's World* magazine. She writes about the important things in life: her family and her faith. E-mail her at Dianestark19@yahoo.com.

Mary Beth Sturgis is happily retired with her husband, Ed. She was previously in *Chicken Soup for the Soul: Messages from Heaven*.

JC Sullivan believes that in addition to her brother's fabulous question, the best advice she ever got was, "Go for it." Break your dream into smaller goals, take steps daily, ask those who have done it. Then momentum happens. Remember, your dream is someone else's reality. Which makes it attainable.

Kamia Taylor has been writing since she was a very young child, and spent over twenty years drafting legal documents. She now lives on an organic farm and wildlife sanctuary with eight rescued dogs, enjoying nature, continuing to write and trying to make sense of her earlier life.

Stephanie Welcher Thompson found her passion at midlife as a mother and writer. Wife to Michael and Mom to Micah, she's a contributing editor for *Guideposts* and *Angels on Earth* magazines. Her stories have appeared in more than a dozen *Chicken Soup for the Soul* books.

Ed VanDeMark is a retired administrator of governmental programs. He served one tour of duty with the U.S. Navy. He is married to Linda and they have three adult children and nine grandchildren. He writes short, often humorous, stories and is nearing the completion of his second book.

Miriam Van Scott is an author and photographer who works in a variety of media, including print, television and online content. Her books include *Song of Old, Encyclopedia of Hell, Candy Canes in Bethlehem* and the *Shakespeare Goes Pop!* series. For clips, photos and to learn more visit miriamvanscott.com.

Rachel Flynn Walker is delighted to share that the hotel she works at is back to being an uplifting, harmonious environment! She is thankful for Amy Newmark's advice, as it helped her navigate a difficult time of transition.

Susan Walker has the free-spirited soul of a gypsy, and the heart of a warrior. An Air Force veteran, she loves telling a story that will touch her readers. She lives in central Texas with a muse who demands lots of time off to play between books and snacks. Lots of snacks.

Jude Walsh writes memoir, personal essay, and self-help. Her writing is published in numerous literary magazines and anthologies, including *The Magic of Memoir* (2016) and *Chicken Soup for the Soul: Inspiration for Teachers* (2017). She lives in Dayton, OH with her son and three lively dogs. Learn more at www.judewalsh-writer.com.

Roz Warren is the author of *Our Bodies, Our Shelves: A Collection of Library Humor.* She writes for everyone from *The New York Times* to *Funny Times*, and has been featured on both the *Today* and *Morning Edition.* This is the sixth time her work has appeared in a *Chicken Soup for the Soul* book.

Rebecca Waters has been a writer most of her life. Her first published work was a story in the school newspaper she wrote in second grade. Her first novel, *Breathing on Her Own*, was released in 2014. Her second novel, *Libby's Cuppa Joe* is due out in March of 2019.

Glenice Wilson enjoys nature, table tennis, travel, humour, cross-country skiing, writing, visual arts and music, along with the people and surprises they all offer. She grew up on big sky Manitoba prairie and ventured out to Alberta — living in Edmonton, Jasper, and now back into a farming community at Barrhead, AB.

Ferida Wolff has been writing stories since she was seven. She is the author of seventeen books for young readers and three books for adults. Her latest book for middle grade readers will be out in Fall 2019. She encourages anyone who dreams of writing to work at the craft and not give up.

Luanne Tovey Zuccari lives in Western New York with her husband Paul. She is a retired community outreach coordinator for public schools and co-founder of her county's Mothers Against Drunk Driving community action team. She is also a frequent speaker in her community about the impact of drunk driving.

Meet Amy Newmark

Amy Newmark is the bestselling author, editor-in-chief, and publisher of the *Chicken Soup for the Soul* book series. Since 2008, she has published more than 150 new books, most of them national bestsellers in the U.S. and Canada, more than doubling the number of Chicken Soup for the Soul titles in print today. She is also the author of *Simply Happy*, a crash course in Chicken Soup for the Soul advice and wisdom that is filled with easy-to-implement, practical tips for enjoying a better life.

Amy is credited with revitalizing the Chicken Soup for the Soul brand, which has been a publishing industry phenomenon since the first book came out in 1993. By compiling inspirational and aspirational true stories curated from ordinary people who have had extraordinary experiences, Amy has kept the twenty-five-year-old Chicken Soup for the Soul brand fresh and relevant.

Amy graduated *magna cum laude* from Harvard University where she majored in Portuguese and minored in French. She then embarked on a three-decade career as a Wall Street analyst, a hedge fund manager, and a corporate executive in the technology field. She is a Chartered Financial Analyst.

Her return to literary pursuits was inevitable, as her honors thesis in college involved traveling throughout Brazil's impoverished northeast region, collecting stories from regular people. She is delighted to have

Meet Amy Newmark | 339

come full circle in her writing career — from collecting stories "from the people" in Brazil as a twenty-year-old to, three decades later, collecting stories "from the people" for Chicken Soup for the Soul.

When Amy and her husband Bill, the CEO of Chicken Soup for the Soul, are not working, they are visiting their four grown children and their first grandchild.

Follow Amy on Twitter @amynewmark. Listen to her free podcast — "Chicken Soup for the Soul with Amy Newmark" — on Apple Podcasts, Google Play, the Podcasts app on iPhone, or by using your favorite podcast app on other devices.

Thank You

We owe huge thanks to all of our contributors and fans. We were overwhelmed by the thousands of stories and poems you submitted about the best advice you ever heard. Our Associate Publisher D'ette Corona, our Senior Editor Barbara LoMonaco, and our editors Elaine Kimbler and Ronelle Frankel made sure they read every single one.

Susan Heim did the first round of editing, D'ette Corona chose the perfect quotations to put at the beginning of each story, and editor-in-chief Amy Newmark edited the stories and shaped the final manuscript.

As we finished our work, D'ette Corona continued to be Amy's right-hand woman in creating the final manuscript and working with all our wonderful writers. Barbara LoMonaco and Kristiana Pastir, along with Elaine Kimbler, jumped in at the end to proof, proof, proof. And yes, there will always be typos anyway, so feel free to let us know about them at webmaster@chickensoupforthesoul.com and we will correct them in future printings.

The whole publishing team deserves a hand, including Executive Assistant Mary Fisher, Senior Director of Marketing Maureen Peltier, Senior Director of Production Victor Cataldo, and our graphic designer Daniel Zaccari, who turned our manuscript into this beautiful book.

Changing your life one story at a time®
www.chickensoup.com